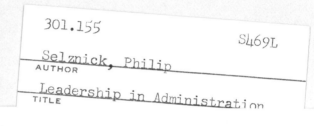

Leadership in Administration

A Sociological Interpretation

Leadership in Administration

A Sociological Interpretation

PHILIP SELZNICK

University of California, Berkeley

HARPER & ROW, PUBLISHERS

NEW YORK, EVANSTON, AND LONDON

MANUFACTURED IN THE UNITED STATES OF AMERICA

To Gertrude

Foreword

When the thoughtful American pauses to reflect upon the contrast between his life and that of his opposite number behind the Iron Curtain, and asks himself why it is that our life is so rich and the other so drab, he must inevitably arrive at the conclusion that the secret lies in the contrasting forms under which society here, and society there, are organized. He will proudly see that it is no mere coincidence that ours, the one which is least planned, and least controlled, is not only the most effective, but the most rewarding. He will find that therein lies the cause itself, the hidden source of all of our good fortune.

Never in history has the world seen the like of our way of life, and the conclusion is inescapable that free men who voluntarily accept leadership outstrip in every aspect of human activity those upon whom direction is arbitrarily imposed. Freedom is therefore not only man's most satisfying experience, but his most reliable working tool.

It is the consent of the governed that is involved. We know this as the basic principle of our form of government, but it is broader than that. It is also the universal method by which we, in America, organize all forms of human effort. Business, production, education, public administration, the Church: they all advance toward their objectives as institutions through the unifying force of leadership that is willingly followed by free men. Conversely, the continuity of leadership rests with us solely upon meritorious performance. That which is unworthy will inevitably be changed.

It is to this concept of organization through leadership, as distinguished from authoritarian control, that this stimulating book is addressed.

Businessmen will find that it will broaden their intellectual horizons. It will bring them face to face with old ideas which they may have failed to reason through, but of which they have been instinctively aware. They will see familiar concepts brought into sharper focus, and set against a philosophical background. They will sense the importance of goals, for themselves and for their institutions, and will weigh the relationship of a standard of values to institutional performance. They will have a deeper understanding of the amazing resiliency and responsiveness to development in a changing world that the leadership principle provides. They will be encouraged to bring sharp self-criticism to the fulfillment of their daily tasks. They will have better insight into why they do what they do, and will advance toward the creation of their own philosophy of leadership.

CLARENCE B. RANDALL

May 24, 1957

Preface

This essay outlines a perspective for the study of leadership in administrative organizations. It was written in the conviction that more reflective, theoretical discussion is needed to guide the gathering of facts and the diagnosis of troubles. This subject, like the larger study of government and society, requires our profoundest intellectual concern. We shall not find any simple prescriptions for sound organizational leadership; nor will it be purchased with a bag of tricks and gadgets. It requires nothing less than the proper ordering of human affairs, including the establishment of social order, the determination of public interest, and the defense of critical values. Thus conceived, our inquiry has ancient roots. The main problems and issues have been known for a long time, although they need to be restated for the purposes of administrative theory.

This essay was begun while I was associated with The RAND Corporation, and I am deeply grateful to my former colleagues there for providing a creative and challenging intellectual environment. Many others have also been helpful, especially Chester I. Barnard, Herbert Blumer, Leonard Broom, Burton R. Clark, Martin Diamond, Paul Jacobs, Sheldon L. Messinger, Rollin B. Posey, Gertrude J. Selznick,

Herbert A. Simon, and Harold Stein. The fact that I have included some critical comments on Simon's point of view in no way detracts from my great appreciation for his contribution to our common understanding. I am grateful to Dwight Waldo for his persistent and sympathetic encouragement, and to the late Edward Boehm, who gave generously of his long experience and practical insight.

P. S.

Berkeley, California
November, 1956

Contents

CHAPTER THREE

CHAPTER FOUR

CHAPTER FIVE

ONE

Introduction

The nature and quality of leadership, in the sense of states-manship, is an elusive but persistent theme in the history of ideas. Most writers have centered their attention on *political* statesmen, leaders of whole communities who sit in the high places where great issues are joined and settled. In our time, there is no abatement of the need to continue the great discussion, to learn how to reconcile idealism with expediency, freedom with organization.

But an additional emphasis is necessary. Ours is a pluralist society made up of many large, influential, relatively autonomous groups. The United States government itself consists of independently powerful agencies which do a great deal on their own initiative and are largely self-governing. These, and the institutions of industry, politics, education, and other fields, often command large resources; their leaders are inevitably responsible for the material and psychological well-being of numerous constituents; and they have become increasingly *public* in nature, attached to such interests and dealing with such problems as affect the welfare of the entire community. In our society the need for statesmanship is widely diffused and beset by special problems. An understanding of leadership in both public and private organizations must have a high place on the agenda of social inquiry.

The scientific study of large organizations is certainly not neglected. Much has been learned in the fields of industrial management and public administration. Recent years have seen a lively interest in new approaches to scientific management and in the development of a "theory of organization." Among students of political science, sociology, economics, and business administration there is a steady search for fresh ways of looking at organization, for new "models" to help us achieve a better use of human resources and a more adequate understanding of decision-making.

Much of this interest has quite practical roots. The question most often asked or implied is: How can we make our organizations more *efficient?* How can we improve incentives, communication, and decision-making so as to achieve a smoother-running operation? How can we do the job most surely and at the least cost? This is a necessary and reasonable quest, for there is no doubt that most organizations operate at levels well below their potential capacity.

But does a preoccupation with administrative efficiency lead us to the knottiest and most significant problems of leadership in large organizations? Should efficiency be the central concern of the president of a university or a large business, the head of a government agency or the director of a voluntary association? Are we getting at what is truly basic in the experience of institutional leaders? Are we helping to improve the self-knowledge—and thereby the competence—of men charged with leadership responsibilities? Are we able to link the development of managerial skills to the larger problems of policy? This essay is an attempt to deal with these questions by exploring the nature of critical decisions and of institutional leadership.

As we ascend the echelons of administration, the analysis of decision-making becomes increasingly difficult, not simply because the decisions are more important or more complex, but because a new "logic" emerges. The logic of efficiency applies most clearly to subordinate units, usually having rather clearly defined operating responsibilities, limited discretion, set communication channels, and a sure position in the command structure. At these lower levels we may expect to find effective use of rather simple devices for increasing efficiency and control; and it is here that scientific techniques of observation and experiment are likely to be most advanced and most successful.

The logic of efficiency loses force, however, as we approach the top of the pyramid. Problems at this level are more resistant to the ordinary approach of management experts. Mechanical metaphors—the organization as a "smooth running machine"—suggest an overemphasis on neat organization and on efficient techniques of administration. It is probable that these emphases induce in the analyst a trained incapacity to observe the interrelation of policy and administration, with the result that the really critical experience of organizational leadership is largely overlooked. This may explain the coolness with which organizational studies are often received by leading administrators, particularly when these studies deal with top command and staff areas. Much of this coolness undoubtedly stems from a natural reaction against proposed changes which may threaten vested interests. Yet there is also a feeling among administrators that the studies offered are naïve and irrelevant, perhaps because they apply a logic which does not adequately reflect the real problems that the administrator himself must face.

The search for a fresh approach to administration has led to a considerable interest in "human relations." This interest has brought about a wider understanding of why people work and how they get along together, particularly in small-scale group settings. The characteristics of small groups, especially the psychological aspects of communication and perception, have received much emphasis. There is no doubt that this work can and does tell us much about the human problems of participation in organizations. But the observer of large enterprises, if he tries to see them whole, is left with a sense of inadequacy. He feels a need to look beyond personal relations to the larger patterns of institutional development. Yet he knows also that no social process can be understood save as it is located in the behavior of individuals, and especially in their perceptions of themselves and each other. The problem is to link the larger view to the more limited one, to see how institutional change is produced by, and in turn shapes, the interaction of individuals in day-to-day situations. The closer we get to the areas of far-reaching decision, the greater is the need for this deeper and more comprehensive understanding of social organization.

The argument of this essay is quite simply stated: *The executive becomes a statesman as he makes the transition from administrative management to institutional leadership.*

This shift entails a reassessment of his own tasks and of the needs of the enterprise. It is marked by a concern for the evolution of the organization as a whole, including its changing aims and capabilities. In a word, it means viewing the organization as an institution. To understand the nature of institutional leadership, we must have some notion of the meaning and significance of the term "institution" itself.

Organizations and Institutions

The most striking and obvious thing about an administrative organization is its formal system of rules and objectives. Here tasks, powers, and procedures are set out according to some officially approved pattern. This pattern purports to say how the work of the organization is to be carried on, whether it be producing steel, winning votes, teaching children, or saving souls. The organization thus designed is a technical instrument for mobilizing human energies and directing them toward set aims. We allocate tasks, delegate authority, channel communication, and find some way of co-ordinating all that has been divided up and parceled out. All this is conceived as an exercise in engineering; it is governed by the related ideals of rationality and discipline.

The term "organization" thus suggests a certain bareness, a lean, no-nonsense system of consciously co-ordinated activities.[1] It refers to an *expendable tool,* a rational instrument engineered to do a job. An "institution," on the other hand, is more nearly a natural product of social needs and pressures—a responsive, adaptive organism. This distinction is a matter of analysis, not of direct description. It does not

[1] C. I. Barnard, *The Functions of the Executive* (Cambridge: Harvard University Press, 1938), p. 73.

mean that any given enterprise must be either one or the other. While an extreme case may closely approach either an "ideal" organization or an "ideal" institution, most living associations resist so easy a classification. They are complex mixtures of both designed and responsive behavior.

When we say that the Standard Oil Company or the Department of Agriculture is to be studied as an institution, we usually mean that we are going to pay some attention to its history and to the way it has been influenced by the social environment. Thus we may be interested in how its organization adapts itself to existing centers of power in the community, often in unconscious ways; from what strata of society its leadership is drawn and how this affects policy; how it justifies its existence ideologically. We may ask what underlying need in the larger community—not necessarily expressed or recognized by the people involved—is filled by the organization or by some of its practices. Thus, the phrase "as a social institution" suggests an emphasis on problems and experiences that are not adequately accounted for within the narrower framework of administrative analysis.

Perhaps a classic example is the analysis of a political constitution as an institution. In such an inquiry the social and cultural conditions (class structure, traditional patterns of loyalty, educational level, etc.) that affect its viability are studied. We see how the formal charter is given life and meaning by the informal "social constitution" in which it is imbedded. When the latter is absent, the constitution is likely to be weak and ineffective. Giving life to a constitution is partly a matter of achieving general consensus regarding proper ways of winning power and making laws.

But much more is also involved. The working of the American constitutional order cannot readily be grasped without understanding the function of the party system in accommodating diverse interests, in blunting the edge of ideological conflicts, in winning for the community a progressive erasure of old issues as new ones arise. Proposals to change the parties into single-minded ideological instruments strike at the institutional basis of the political order. These and similar problems have long been recognized. It is important, however, to make the transition from these great constitutional issues to the less dramatic problems of administration that also arise from the interplay of formal or legal systems and their social environments.

An awareness of the social setting of administrative activity goes beyond "public relations." The latter phrase suggests practices that leave the organization intact, essentially what it has always been, using routine devices for smoothing over difficulties with groups on whom it is dependent. Indeed, much is accomplished in this way. But when an enterprise begins to be more profoundly aware of dependence on outside forces, its very conception of itself may change, with consequences for recruitment, policy, and administrative organization at many levels. As a business, a college, or a government agency develops a distinctive clientele, the enterprise gains the stability that comes with a secure source of support, an easy channel of communication. At the same time, it loses flexibility. The process of institutionalization has set in.

The relation of an organization to the external environment is, however, only one source of institutional experience. There is also an internal social world to be considered. An organization is a group of living human beings. The formal or official design for living never completely accounts for what the participants do. It is always supplemented by what is called the "informal structure," which arises as the individual brings into play his own personality, his special problems and interests. Formal relations co-ordinate roles or specialized activities, not persons. Rules apply to foremen and machinists, to clerks, sergeants, and vice-presidents, yet no durable organization is able to hold human experience to these formally defined roles. In actual practice, men tend to interact as many-faceted persons, adjusting to the daily round in ways that spill over the neat boundaries set by their assigned roles.

The formal, technical system is therefore never more than a part of the living enterprise we deal with in action. The persons and groups who make it up are not content to be treated as manipulable or expendable. As human beings and not mere tools they have their own needs for self-protection and self-fulfillment—needs that may either sustain the formal system or undermine it. These human relations are a great reservoir of energy. They may be directed in constructive ways toward desired ends or they may become recalcitrant sources of frustration. One objective of sound management practice is to direct and control these internal social pressures.

The relations outlined on an organization chart provide a framework within which fuller and more spontaneous human behavior takes place. The formal system may draw upon that behavior for added strength; it will in its turn be subordinated to personal and group egotism. Every official and employee will try to use his position to satisfy his psychological needs. This may result in a gain for the organization if he accepts its goals and extends himself in its interests. But usually, even in the best circumstances, some price is paid in organizational rigidity.

Similarly, when a technically devised organizational unit becomes a social group—a unity of persons rather than of technicians—newly deployable energy is created; but this, too, has inherently divisive and frustrating potentialities. For the unity of persons breaks through the neat confines of rational organization and procedure; it creates new strivings, primarily for the protection of group integrity, that exert an unceasing influence on the formal pattern of delegation and control. This search for security and fulfillment is reflected in the struggle of individuals for place and preferment, in rivalry among units within the organization, and in commitment to ingrained ways of behaving. These are universal features of organizational life, and the problems they raise are perennial ones.

Of these problems, organizational rivalry may be the most important. Such rivalry mobilizes individual egotism while binding it to group goals. This may create a powerful force, threatening the unity of the larger enterprise. Hence it is that within every association there is the same basic constitutional problem, the same need for an accommodative balance between fragmentary group interests and the aims of the whole, as exists in any polity. The problem is aggravated in a special-purpose enterprise because the aims of the whole are more sharply defined, and therefore more vulnerable to divisive activity, than in the natural community.

Organizational rivalry has received a great deal of attention in connection with efforts to unify the United States military establishment. This case is especially instructive, because throughout the discussion the positive value of competition among military agencies has been emphasized. The rivalry in question here does not pertain primarily to combat or low-echelon units, but rather to "headquarters" competition involving the struggle for funds and prestige among the services.

What arrangements, it is asked, will best protect legitimate competition among military services, yet maintain the needed integration of strategic and tactical planning? This broad question depends in turn on others: Who are the key participants in various kinds of organizational rivalry? Of what value is integrated training and should it take place at low levels or at high levels in the command structure? Do weak technical services need special protection against stronger rivals? What can this protection consist of? These and many similar "constitutional" problems arise because of the natural tendency for parochial, self-protective interests of subordinate individuals and groups to be given an undue priority. As in all constitution-making, the problem is to fit this spontaneously generated competition into a framework that will hold it to the interests of the whole.

Once we turn our attention to the emergence of natural social processes within a formal association, and the pressure of these on policy, we are quickly led to a wide range of interesting questions. Thus, the tendency for a group to develop fixed ways of perceiving itself and the world, often unconsciously, is of considerable importance. With this sort of problem in mind, a study of a military intelligence agency, for example, can go beyond the more routine aspects of administrative efficiency. The study should also consider whether any institutional factors affect the ability of the agency *to ask the right questions*. Are its questions related to a general outlook, a tacit image of itself and its task? Is this image tradition-bound? Is it conditioned by long-established organizational practices? Is there a self-restricted outlook due to insecurities that motivate a safe (but narrow and compartmentalized) concept of military intelligence? A study of these problems would explore the conditions under which organizational self-protection induces *withdrawal* from rivalry rather than participation in it. More needs to be known about such pathological withdrawal for it, too—no less than excessive rivalry itself—may frustrate the rational development of organizations and programs.

The dynamics of organizational rivalry—not the mere documentation of its existence—has received very little systematic attention. This is a good example of an area of experience not adequately accounted for within the conceptual framework of administrative analysis. Organizational struggles are usually thought of as adventitious and subversive. This outlook inhibits the development of a body of knowledge *about* organizational rivalry, e.g., stating the conditions and consequences of factional victory, defeat, and withdrawal, or indicating the way external pressures on an organization are reflected in internal controversy.

A similar sensitivity to internal social needs is assumed when we raise the issue in an even more delicate form: Does the conventional organization of military services according to distinctive weapons result in the espousal of self-serving strategies? If there is an intimate relation between strategy and capability, then the strategically unguided development of weapons may create ultimately undesirable commitments to strategies that depend on these weapons. Is it not worth inquiring whether the ability to adapt military planning—including, especially, research and development—to politically significant goals is not inhibited by this organization of the services? The tendency to emphasize methods rather than goals is an important source of disorientation in all organizations. It has the value of stimulating full development of these methods, but it risks loss of adaptability and sometimes results in a radical substitution of means for ends. Leaders may feel more secure when they emphasize the exploitation of technical potentialities, but the difficult task of defining goals and adapting methods to them may be unfulfilled. This is so because the definition of goals requires an appraisal of many co-ordinate objectives —for example, political as well as military—whereas technical development can be more comfortably single-minded.

Taking account of both internal and external social forces, institutional studies emphasize the *adaptive* change and evolution of organizational forms and practices. In these studies the story is told of new patterns emerging and old ones declining, not as a result of conscious design but as natural and largely unplanned adaptations to new situations. The most interesting and perceptive analyses of this type show the organization responding to a problem posed by its history, an adaptation significantly changing the role and character of the organization. Typically, institutional analysis sees legal or formal changes as recording and regularizing an evolution that has already been substantially completed informally.

Thus the emergence of the Operations Division as General Marshall's command post, eclipsing other sections of the General Staff, is an important theme in Cline's institutional history of that agency.[2] In this work we see the contending forces, the changing problems of command, the informal accommodations of interest and power, all contributing to a developing pattern that was largely "in the cards." A similar study of the present Joint Chiefs of Staff organization would attempt to discern the direction of its evolution, keeping in mind as a hypothesis the potential emergence of a single chief for all the services. Such an analysis of a Research and Development Board would take account of the inherent instability of advisory bodies, the pressures for integration into the military command structure and for providing an immediate operational pay-off, as well as the possibilities of allaying these pressures without sacrificing the basic character of the agency.[3] Throughout, emphasis is on the group processes at work—how they generate new problems and force new adaptations.

This emphasis on adaptive change suggests that in attempting to understand large and relatively enduring organizations we must draw upon what we know about natural communities. In doing so we are led to consider such matters as the following:

[2] Ray S. Cline, *Washington Command Post: The Operations Division* (Washington, D.C.: Office of the Chief of Military History, Department of the Army, 1951).

[3] Although realistic studies of such organizations are not readily feasible (though not excluded) even at much lower echelons, historical analyses of similar but less "sensitive" agencies can provide a more adequate basis for organization planning. A program of case studies, guided by theoretical sophistication and alertness to significant problems, can provide the data needed. An important beginning along these lines has been made by the Inter-University Case Program under the direction of Harold Stein. See his *Public Administration and Policy Development* (New York: Harcourt, Brace, 1952).

1. The development of administrative ideologies as conscious and unconscious devices of communication and self-defense. Just as doctrinal orthodoxies help natural communities to maintain social order, so, too, in administrative agencies, technical programs and procedures are often elaborated into official "philosophies." These help to build a homogeneous staff and ensure institutional continuity. Sometimes they are created and manipulated self-consciously, but most administrative ideologies emerge in spontaneous and unplanned ways, as natural aids to organizational security. A well-formulated doctrine is remarkably handy for boosting internal morale, communicating the bases for decisions, and rebuffing outside claims and criticisms.

2. The creation and protection of elites. In the natural community elites play a vital role in the creation and protection of values.[4] Similarly, in organizations, and especially those that have or strive for some special identity, the formation of elites is a practical problem of the first importance. Specialized academies, selective recruiting, and many other devices help to build up the self-consciousness and the confidence of present and potential leaders. However, again as in the natural community, counter-pressures work to break down the insulation of these elites and to warp their self-confidence. A problem of institutional leadership, as of statesmanship generally, is to see that elites do exist and function while inhibiting their tendency to become sealed off and to be more concerned with their own fate than with that of the enterprise as a whole. One answer, as in the Catholic Church, is to avoid selectivity in the *choice* of leaders while emphasizing intensive indoctrination in their

[4] See pp. 119–130.

training. The whole problem of leadership training, and more generally of forming and maintaining elites, should receive a high priority in scientific studies of organization and policy.

3. The emergence of contending interest-groups, many of which bid for dominant influence in society. The simple protection of their identity, and the attempt to control the conditions of existence, stimulate the normal push and pull of these groups; and the bid for social dominance is reflected in the crises that signify underlying shifts in the distribution of power. The same natural processes go on within organizations, often stimulating the rivalry of formal administrative units, sometimes creating factions that cut across the official lines of communication and command. Here, too, there is normal day-to-day contention, and there is the attempt to become the dominant or "senior" unit, as when a personnel department replaces an accounting division as the source from which general managers are recruited; or when a sales organization comes to dominate the manufacturing organization in product design. These changes cannot, however, be accounted for as simply the products of bureaucratic maneuver. The outcome of the contest is conditioned by a shift in the character and role of the enterprise. Many internal controversies, although stimulated by rather narrow impulses, provide the channels through which broader pressures on the organization are absorbed.

The natural tendencies cited here—the development of defensive ideologies, the dependence of institutional values on the formation and sustaining of elites, the existence of internal conflicts expressing group interests—only illustrate the many elements that combine to form the social structure of an organization. Despite their diversity, these forces have a unified effect. In their operation we see the way group values are formed, for together they define the commitments of the organization and give it a distinctive identity. In other words, to the extent that they are natural communities, organizations have a history; and this history is com- pounded of discernible and repetitive modes of responding to internal and external pressures. As these responses crystal- lize into definite patterns, a social structure emerges. The more fully developed its social structure, the more will the organization become valued for itself, not as a tool but as an institutional fulfillment of group integrity and aspira- tion.

Institutionalization is a *process*. It is something that hap- pens to an organization over time, reflecting the organi- zation's own distinctive history, the people who have been in it, the groups it embodies and the vested interests they have created, and the way it has adapted to its environment. For purposes of this essay, the following point is of special importance: The degree of institutionalization depends on how much leeway there is for personal and group interac- tion. The more precise an organization's goals, and the more specialized and technical its operations, the less op- portunity will there be for social forces to affect its develop- ment. A university has more such leeway than most busi- nesses, because its goals are less clearly defined and it can give more free play to internal forces and historical adapta- tion. But no organization of any duration is completely free of institutionalization. Later we shall argue that leadership is most needed among those organizations, and in those periods of organizational life, where there is most freedom from the determination of decisions by technical goals and methods.

In what is perhaps its most significant meaning, "to institutionalize" is to *infuse with value* beyond the technical requirements of the task at hand. The prizing of social machinery beyond its technical role is largely a reflection of the unique way in which it fulfills personal or group needs. Whenever individuals become attached to an organization or a way of doing things as persons rather than as technicians, the result is a prizing of the device for its own sake. From the standpoint of the committed person, the organization is changed from an expendable tool into a valued source of personal satisfaction. Some manifestations of this process are quite obvious; others are less easily recognized. It is a commonplace that administrative changes are difficult when individuals have become habituated to and identified with long-established procedures. For example, the shifting of personnel is inhibited when business relations become personal ones and there is resistance to any change that threatens rewarding ties. A great deal of energy in organizations is expended in a continuous effort to preserve the rational, technical, impersonal system against such counter-pressures.

Less generally recognized is the effect of this personal involvement on the rational choice of methods and goals. We have already hinted at the importance of "self-images" in, say, restricting the outlook of military-intelligence and similar agencies. These self-images are natural products of organizational experience. They provide the individual with an ordered approach to his day-to-day problems, a way of responding to the world consistently yet involuntarily, in accordance with approved perspectives yet without continuous reference to explicit and formalized rules. This consistent outlook or orientation is indicated when organizational names are applied to individuals as labels for characteristic ways of thinking and working, as when we speak of a "regular army" or a "Foreign Service" man. By long habituation, sometimes also as a result of aggressive indoctrination, the individual absorbs a way of perceiving and evaluating his experience. This reduces his anxiety by lending the world of fact a familiar cast; and it helps assure an easy conformity with established practice.

As in the case of all institutionalization, the development and transmission of self-images is useful but potentially frustrating. To mold the minds of individuals according to a definite pattern creates a homogeneous organization, and this is an enormous aid to communication. A broad context of "understood" meanings ensures that in the performance of assigned tasks the spirit as well as the letter will be observed. Similarly, emotional identification with the organization creates resources of energy that may increase day-to-day effort and, especially, be summoned in times of crisis or threat. But these commitments are costly. They bind the organization to specific aims and procedures, often greatly limiting the freedom of the leadership to deploy its resources, and reducing the capacity of the organization to survive under new conditions.

The test of infusion with value is *expendability*. If an organization is merely an instrument, it will be readily altered or cast aside when a more efficient tool becomes available. Most organizations are thus expendable. When value-infusion takes place, however, there is a resistance to change. People feel a sense of personal loss; the "identity" of the group or community seems somehow to be violated; they bow to economic or technological considerations only reluctantly, with regret. A case in point is the perennial effort to save San Francisco's cable cars from replacement by more economical forms of transportation. The Marine Corps has this institutional halo, and it resists administrative measures that would submerge its identity. In 1950, President Truman became irritated with political pressure favoring Marine Corps membership on the Joint Chiefs of Staff. He wrote a letter calling the Marines the Navy's "police force" and likening their "propaganda machine" to Stalin's. This raised a storm of protest which ended with a presidential apology.

From the standpoint of social systems rather than persons, organizations become infused with value as they come to symbolize the community's aspirations, its sense of identity. Some organizations perform this function more readily and fully than others. An organization that does take on this symbolic meaning has some claim on the community to avoid liquidation or transformation on purely technical or economic grounds. The Marine Corps has this halo far more than other military units and is correspondingly less expendable.

All this is a relative matter and one of degree. With respect to the national community most of the many thousands of organizations in the country are not highly valued for themselves, although certain principles on which they are based, such as free speech or competition, may have deep cultural roots. On the other hand, special groups, such as college alumni, are often urged to keep some organization from dying for lack of support. For the group that participates directly in it, an organization may acquire much institutional value, yet in the eyes of the larger community the organization may be readily expendable.

Both personal and social commitments combine to weaken the purely technical significance of organizations. Beginning as a tool, the organization derives added meaning from the psychological and social functions it performs. In doing so it becomes valued for itself. To be sure, the personal and group bonds that make for institutionalization are not wholly separable. As the individual works out his special problems, seeking his own satisfactions, he helps to tie the organization into the community's institutional network. Personal incentives may spark this absorption, and provide the needed energy; but its character and direction will be shaped by values already existent in the community at large. Similarly, although organizational controversy may be directly motivated by narrow personal and group aims, the contending programs usually reflect ideological differences in the larger arena. In this way, the internal struggle for power becomes a channel through which external environmental forces make themselves felt. This is, indeed, a classic function of the American political party system; but less formal and recognized groupings within administrative organizations follow the same pattern. Organizations do not so much create values as embody them. As this occurs, the organization becomes increasingly institutionalized.

The transformation of expendable technical organizations into institutions is marked by a *concern for self-maintenance*.

A living association blends technical aims and procedures with personal desires and group interests. As a result, various elements in the association have a stake in its continued existence. Moreover, the aims of the organization may require a certain permanence and stability. There is a need to accommodate internal interests and adapt to outside forces, in order to maintain the organization as a "going concern," minimize risks, and achieve long-run as well as short-run objectives. An important sign of this development is that the leaders become security-conscious and are often willing to sacrifice quick returns for the sake of stability. The history of the labor movement is replete with efforts to win union security through provisions for compulsory membership and automatic deduction of dues payments from wages. These objectives look to the long-run maintenance of the union rather than to immediate gains for the members.

There is a close relation between "infusion with value" and "self-maintenance." As an organization acquires a self, a distinctive identity, it becomes an institution. This involves the taking on of values, ways of acting and believing that are deemed important for their own sake. From then on self-maintenance becomes more than bare organizational survival; it becomes a struggle to preserve the uniqueness of the group in the face of new problems and altered circumstances.

To summarize: organizations are technical instruments, designed as means to definite goals. They are judged on engineering premises; they are expendable. Institutions, whether conceived as groups or practices, may be partly engineered, but they have also a "natural" dimension. They are products of interaction and adaptation; they become the receptacles of group idealism; they are less readily expendable.

Some Premises about Leadership

Leadership is not a familiar, everyday idea, as readily available to common sense as to social science. It is a slippery phenomenon that eludes them both. What leaders do is hardly self-evident. And it is likely that much failure of leadership results from an inadequate understanding of its true nature and tasks. Most of this essay will be devoted to identifying and analyzing the chief functions of institutional leadership. By way of introduction, however, it may be helpful to state a few simple guiding ideas here.

1. *Leadership is a kind of work done to meet the needs of a social situation.* Possibly there are some individuals more likely to be leaders than others, possessed of distinguishing personal traits or capacities.[5] Whether or not this is so, we shall here be concerned with leadership as a specialized form of activity, a kind of work or function. Identifying what leaders do certainly bears on (and is perhaps indispensable to) the discovery of requisite personal attributes; but the questions are of a different kind and may be treated separately.

To know the nature of the work done by leaders, we must know something about the social situations they are called upon to handle. This immediately suggests that there must

[5] This problem has received considerable attention, with largely negative but still inconclusive results. See Ralph M. Stogdill, "Personal Factors Associated with Leadership: A Survey of the Literature," *J. Psychology*, 1948, **25**: 35–71; also William O. Jenkins, "A Review of Leadership Studies with Particular Reference to Military Problems," *Psychological Bulletin*, 1947, **44**: 54–77.

be a very wide variety of activities associated with leadership.[6] However, it does not follow that the *nature* of leadership varies with each social situation. If that were so, there would be nothing determinate about it; its study would be a scientific blind alley. In fact, of course, we must assume that significant leadership patterns are relatively few; and that these patterns are related to *types* of social situations. This means that certain very general activities of leaders— e.g., facilitating communication within the group—reflect equally general characteristics of all human groups; and that the functions of leadership will be understood only as we develop a better understanding of the main types of groups and the recurrent problems they face. In other words, a theory of leadership is dependent on a theory of social organization.

We shall not be concerned here with all leadership, but with leadership in large-scale organizations. This will require some consideration of the nature of such enterprises, including the characteristic problems that arise within them.

[6] Indeed, the current literature on this subject, in part as a reaction against the "trait" approach, in part due to the influence of "situational" or "field" theory in social psychology, has made this a central conclusion. Thus Jenkins, *op. cit.,* p. 75, finds: "Leadership is specific to the particular situation under investigation. Who becomes the leader of a given group engaging in a particular activity and what the leadership characteristics are in the given case are a function of the specific situation, including the measuring instruments employed. There is a wide variation in the characteristics of individuals who became leaders in similar situations, and even greater divergence in leadership in different situations." But note the following by Stogdill, *op. cit.,* p. 65: "The evidence suggests that leadership is a relation that exists between persons in a social situation, and that persons who are leaders in one situation may not necessarily be leaders in other situations. Must it then be assumed that leadership is entirely incidental, haphazard, and unpredictable? Not at all. The very studies which provide the strongest arguments for the situational nature of leadership also supply the strongest evidence indicating that leadership patterns as well as non-leadership patterns of behavior are persistent and relatively stable."

It will be necessary to understand the institutional aspects of large-scale organizations, for the central argument will stress the close connection between these aspects and the key functions of leadership. Although institutional leadership must share the general characteristics of all leadership, we shall not deal with the latter problem directly.

2. *Leadership is not equivalent to office-holding or high prestige or authority or decision-making.* It is not helpful to identify leadership with whatever is done by people in high places. The activity we have in mind may or may not be engaged in by those who are formally in positions of authority. This is inescapable if we are to develop a theory that will be useful in diagnosing cases of inadequate leadership on the part of persons in authority. If this view is correct, it means that only some (and sometimes none) of the activities of decision-makers are leadership activities. Here again, understanding leadership requires understanding of a broader social process. If some types of decisions are more closely related to leadership activities than others, we should learn what they are. To this end in this analysis let us make a distinction between "routine" and "critical" decision-making.

3. *Leadership is dispensable.* The word "leadership" has its own halo, easily inviting the tacit assumption that, being a good thing, it is always in order. It may indeed be that all human groups require at all times *some* leadership activities. But if leadership is anything determinate, we should know how to distinguish its presence from its absence; similarly, if there are some social situations that especially require leadership, we should know how to tell them apart from other social situations. The idea is de-

veloped in this essay that leadership is not equally necessary in all large-scale organizations, or in any one at all times, and that it becomes dispensable as the natural processes of institutionalization become eliminated or controlled. This will provide some clues to the general conditions that call for leadership decisions.

These premises emphasize the futility of attempting to understand leadership apart from the broader organizational experience of which it is a phase. A theory of leadership will necessarily reflect the level of sophistication we have reached in the study of organization. We are dealing with an activity, with a function, with work done; we can make no more sense of it than is allowed by our understanding of the field within which that activity takes place.

The Default of Leadership

When institutional leadership fails, it is perhaps more often by default than by positive error or sin. Leadership is lacking when it is needed; and the institution drifts, exposed to vagrant pressures, readily influenced by short-run opportunistic trends. This default is partly a failure of nerve, partly a failure of understanding. It takes nerve to hold a course; it takes understanding to recognize and deal with the basic sources of institutional vulnerability.

One type of default is the failure to set goals. Once an organization becomes a "going concern," with many forces working to keep it alive, the people who run it can readily escape the task of defining its purposes. This evasion stems partly from the hard intellectual labor involved, a labor that often seems but to increase the burden of already onerous daily operations. In part, also, there is the wish to avoid conflicts with those in and out of the organization who would be threatened by a sharp definition of purpose, with its attendant claims and responsibilities. Even business firms find it easy to fall back on conventional phrases, such as that "our goal is to make profit," phrases which offer little guidance in the formulation of policy.

A critique of leadership, we shall argue, must include this emphasis on the leader's responsibility to define the mission of the enterprise. This view is not new. It is important because so much of administrative analysis takes the goal of the organization as given, whereas in many crucial instances this is precisely what is problematic. We shall also suggest that the analysis of goals is itself dependent on an understanding of the organization's social structure. In other words, the purposes we have or can have depend on what we are or what we can be. In statesmanship no less than in the search for personal wisdom, the Socratic dictum—know thyself—provides the ultimate guide.

Another type of default occurs when goals, however neatly formulated, enjoy only a superficial acceptance and do not genuinely influence the total structure of the enterprise. Truly accepted values must infuse the organization at many levels, affecting the perspectives and attitudes of personnel, the relative importance of staff activities, the distribution of authority, relations with outside groups, and many other matters. Thus if a large corporation asserts a wish to change its role in the community from a narrow emphasis on profit-making to a larger social responsibility (even though the ultimate goal remains some combination of survival and profit-making ability), it must explore the implications of such a change for decision-making in a wide variety of organizational activities. We shall stress that the task of building special values and a distinctive competence into the organization is a prime function of leadership.

In this sense, the leader is an agent of institutionalization, offering a guiding hand to a process that would otherwise occur more haphazardly, more readily subject to the accidents of circumstance and history. This is not to say that the leader is free to do as he wishes, to mold the organization according to his heart's desire, restrained only by the quality of his imagination and the strength of his will. Self-knowledge means knowledge of limits as well as of potentialities.

The default of leadership shows itself in an acute form when *organizational* achievement or survival is confounded with *institutional* success. To be sure, no institutional leader can avoid concern for the minimum conditions of continued organizational existence. But he fails if he permits sheer organizational achievement, in resources, stability, or reputation, to become the criterion of his success. A university led by administrators without a clear sense of values to be achieved may fail dismally while steadily growing larger and more secure.

Finally, the role of the institutional leader should be clearly distinguished from that of the "interpersonal" leader. The latter's task is to smooth the path of human interaction, ease communication, evoke personal devotion, and allay anxiety. His expertness has relatively little to do with content; he is more concerned with persons than with policies.

His main contribution is to the efficiency of the enterprise. The institutional leader, on the other hand, *is primarily an expert in the promotion and protection of values.* The interpretation that follows takes this idea as a starting point, exploring its meaning and implications.

TWO

Routine and Critical Decisions

"Decision-making" is one of those fashionable phrases that may well obscure more than it illuminates. It has an air of significance, of reference to important events; and the mere use of the phrase seems to suggest that something definite has been scientifically isolated. But decisions are with us always, at every level of experience, in every organism. The general features of all choice, or of all social choice, may some day be convincingly stated. But it will still be necessary to distinguish the more and the less trivial; and, if there is any order in this phenomenon, to identify some kinds of decision, linking them to the distinctive problems or situations out of which they arise. Here we are concerned with leadership in large organizations. Is there a special kind of experience that underlies and prompts leadership decisions?

A Psychological Analogy

Let us consider the work of two psychologists, each a student of individual behavior. One of these directs his attention to what may be called "routine" psychological processes. He is biologically oriented, usually experimental in method, and interested in the basic psychophysical aspects of behavior. He belongs to the group of psychologists most closely associated with "human engineering," developing useful information on tolerance levels, error, learning, and such related matters as affect the responses of all human beings, in measurable ways, to various types of work and control situations.

Our second man is called a "clinical" psychologist. This term refers directly to method but indirectly to subject-matter. The clinical psychologist is interested in such matters as emotional development and character structure. The methods he uses, such as the depth interview and projective tests, are more obscure and uncertain than those of the experimental psychologist, though the methodological gap is closing. He is more likely to be concerned with disorders, especially those that are "functional" rather than somatic. Above all, the clinical psychologist is distinguished by an interest in the change and growth of total personalities. To the extent that he is concerned with somatic processes, it is not for their own sake, but only as they bear on problems of emotion and character.

The difference between these two broad areas of psychological inquiry is not accidental. The needs of theory and practice created it. But this does not mean that the boundaries are hard and fast. And there are some signs that the difference will ultimately be erased. Our purpose is not to enter the debate among psychologists but to learn from it. This lesson may be that a similar evolution can be expected in the study of organization and decision-making.

The literature of organization analysis is largely concerned with routine processes. "Routine" need not mean unimportant, nor lacking in research interest. Rather, it refers to the solution of day-to-day problems for their own sake. Studies of communication and command channels, work simplification, personnel selection, morale-building techniques, team organization, conference methods, and similar matters, are of this sort. They have to do with the conditions necessary to keep organizations running at efficient levels. They are "technical" in the sense that experts may be employed (and usually are, in large organizations) to take care of these functions, and, indeed, to make them routine. It is in this area that experimental methods are most applicable since small groups of employees may be studied within a controlled design. Here the emphasis is on orderly process, on smooth functioning.

Routine functions include not only the older techniques of management but also those born of the newer "human relations" perspective. We learn from the latter that authority and communication must be broadly understood to take account of the social psychology of obedience, perception, and co-operation. This is the burden of much new thinking and research on organization, including such major contributions as C. I. Barnard's *The Functions of the Executive,* as well as the more experimental studies of group dynamics specialists in social psychology.

If we search for the proper counterpart of the clinical psychologist in organization studies, we shall not find him among the human relations experts. Nothing in the logic of their approach turns them to *the dynamic .adaptation of the total organization to internal strivings and external pressures.* But it is just such a "dynamic adaptation" of total personality that defines the main interest of the "clinical" psychologist, particularly if he accepts psychoanalytic premises.[1] Let us inspect the key terms of this formulation a bit more closely, especially the words "dynamic" and "total."

Psychoanalysis is referred to as "dynamic" psychology because it "explains mental phenomena as the result of the interaction and counteraction of forces."[2] This general emphasis on inner need, environmental pressure, and a mediating structure, is shared by other related psychologies, but the Freudians have developed the most complete model. In this view, the personality is an adaptive, equilibrium-seeking organism; but this process is not a smooth continuum of adjustment; there are breaks in the continuum, as, in response to threat, there is a turning inward to reconstruct the self, sometimes in pathological ways. The ego, as "mediator between the organism and the outer world,"[3] draws upon a defensive armory to control inner strivings, as in repression, or to alter the relation between organism and environment, as in regressive withdrawal. These "dynamisms," as they are sometimes called, are associated with persistent modifications of the personality; hence they affect future modes of response.

---

[1] This analogy is of course not offered as proof, but as an aid to reflection; nor does the argument require any literal treatment of organizations as "persons." Rather, we may find that personalities and organizations are particular embodiments of the same *type* of natural system, hence may be analyzed with logically similar tools. Reference to "psychoanalytic psychology" here includes all who work with the main tools developed by Freud, not just to the orthodox Freudians.

[2] Otto Fenichel, *The Psychoanalytic Theory of Neurosis* (New York: Norton, 1945), p. 11.

[3] *Ibid.*, p. 16.

Drawing on general psychoanalytic theory, Erich Fromm distinguishes "static" and "dynamic" adaptation:

By static adaptation we mean such an adaptation to patterns as leaves the whole character structure unchanged and implies only the adoption of a new habit. An example of this kind of adaptation is the change from the Chinese habit of eating to the Western habit of using fork and knife. A Chinese coming to America will adapt himself to this new pattern, but this adaptation in itself will have little effect on his personality; it does not arouse new drives or character traits.[4]

This may be compared with the idea of routine psychological processes suggested above. Static adaptation is not static, strictly speaking: it is, one might say, "everyday" dynamics. It is routine learning, and the study of it centers on such factors as motivation, practice, etc. It is ordinary, responsive behavior, subject to such normal tendencies as stimulus generalization. Most human responses are of this routine sort. It is natural that, wherever the training and control of large numbers is involved, as in industrial or military life, the students of these processes will have the major role.

Yet certain critical areas of experience belong to a different realm:

By dynamic adaptation we refer to the kind of adaptation that occurs, for example, when a boy submits to the commands of his strict and threatening father—being too much afraid of him to do otherwise—and becomes a "good" boy. While he adapts himself to the necessities of the situation, something happens in him. He may develop an intense hostility against his father, which he represses, since it would be too dangerous to express

[4] Erich Fromm, *Escape from Freedom* (New York: Rinehart, 1941), p. 15.

it or even to be aware of it. This repressed hostility, however, though not manifest, is a dynamic factor in his character structure. It may create new anxiety and thus lead to still deeper submission; it may set up a vague defiance, directed against no one in particular but rather toward life in general. While here, too, as in the first case, an individual adapts himself to certain external circumstances, this kind of adaptation creates something new in him, arouses new drives and new anxieties. Every neurosis is an example of this dynamic adaptation.[5]

"Dynamic" here connotes more than simple activity, change, or growth. It suggests certain impelling forces that have a quite different origin and role from the routine tissue tensions of hunger, toothache, and sex. In dynamic adaptation, there is no simple one-to-one relation between an isolated stimulus and its response, a particular drive and its satisfaction, even if one accepts the idea that to some degree the total organism is implicated in all responsive behavior. The point is not the degree of involvement, but the reconstruction of need, the change in posture and strategy, the commitment to new types of satisfaction.

The relevance of these remarks for organizational theory is not far to seek. "Static adaptation" occurs in organizations as well as in personalities. The day-to-day functioning of the organization requires the continuous solution of problems. For the most part, the existing structure—both the informal human relations and the more formal patterns of communication and control—is competent to meet issues as they arise *without internal crisis*. As the daily work proceeds, changes occur, but normally these do not significantly affect the nature of the enterprise or its leadership.

[5] *Ibid.*, pp. 15–16.

Even changes in top personnel may not be significant, if succession is orderly and fundamental policy is firmly established. The corporation grinds out sales and products; the union continues its ceaseless round of negotiations; the government agency extends approved services to assigned publics. Within broad limits, we sometimes say, these large organizations "run themselves"; yet we understand that this holds only for routine activity. In organizational life, just as in individual behavior, this routine functioning and adaptation is quantitatively preponderant. And the proper tooling of everyday activity is a legitimate and necessary preoccupation of management.

Yet in organizations, too, it is plainly necessary to focus attention on dynamics, to study less routine kinds of adaptation. There is a vital sector of organizational experience that cannot be understood as simple problem-solving in which the organization remains essentially intact. Rather, in this sector we find such adaptations of leadership to the interplay of internal and external forces as result in basic institutional changes. This is the area of "character-defining" commitments, which affect the organization's capacity to control its own future behavior. The range of discretion becomes limited, often in unanticipated ways; or it may be significantly broadened. For example, a government agency may adapt itself to a potentially hostile clientele by appointing representatives of the clientele to the agency staff. This has far-reaching consequences for policy, and is not understandable as simple "economic" personnel procurement.

In organizations, "dynamic adaptation" takes place in the shadowy area where administration and policy meet. We must take this, not in the obvious sense that administrative devices execute and form policy, but rather in the sense that organizational processes profoundly influence the kinds of policy that can be made, and policy in turn shapes the machinery of organization in ways that cannot be accounted for on the premises of efficient functioning. At the same time, this is precisely the area of "critical experience" upon which we wish to focus.

When we discuss the bearing of military unification on strategy, the social composition of administrative staffs, the restrictive consequences of administrative alliances, the abandonment of old agencies for new ones, the relation of autonomy to the defense of a program, the unorthodox administrative practices of Franklin Roosevelt, and similar matters, we find ourselves outside the area where administration can be made routine. We are squarely in the field where leadership counts and where managerial *expertise* is of secondary importance.

The term "leadership" connotes critical experience rather than routine practice. This is suggested in the following comment by Barnard:

> The overvaluation of the apparatus of communication and administration is opposed to leadership and the development of leaders. It opposes leadership whose function is to promote appropriate adjustment of ends and means to new environmental conditions, because it opposes change either of status in general or of established procedures and habitual routine. This overvaluation also discourages the development of leaders by retarding the progress of the abler men and by putting an excessive premium on routine qualities.[6]

[6] C. I. Barnard, *Organization and Management* (Cambridge: Harvard University Press, 1948), pp. 240 f.

However, it is easy to overemphasize the *personal* element. While personal qualities are important, and reflect differences in self-conception, too much attention to them may obscure the essential distinction. Even the person free of "routine qualities" may in fact be performing a routine function if he devotes his main energy to greasing the wheels of organization, albeit in human terms. In thinking of leadership, we too often have in mind the personal relation of leader and follower, especially as it involves such psychological mechanisms as identification. This emphasis leads us away from the role of leadership in the making of critical decisions.

It is in the realm of policy—including the areas where policy-formation and organization-building meet—that the distinctive quality of institutional leadership is found. Ultimately, this is the quality of statesmanship which deals with current issues, not for themselves alone but according to their long-run implications for the role and meaning of the group. Group leadership is far more than the capacity to mobilize personal support; it is more than the maintenance of equilibrium through the routine solution of everyday problems; it is the function of the leader-statesman—whether of a nation or a private association—to define the ends of group existence, to design an enterprise distinctively adapted to these ends, and to see that that design becomes a living reality. These tasks are not routine; they call for continuous self-appraisal on the part of the leaders; and they may require only a few critical decisions over a long period of time. "Mere speed, frequency, and vigor in coming to decisions may have little relevance at the top executive level, where a man's basic contribution to the enterprise may turn on his making two or three significant decisions a year."[7] This basic contribution is not always aided by the traits often associated with psychological leadership, such as aggressive self-confidence, intuitive sureness, ability to inspire.

The Concept of Organization Character

Our general perspective may be clarified further if we continue the psychological analogy. In particular, the process of "character-formation" seems worth exploring for the insights it may yield to students of institutionalization and critical decision-making. When we have seen the connection between these two phenomena we shall be in a better position to analyze the nature and tasks of institutional leadership.

The idea of "character" as used by personality analysts is not altogether clear, but its usefulness is scarcely in doubt. There seems to be general agreement on four attributes.

First, character is a *historical* product. "The character as a whole," writes Fenichel, "reflects the individual's historical development."[8] Character is the "ego's habitual ways of reacting." In this sense every individual has a unique character.

Second, character is in some sense an *integrated* product, as is suggested by the term "character-structure." There is a discoverable pattern in the way the ego is organized; and the existence of such a pattern is the basis of character analysis.

Third, character is *functional,* in the sense that it is no mere accidental accretion of responsive patterns. Character

[7] E. P. Learned, D. N. Ulrich, and D. R. Booz, *Executive Action,* Harvard University Graduate School of Business Administration, Boston, 1951, p. 57.

[8] Otto Fenichel, *The Psychoanalytic Theory of Neurosis* (New York: Norton, 1945), p. 470.

development fulfills a task set by the requirements of personality organization: the defense of the individual against inner and outer demands which threaten him. "Biologically speaking, character formation is an autoplastic function. In the conflict between instinct and frustrating outer world, and motivated by the anxiety arising from this conflict, the organism erects a protection mechanism between itself and the outer world." [9] Whatever the special content of varying theories of character-formation, they share an emphasis on the *reconstruction of the self* as a way of solving anxiety-laden problems.

Fourth, character is *dynamic* in that it generates new strivings, new needs and problems. It is largely through the identification of these needs that diagnosis proceeds, as when the discovery of excessive dependency or aggressiveness suggests that the patient has a particular type of character-structure.

Now let us compare these attributes of character with the discussion above of how organizations become institutions. The following points were emphasized there:

1. The technical, rational, impersonal, task-oriented formal system (the "organization") is conditioned by the responsive interaction of persons and groups.

2. In the course of time, this responsive interaction is patterned. A social structure is created. This patterning is *historical,* in that it reflects the specific experiences of the particular organization; it is *functional* in that it aids the organization to adapt itself to its internal and external social environment; and it is *dynamic,* in that it generates new and active forces, especially internal interest-groups

[9] Wilhelm Reich, *Character-Analysis,* New York, 1949, p. 159.

made up of men committed to particular jobs or policies.

3. Organizations become institutions as they are *infused with value,* that is, prized not as tools alone but as sources of direct personal gratification and vehicles of group integrity. This infusion produces a distinct identity for the organization. Where institutionalization is well advanced, distinctive outlooks, habits, and other commitments are unified, coloring all aspects of organizational life and lending it a *social integration* that goes well beyond formal co-ordination and command.

The study of organizational character-formation is, then, a phase of institutional analysis. Here the emphasis is on the embodiment of values in an organizational structure through the elaboration of commitments—ways of acting and responding that can be changed, if at all, only at the risk of severe internal crisis. As in the case of individuals, the emergence of organizational character reflects the irreversible element in experience and choice. A great deal of management practice, as in the hiring of personnel, may be viewed as an effort to hold down the number of irreversible decisions that must be made. On the other hand, a wise management will readily limit its own freedom, accepting irreversible commitments, when the basic values of the organization and its direction are at stake. The acceptance of irreversible commitments is the process by which the character of an organization is set.

We have suggested that "critical" experience is closely related to organizational self definition and self-reconstruction. This experience reflects the "open-endedness" of organizational life—the existence of alternative ways of responding and changing. Critical experience calls for leadership.

Experience is less critical, and leadership is more dispensable, when the range of alternatives is limited by rigid technical criteria. The more limited and defined the task, the more readily can technical criteria prevail in decision-making. That is one reason why critical experience increases as we ascend the echelons of administration, where decisions based on broader interests must be made. But when the organization is not so limited, when it has the leeway to respond in alternative ways, there is room for character-formation, which enters to give structure to precisely this area of freedom.[10] Hence leadership, character, and critical decision-making are linked as aspects of the same basic phenomenon: the institutionalization of organizational life.

Perhaps the most obvious indicator of organizational character as a palpable reality is the abandonment of old organizations and the creation of new ones when changes in general orientation seem required. A new program does not always call for a new organization, but where a new point of view is to be embodied, there is often recourse to a fresh start. The fear is that the character of the old organization will create resistances to the full development of the new program. In practical terms, this usually means that the

[10] Cf. Karl W. Deutsch, "Communication in Self-Governing Organizations," in *Freedom and Authority in Our Time* (New York: Harper, 1953): "The importance of memory is the greater, and the effects of its loss the more severe, because a functioning memory implies the probability of eventual *individuation*. Two organizations might set out with exactly the same structure, and yet the different experiences from the outside world would eventually produce different stocks of memories in each, and eventually different kinds of behavior even in the presence of identical stimuli. Then such organizations might function in some respects similarly to individuals with peculiarities of personality; and as their memory-guided behavior might influence their intake of subsequent memories, such organizations might be capable of considerable internal evolution" (p. 275).

new program, even if accepted in good faith, may be threatened by personnel or budgetary procedures, and by many other operating routines that are uncongenial to it. An organization requiring considerable flexibility in personnel practice may find itself seriously hampered as part of a larger enterprise that must, considering the interests of the whole, enforce more rigid standards. Or, where long-established habits of work prevail, a new program may find itself quickly redefined into terms that sustain the received patterns. Issues of this sort were involved when the Roosevelt administration set up many new agencies, as in agriculture, instead of channeling new programs through existing organizations.

Character as Distinctive Competence

In studying character we are interested in the *distinctive competence or inadequacy* that an organization has acquired. In doing so, we look beyond the formal aspects to examine the commitments that have been accepted in the course of adaptation to internal and external pressures.

For purposes of illustration, let us examine briefly two rather different organizational experiences which have been previously investigated and reported, and in which the phenomenon considered here was studied. We may then consider some further applications and theoretical implications.

1. *Policy and character in the TVA experience.* In a study of the Tennessee Valley Authority,[11] the policy of channeling a federal program through local agencies was examined.

[11] Philip Selznick, *TVA and the Grass Roots* (Berkeley and Los Angeles: University of California Press, 1949).

In particular, the agricultural activities of the Authority were carried out in co-operation with the Extension Services of the land-grant colleges in the seven Valley states. This co-operation was extensive; in effect, the Extension Service organizations became the operating arm of the TVA in the agricultural field. In assessing the consequences of this arrangement, it was necessary to inquire into such commitments of the Extension Services as (1) might affect the way in which the TVA agricultural program was administered, and (2) might have a broader influence on policy-making in the TVA as a whole.

The "character" of the Extension Service was reflected in the following set of related commitments: (1) The involvement of the county agricultural agent in "courthouse" politics; (2) the intimate relation between the Extension Service and the American Farm Bureau Federation; (3) a tendency of the extension agents to deal with the relatively more prosperous elements of the local farm population and to reflect certain dominant attitudes, such as those toward farm tenancy; (4) a shift in the role of the Extension Service from a primarily educational emphasis to the acceptance of responsibility for "action" programs. These and related commitments, it was found, significantly affected the ability of the TVA to achieve an agricultural program that would be free of restrictive pressures. In addition, the TVA's commitment to the Extension Service involved it in the national struggle for control of the U.S. agricultural programs, drawing it into the Farm Bureau camp. Further, the commitment created a group *inside* TVA that defended general Extension Service attitudes and objectives and successfully exerted pressure on other TVA programs, e.g., forcing revision of the policy reserving a strip of land around the reservoirs for public access and for recreation and conservation activities.

On the other hand, the TVA purchased a considerable advantage with these concessions. It gained the support of important local interests and of a powerful national lobby. These defended not only the agricultural program but TVA as a whole. In this way, by modifying its agricultural program and certain broad social policies, the Authority was able to ward off threatened dismemberment and to gain time for the successful development of its key activity —the expansion of electric power facilities.

The critical decisions taken here—not necessarily consciously—had little to do with efficient operation as such.[12] They were intimately related to the way the Extension Services had become *institutionalized* and had absorbed commitments to personnel, practices, and group interests. These commitments, taken together, formed the relevant character of the Extension Services. This in turn defined the capacity of these agencies to aid the TVA's adaptation to its area of operations; but it also made them something other than innocent collaborators in the administration of a technical program. Both advantages and disadvantages for

[12] However, even apparently routine matters of administrative procedure had to be assessed against the general background discussed here. Thus the choice between a contractual arrangement that would call for a lump-sum grant by TVA to the colleges, as against reimbursement for detailed items of expenditure, could not be understood apart from the aim of giving the Extension Services maximum freedom. The policy adopted—of reimbursement for detailed items—though superficially suggesting a measure of control by the Authority, in fact was congenial to the loose arrangement desired. A lump-sum grant procedure invites inspection of other kinds of detail, including work planning and fiscal controls within the recipient agency, to say nothing of the possibility of instituting a requirement that the colleges match sums contributed by the TVA to the co-operative program.

TVA derived from the institutional aspects of the Extension Services.

The emergent character of the TVA itself, of course, was significantly influenced by its own interaction with the land-grant college system. As a result of this interaction, the Authority absorbed commitments to an ideology and to specific institutions that modified its role as a New Deal agency.

2. *Bolshevik character-definition.* A study of the Bolshevik type of party also led to the investigation of organizational character-formation.[13] The distinctive competence of the Bolshevik "combat" party lies in its ability to transform members of a voluntary association into disciplined and deployable agents. This requires the building of an organization that can be oriented to the continuous conquest of power in all areas of social life. Such an organization cannot be created by verbal resolutions alone. Special measures must be taken to "Bolshevize" the organization, that is, to see that its own commitments—to structure, personnel, and doctrine—are so firmly set as to be virtually irreversible.

One problem confronting the Communists over a number of years was the repudiating of socialist methods of organization and activity. The Communist organizations were formed as offshoots of the socialist parties. They brought with them a heritage which had to be eradicated if a new type of organization adapted to the continuous struggle for power—especially in industry rather than in the electoral arena—was to be built. These alterations in-

[13] Philip Selznick, *The Organizational Weapon* (New York: McGraw-Hill, 1952).

cluded an overhauling of the party structure itself, to do away with the older territorial divisions adapted to the running of election campaigns, and to substitute a much more flexible party unit capable of facilitating control in key industries. In addition, the older social-democratic attitude toward leadership was changed. The status of the full-time party official was greatly enhanced, and measures were instituted to control middle-class leaders whose life-commitment to the party was not complete. This reorientation could not be simply formal, but demanded a restructuring of the attitudes and actions of the membership. The habits of political activity are not easily altered when established in the course of years of effort; so, too, with the attempt to increase the stature of the full-time official and to alter the relation of the ideological leader to the party. These attitudes toward leadership and proper methods of work help to form the character of the organization as a whole.

Another aspect of organizational character-definition is control over the *social composition* of the membership. It is evident that where the class, family, sectional, or ethnic origins of personnel are uncontrolled, unanticipated consequences for decision-making may ensue. Organizations that are self-conscious about their characters—an officers' corps, an elite school, etc.—normally attempt to control composition by being selective, so that only persons having appropriate social origins are accepted. The Communists are likewise concerned about composition but are not able to be completely selective. As a consequence, they must devise special measures for the reorientation of personnel whose origins may raise doubts as to reliability and utility. Such doubts arise especially in the relation of the party to members recruited from among doctors, writers, teachers, and other professionals. The party meets this organizational problem by *recruiting selectively* among professionals, establishing more rigorous criteria for admission than in the case of industrial workers; by *intensive education,* insisting on a compulsory schedule of indoctrination through discussion groups, party schools, and literature oriented to intellectuals; and by involving the intellectual in *mass work,* e.g., by assigning him to work with a group of Communists in a trade-union, acting as secretary or educational director. These practices reflect the need to shape the commitments of personnel where these are not already established by the individual's earlier life-experience. The problem is especially acute, of course, for any organization, such as the Bolshevik type of party, which seeks to induce an esoteric reorientation and therefore cannot depend on the ordinary machinery of education in the community at large.

The TVA and Bolshevik experiences are of course widely different. Yet in each there is an emergent institutional pattern that decisively affects the competence of an organization to frame and execute desired policies. Commitments to ways of acting and responding are built into the organization. When integrated, these commitments define the "character" of the organization. Of the two cases, the Bolshevik experience is perhaps the more instructive, for it points to a distinctive *type,* not simply a unique accretion of rigidities or capabilities. The Bolshevik type of party has a *generalized* character as well as a historical uniqueness. It is a new *kind* of party, a "combat" party, one capable of deploying members as disciplined agents in a far-flung struggle for power.

The point may be further clarified if we compare the Democratic and Republican parties in the United States. In the same sense that each individual has a unique character, these parties have historically conditioned differences. Though they are different, these parties share significant capabilities and limitations. They are parties of the same *type*—committed to electoral victory in the short run, decentralized, capable of absorbing new ideas and social forces, incapable of making many demands upon a weakly involved party membership.

When we speak of "commitment" here we mean more than merely verbal assent or even ideological attachment. Thus "commitment to the short run" refers to the actual interests of those who man the party organization—their personal stake in victory or defeat. It is conceivable that a long period out of power may shift control of one of the parties into the hands of men who, though they might like to win, do not really have to win. Such men might be able to afford the luxury of losing elections while retaining the comforting purity of the party leadership and its principles. A shift of this kind at the local level would tend to change the nature of the party from a majority-forming agency, receptive to change and compromise, into a more narrowly ideological instrument.

The Bolshevik "combat" party is a different kind of institution. It is not committed to short-run electoral victory; it establishes maximal control over the individual, creating a membership deployable outside of politics proper (e.g., in trade-unions); it achieves a tight doctrinal unity and is incapable of any but tactical accommodations. Though each is a political organization dedicated to the achievement of power, it is impossible without severe distortion to classify the Bolshevik type of party with the parties of Western parliamentarism.

In each of these cases, we have emphasized the emergence of special capabilities and limitations as institutionalization proceeds. And indeed, as a practical matter, the assessment of organizations necessarily scrutinizes this element of competence or disability. During the controversy over military unification referred to above, the Navy Department emerged as the defender of subtle institutional values and tried many times to formulate the distinctive characteristics of the various services. The naval leaders emphasized the special sensitivities each had acquired as a result of long historical development. Thus in the published diary of the first Secretary of Defense we read:

[Gruenther] made the observation that there was a fundamental difference in thinking between Army and Navy on the question of a Staff versus Committee system of arriving at decisions. I concurred, but I said the difference went deeper than that—for example, the vast difference in the conduct of war on land masses and the kind of war that was fought in the Pacific; the inherent organizational differences between Army and Navy derived from the fact that the smallest unit the Army could employ was a division, whereas the Navy was accustomed to operating either a single PT or a task force of a thousand ships, and for that reason had to be flexible. Gruenther admitted that there was this basic difference, both as regards the character of war and the character of organization.[14]

Other Navy spokesmen attempted to distinguish between the Army as a "manpower" organization and the Navy as a finely adjusted system of technical, engineering skills—a "machine-centered" organization. Faced with what it perceived as a mortal threat, the Navy became highly self-conscious about its distinctive competence, although many of the formulations offered had the ring of partisan improvisation.

The idea of distinctive competence is not necessarily restricted to the outcome of an organization's peculiar adaptation to its own special purposes and programs. A somewhat more general competence may develop, as when we say that a firm is good at marketing but less successful in production. Many organizations, though they have different objectives, face similar problems and become adapted to solving those problems. Thus some groups have in common the need to mobilize and control volunteer units, whether for fundraising, political action, or fire-fighting. Analyzing these common problems may yield a better way of classifying organizations than focusing attention on similarities in structure or in aims.

The distinctive competence to do a *kind* of thing is in question when we ask whether an agency is well adapted to carrying out an "action" program. This has little to do with routine administrative efficiency; rather, it reflects the general orientation of personnel, the flexibility of organiza-

[14] Walter Millis (ed.), *The Forrestal Diaries* (New York: Viking, 1951), pp. 314–315. Note also the assessment of general orientation in John J. McCloy's comment on Air Force attitudes toward close air support, quoted herein on p. 72.

tional forms, and the nature of the institutional environment to which the organization is committed. In the mid-thirties, the assessment of the Extension Service's capacity to serve as a field force for new Federal agricultural programs turned on these matters, an assessment that led to the creation of new organizations in the belief that these would be better adapted to an aggressive program of government intervention.

The debate over the Department of State's suitability as a psychological warfare agency has required a similar appraisal, involving such questions as: (*a*) Does the training of Foreign Service officers result in a passive orientation, a disposition to wait for something to happen rather than to go out to meet it? (*b*) Is the Department able to maintain enough freedom from the pressure of day-to-day opinion to enable it to develop strategic plans objectively? Efforts to retain the Foreign Service as a distinctive unit having claims to esoteric skills probably reflect this concern. (*c*) Can the same leadership that must develop a policy of accommodation to hostile powers create the organizational conditions necessary for a dynamic program of "psychological warfare"? (*d*) Given the need for close integration between foreign policy decisions and propaganda, will this integration be better achieved with a psychological warfare organization *inside* the Department of State—hence theoretically "closer" to policy-formation—or do conflicts of function within the Department make it likely that performance will be better when the psychological warfare agency is independent of the Department and able to exert pressure upon it? In other words, do the commitments of the Department to established outlooks and procedures provide a congenial environment for an organization that must mobilize information and skills for day-to-day action on a broad front, of which diplomatic negotiations are only one sector?

In a quite different field, the "action" potentialities of the National Association for the Advancement of Colored People have received some attention.[15] The NAACP has scored its most brilliant successes in the courts, culminating in the Supreme Court ruling against segregation in the public schools. It has not engaged in much mass agitational activity, nor has it been effectively primed for the problems of mobilization and direction which such activity entails. On the whole, the NAACP has tended to follow rather than lead in the field of mass action. The March on Washington· Movement during World War II, the mass pressure for employment of Negroes in Harlem stores, and the bus boycott of 1956 in Montgomery, Alabama, were characteristically organized outside of the NAACP.

The weakness of the organization as a "direct action" group stems from and is reflected in its internal structure as well as in its relations to both the Negro and white communities. Structurally the NAACP has been very much a "headquarters" enterprise; its loosely bound members have functioned mainly as a "tax" base to support the headquarters, much as a government agency is supported by the general taxpayer. Relatively little attention has been paid to local organization and only a few paid regional directors have been employed. Moreover, the organization has close ties to the middle-class white community, from

[15] See Paul Jacobs, "The NAACP's New Direction," *The New Republic,* July 16, 1956.

which it gains money, status, and political allies. Within the Negro community, its base has also been primarily middle class. The result is an organization which cannot easily be called upon to engage in unaccustomed types of action or to support "precipitous" policies.

There were, to be sure, very good reasons for this development, including the exposed position of local people, their dependence on a protected headquarters, and the availability of the courts as channels for constructive change. But whatever the reasons, the emergence of a distinctive competence to win community support for legal action has probably carried with it a distinctive incompetence to take the lead in situations calling for mass action. An effort to change this basic orientation would require substantial changes in leadership and organizational structure, a much greater emphasis on member education, and significant moves to find a new pattern of alliance within both white and Negro communities.

The assessment of industrial firms also requires study of distinctive capabilities and limitations. For example, a commitment to quality of product may be an important determinant of organizational character or institutionalization.

The first boats made by Gar Wood were high quality craft, made of the finest materials by master boat builders. Later, the company decided to mass-produce a comparatively low cost speed boat for wide distribution. It developed that the entire organization found itself unable to cope with the effort to shift commitments. Workmen and shop supervisors alike continued to be preoccupied with high cost quality craftsmanship. Members of the selling staff, too, could not shift emphasis from "snob appeal" to price appeal. The quality commitment was so strong that an entirely new division—operating in a separate plant hundreds of miles away and therefore recruiting from a different labor market—had to be created to do the job successfully.[16]

A radical step was needed to provide organizational conditions congenial to the execution of a new policy. This was not a problem to which narrow criteria of organization engineering could be applied. It required an assessment of the built-in capabilities and limitations of the organization, that is, of its character as shaped by institutionalization.

In his study of the retailing activities of Sears, Roebuck and Co., Moore has used a similar concept of organization character. "The character of a store," he writes, "just like the character of an individual, is determined by what it does, but obviously what it does depends on the limits of its own resources, how it fits into the already established community, and how it comes to be regarded by the general public. All of this is a mutually interacting complex, involving growth, development, and fortuitous circumstances as well as conscious planned effort." [17]

Moore reminds us that Sears' retailing grew out of an already established mail-order business:

Prior to the birth of retailing, Sears, Roebuck and Company was capable of selling a quarter of a billion dollars worth of merchandise *sight unseen*. It was nationally known; and it al-

[16] From unpublished notes by the late Edward Boehm, formerly a Vice-President of Gar Wood Industries.

[17] David G. Moore, "Managerial Strategies and Organization Dynamics in Sears Retailing" (Unpublished doctoral dissertation, University of Chicago, 1954), p. 45. For a discussion of policy and organization character, see Selznick, *TVA and the Grass Roots*, pp. 181 ff.

ready had an institutional quality. Opening up Sears stores was like bringing the catalogue to life. . . . While Sears retailing took advantage of the Sears name, it also geared itself to the growth and development of large urban centers and the increasing use of the automobile. The development of the parking-lot, single-stop, family store located in an easily accessible place away from the center of town was Sears' strategic answer to the problem of competition in the central shopping district. It simply took advantage of the growth of the city and the development of the family automobile. More than this, the outlying location fitted its character as a retail store much better than competing in a downtown location. A Sears retail store is not typically a dominant store like Marshall Field's or J. L. Hudson's. Its character lies somewhere between a large neighborhood store and a downtown department store. Executives of large retailing establishments like those connected with the Associated Merchandising Corporation do not regard Sears as a department store in the full sense of the word. The distinction is not quite clear, but perhaps they are making reference to the fact that Sears is not, typically, a downtown store, handling a complete line of merchandise, and doing its own buying, or, for that matter carrying its whole merchandising and sales promotion load. It is more akin to an expanded auto store or electrical accessory store from the AMC point of view.[18]

The formation of an institution is marked by the making of value commitments, that is, choices which fix the assumptions of policymakers as to the nature of the enterprise—its distinctive aims, methods, and role in the community. These character-defining choices are not made verbally; they may not even be made consciously. When such com-

[18] Moore, *op. cit.*, pp. 49–50.

mitments are made, the values in question are actually built into the social structure, as in the case of the Gar Wood craftsmen just cited, or when the special weight or status accorded to one division in a business or government agency reflects and sustains a major policy decision.

Policy and Critical Decision

Decisions affecting institutional development are critical decisions. When made consciously they reflect or constitute "policy" in its traditional sense. However, the word "policy" is often used rather loosely in administrative circles and is applied to any rule or course of action designed to guide specific decisions. Thus we may hear of vacation policies, or promotion policies, irrespective of whether or not these bear on the creation or preservation of key values. Such usage is unfortunate to the extent that it blurs the distinction between routine and critical experience.

Among students of public administration, the need to distinguish analytically between policy-making and policy-serving decisions has long been recognized. This is reflected in the separation of "policy" and "administration," the former denoting aims and rules formulated by a legislature or other political body, the latter reserved for technical, executive, policy-serving functions. There is growing awareness, however, that this separation of policy and administration can obscure the truth.[19] At the same time, the term "basic policy" suggests something more than mere permanence; it has long-run implications for the organization,

[19] See Dwight Waldo, *The Administrative State* (New York: Ronald, 1948), pp. 123 ff.; also Albert Lepawsky, *Administration* (New York: Knopf, 1949), Chap. III.

not merely in being permanent, but even more in deciding central aims and distinctive methods.

In asserting the continuity of policy and administration, we are saying that certain organizational practices can enter the critical experience of leadership. These practices and the attitudes associated with them help to shape the key values in the organization, and especially the distribution of the power to affect these values.[20]

1. Decisions regarding the *recruitment of personnel* may become part of critical experience. This occurs when selection must take account of more than technical qualification, as when leading individuals are chosen for their personal commitment to precarious aims or methods. Not only cabinet ministers, but the heads of quite subordinate sections of an organization may be screened in this way. In business it may be important to have an executive who is "sales-minded" or "research-minded" or "production-minded." It may at times be useful to recruit whole staffs from a particular social milieu, in order to increase the chances that a given set of policies will become meaningful and effective guides to behavior. Where functions can be narrowly and technically defined, this type of recruitment is often unnecessary, and recruitment policy will not occupy a central place in the attention of leadership. But where the social composition of the staff significantly affects the interplay of policy and administration, personnel selection cannot be dealt with as routine management practice.

[20] "Value" here is not used in a very general sense, such as "object of any interest," but rather to denote something which in the given organization is taken as an end in itself. Note also that not all power distribution is relevant, but only that which can affect these values. This excludes the controlled delegation of authority, save as incidental discretion may influence the emergent character of the organization.

2. *Training of personnel* may also enter the critical experience of leadership. Where implementation of policy depends to any considerable extent on the attitudes and ways of thinking of personnel, an effort must be made to translate policy into an "organization doctrine" and to inculcate these ideas wherever necessary. Indoctrination becomes critically important when policies are insecure. This occurs if policies are new and meet resistance—as when union recognition and collective bargaining require the education of foremen—or when a policy based on the integration of ideas (e.g., politico-military) is likely to be emasculated because those ideas are only superficially accepted or understood. Policymakers must take account of the capacity of a given organization to absorb a point of view. The reconstruction of an organization to make it an adequate vehicle for an insecure or precarious policy has its own logic, demanding the close attention of leadership.

3. Organization-building is also intimately related to policy in the establishment of a system for *the representation of internal group interest*. The function of a leader, at whatever level, is in part to promote and defend the interests of his unit. When freedom to do this is allowed, the top leadership, responsible for the organization as a whole, can feel assured that the values entrusted to the unit will be effectively promoted and defended. This must, of course, be combined with effective co-ordination. But co-ordination involves more than harmonious action. It also consists of "constitutional" procedures for creating balanced representation and for adjudicating conflicts. Such conflicts, given a basic loyalty to the whole enterprise, are taken as normal rather than pathological. They are not routine, for

they reflect the open-endedness of institutional life. Organization controversy—whatever its real source—tends to raise issues that bear heavily on the evolution of key values, if for no other reason than to justify the struggle for group prestige and personal power. Indeed, a system of internal "checks and balances" is in part a way of insuring that policy issues are automatically thrust to the top for scrutiny and action. The problems of co-ordination, seen as the interplay of values, power, and organizational practice, form a major part of the critical experience of institutional leadership.

4. *Co-operation with other organizations* is another field of administrative action fraught with policy implications. Co-operation threatens a loss of control, since commitments in action tend to spill over the limits of verbal agreement. Indeed, a proposal for (or resistance to) co-operation very often reflects a strategy for organizational aggrandizement or protection at least as much as it does an interest in the program to be furthered. Within limits, this is no sign of evil or selfish design, but a natural function of leadership. Proposals for co-operation in a particular area must be examined to see whether in action they will generate unwanted consequences for other parts of a program or for the organization as a whole. This cannot be decided merely by examining the terms of an agreement. The consequences for public opinion, access to clientele, personnel selection, and the establishment of precedents and entrenched organizational machinery must be studied. This entails, in effect, considering *the power implications of co-operation,* not necessarily for the sake of power as such, but because the development and implementation of policy requires it.

These illustrations bear on the distinction between routine and critical experience, as well as on the corollary difference between static and dynamic adaptation. Routine experience works out the detailed applications of established canons. Sometimes virtually everything about an organization can be routine, including the formulation of general rules, if there is little leeway for self-definition and policies are derived automatically from precedent, authority, or technical considerations. That is why, for the bare continuity of organizational existence, leadership is often dispensable. But where leadership is required, as in the examples cited, the problem is always *to choose key values and to create a social structure that embodies them.*[21] The task of building values into social structure is not necessarily consistent, especially in early stages, with rules of administration based on economic premises. Only after key choices have been made and related policies firmly established can criteria of efficient administration play a significant role. Even then, the smooth-running machine must accept disturbance when critical problems of adaptation and change arise.

These examples suggest dynamic rather than static adaptation. The latter embraces changes that do not affect the central (self-defining) aims or methods of the enterprise. But such aims or methods are precisely what may be at stake in selective recruitment, the inculcation of core attitudes, the representation of interests, and administrative co-operation. Any of these processes may take place unconsciously, or at least outside of the attention of policy-

[21] This may be compared with individual moral experience, wherein the individual existentially "chooses" self-defining values and strives to make himself an authentic representative of them, that is, to hold them genuinely rather than superficially.

makers, so that consequences for organization character may be unanticipated and uncontrolled. Indeed, it might be useful to reserve the idea of dynamic vs. static adaptation for unconscious organizational adjustments, preserving more closely the analogy to similar processes in psychology.

The Functions of Institutional Leadership

We have argued that policy and administration are interdependent in the special sense that certain areas of organizational activity are peculiarly sensitive to policy matters. Because these areas exist, creative men are needed —more in some circumstances than in others—who know how to transform a neutral body of men into a committed polity. These men are called leaders; their profession is politics.

A political orientation is greatly needed if we are to reach a proper understanding of institutional leadership. But this orientation should not be too narrowly identified with the struggle for power. The link between "polity" and "politics" must constantly be kept in mind. To be sure, the political process always involves an actual or potential contest of wills, but it also includes the continuous redefinition of public interest and the embodiment of those definitions in key institutions. The German term *Politik*, as distinguished from *Verwaltung*, nonpolitical administration, has some of these connotations. *Politik* is not so much concerned with technical efficiency as with decisions that are open and potentially controversial. While at any given moment there may be consensus, this does not signify indifference. *Verwaltung*, on the other hand, does deal with areas of indifference. Some matters (*Politik*) are part of critical experience because they affect the way the group's character is formed, whereas other matters (*Verwaltung*) are constant despite changes in character. The existence of a contest of wills is prima facie evidence (though not conclusive) that political issues in this sense have been raised. This holds for all organizations that have freedom of self-definition, not just for public agencies.

Leadership sets goals, but in doing so takes account of the conditions that have already determined what the organization can do and to some extent what it must do. Leadership creates and molds an organization embodying—in thought and feeling and habit—the value premises of policy. Leadership reconciles internal strivings and environmental pressures, paying close attention to the way adaptive behavior brings about changes in organizational character. When an organization lacks leadership, these tasks are inadequately fulfilled, however expert the flow of paper and however smooth the channels of communication and command. And this fulfillment requires a continuous scrutiny of how the changing social structure affects the evolution of policy.

The relation of leadership to organizational character may be more closely explored if we examine some of the key tasks leaders are called on to perform:

1. *The definition of institutional mission and role.* The setting of goals is a creative task. It entails a self-assessment to discover the true commitments of the organization, as set by effective internal and external demands. The failure to set aims in the light of these commitments is a major source of irresponsibility in leadership.

2. *The institutional embodiment of purpose.* The task of

leadership is not only to make policy but to build it into the organization's social structure. This, too, is a creative task. It means shaping the "character" of the organization, sensitizing it to ways of thinking and responding, so that increased reliability in the execution and elaboration of policy will be achieved according to its spirit as well as its letter.

3. *The defense of institutional integrity.* The leadership of any polity fails when it concentrates on sheer survival: institutional survival, properly understood, is a matter of maintaining values and distinctive identity. This is at once one of the most important and least understood functions of leadership. This area (like that of defining institutional mission) is a place where the intuitively knowledgeable leader and the administrative analyst often part company, because the latter has no tools to deal with it. The fallacy of combining agencies on the basis of "logical" association of functions is a characteristic result of the failure to take account of institutional integrity.

4. *The ordering of internal conflict.* Internal interest-groups form naturally in large-scale organizations, since the total enterprise is in one sense a polity composed of a number of sub-organizations. The struggle among competing interests always has a high claim on the attention of leadership. This is so because the direction of the enterprise as a whole may be seriously influenced by changes in the internal balance of power. In exercising control, leadership has a dual task. It must win the consent of constituent units, in order to maximize voluntary co-operation, and therefore must permit emergent interest blocs a wide degree of rep-

resentation. At the same time, in order to hold the helm, it must see that a balance of power appropriate to the fulfillment of key commitments will be maintained.

In the chapters to follow, we shall consider the first three of these leadership tasks, with some passing attention to the fourth.

THREE

The Definition of Mission
and Role

We may suppose that to govern is always something of a strain; yet it is surely less demanding to preside over an organization that largely runs itself than to be confronted with the question: What shall we *do?* What shall we *be?* These questions are hard enough in matters of personal guidance; they can be enormously complicated when the character and direction of a polity is at stake.

The institutional leader in his role as goal-setter must confront all of the classic questions that have plagued the study of human aspiration. When is an aim, such as "happiness," specific enough to be meaningful? What is the right role of reason, and of opportunism, in the choice of ends? How may immediate practical goals be joined to ultimate values?

Purpose and Commitment

The aims of large organizations are often very broad. A certain vagueness must be accepted because it is difficult to foresee whether more specific goals will be realistic or wise.[1] This situation presents the leader with one of his most difficult but indispensable tasks. *He must specify and recast the general aims of his organization so as to adapt them, without serious corruption, to the requirements of institutional survival.* This is what we mean by the definition of institutional mission and role.

The term "mission" has a distinctly military flavor, but its meaning is not entirely clear even in that sphere. Emphasis is often placed on the element of *precision* in military assignments of mission. One student of administration has drawn directly on the military analogy in making the point that "a clear statement of purpose universally understood is the outstanding guarantee of effective administration."

On this point military administration taught us a real lesson. With minor exceptions, no activity was initiated by the military without clear definition, a definition cast in terms of purpose, timing, and resources; no organizational unit was set up without a statement of its mission. The success or failure of any man or of any venture was measured against this specific statement of objectives and methods. In administration, God helps those ad-

---

[1] See pp. 5–22, on the distinction between "organization" and "institution" and on the open-endedness of institutional experience. With that discussion in mind, it should be clear that this analysis does not bear on all goal-setting. Here we are dealing with the institutional definition of mission in the sense that this represents an adaptive structuring of aims that cannot be predetermined on a technological basis. Thus the assignment of combat missions becomes increasingly predeterminable as we descend the military echelons. This holds roughly for other enterprises as well.

ministrators who have a clearly defined mission, and thus the beginnings of authority commensurate with their responsibility.[2]

There is surely some undue optimism here, particularly as to the effectiveness with which the missions of high-echelon or noncombat military agencies were specified. Even at lower levels, where no great amount of experience with the type of unit established existed, the use of the word "mission" may have added an aura of clarity that was not justified on closer analysis.

While emphasizing precision and clarity, Gulick also pointed out, however, that administrative failures occurred when there was "no adequate definition of mission *in realistic terms, related to the other activities of the government.*"[3] It appears, indeed, that something more than mere precision is required. Some kind of assessment is necessary before the required clarity can be achieved. And this assessment may itself demand a period of actual experience during which the capabilities of the organization and the pressures of its environment may be tested. If this is so, then *prior* definition of mission—"no organizational unit was set up without a statement of its mission"—is not an indispensable step in organizational planning and, indeed, may result in undue rigidities if prematurely attempted. Our concern here is to emphasize that self-assessment.

In defining the mission of the organization, leaders must take account of (1) *the internal state of the polity:* the strivings, inhibitions, and competences that exist within the organization; and (2) *the external expectations* that de-

[2] Luther Gulick, *Administrative Reflections from World War II*, University of Alabama Press, 1948, p. 77.
[3] *Ibid.* Italics supplied.

termine what must be sought or achieved if the institution is to survive. Let us briefly examine each of these phases.

1. *Internal commitments.* The need to set goals with an eye to the capabilities of the organization and to the irrepressible demands of forces within it, is a problem set for the leadership of any polity, from a great nation, or combination of nations, to the smallest self-sustaining organization.

In international affairs, this problem arose in connection with the definition of "war aims" under conditions of coalition warfare. During World War II, there was much discussion of this issue, particularly among those concerned with the political implications of military operations.[4] It was felt in some quarters that "victory" was too general a term, inadequate to guide the host of decisions, both military and political, that attended the war effort. The plea was for a definition of mission, a statement of aims that would include the wider, nonmilitary (often moral) objectives of the allied powers. Those who stressed these alleged commitments—to democratic forms of government, national self-determination, etc.—were attempting to shape present goals by asserting the claims of an institutional "self" or identity.

The leaders of the joint war effort resisted this attempt to bind their hands. Winston Churchill was especially sensitive to the danger of *premature* self-definition. He did not want to limit the maneuverability of the coalition save for real advantages. He understood that the boundary between apparent and truly binding moral commitments is very fluid; and he undoubtedly recognized as a tactical device the claim of the opposition to hold views that merely

[4] See Hans Speier, *Social Order and Risks of War* (New York: Stewart, 1952), Chap. 29.

reflected the established policy of the community. Commitments to a solidly crystallized public opinion can be very real indeed; but opinions may also be weakly held and readily altered. It is a task of leadership to assess the extent to which even widely held views represent the polity's true self-defining commitments.

In 1940 Churchill insisted against challengers in Parliament that victory was his war aim; and the following year he said: "I have, as the House knows, hitherto consistently deprecated the formulation of peace aims or war aims—however you put it—by His Majesty's Government, at this stage. I deprecate it at this time, when the end of the war is not in sight, when the conflict sways to and fro with alternating fortunes and when conditions and associations at the end of the war are unforeseeable. But a Joint Declaration by Great Britain and the United States is an event of a totally different nature." [5] In resisting the formulation of specific war aims, Churchill was recognizing that changing events might create new obligations and opportunities that would materially affect those aims. At the same time, he accepted the need to do whatever was necessary to establish and maintain an Anglo-American coalition.

"The nature of this war, determined, as it is, by German aggression; the nature of the coalition which Germany has mobilized against herself for a second time in a generation; the respective national contributions to the defeat of Germany by the forces allied against her—all these factors have gone into the making of our war aims." [6] In this passage Speier sums up the argument of his essay, that war

[5] *Ibid.*, quoted on p. 389.
[6] *Ibid.*, p. 395.

aims could not be defined freely on the basis of abstract criteria as to what would be desirable or even effective as propaganda. Such aims were inescapably conditioned by the nature of the warring powers themselves, that is, the commitments they brought with them into the alliance. A leadership that did not undertake this self-assessment, and overlooked these limitations, would open the way to irresponsible adventurism and utopian sentimentality.[7]

Defining the aims of a coalition of sovereign states is of course exceptionally difficult, but it is the same as the basic problem in more familiar organizations. A wise leader faces up to the character of his organization, although he may do so only as a prelude to designing a strategy that will alter it. At the same time, following Churchill, he does not accept restraints unless they are truly conditions of effective action. A university president may have to accept some unwelcome aspects of alumni influence; he would be a poor leader if he did so without knowing whether this dependency was truly part of the institution's character. So too, in foreign affairs, much may be lost by an easy assumption that an American administration "cannot" support

[7] On adventurism, see *ibid.*, p. 388: "It certainly would have been folly to base a decision on their advice, for the political perspective of propagandists is exceedingly short. As experts in political warfare they would not have taken account of the traditions of our foreign policy in the Far East, the lasting interests of this country, the political relations, both at that time and after the defeat of Japan, between Britain and the United States, China and the United States, Russia and the United States. In short, the data and the considerations on which they would have based their advice would have been grotesquely inadequate in view of the great political issues that were affected by the declaration. Statesmen, not propagandists, must make policy." The mark of the statesman, we may add, is his capacity to adapt his aims to the commitments of the polity he leads, that is, to take account of the indirect and long-run consequences of current action for the evolving character of the community or enterprise.

programs abroad that are inconsistent with economic doctrines held by dominant groups at home.

The relation between purpose and institutional commitment is also revealed in the struggle over the missions of the armed services. Here the underlying problem has to do with the capacity of an agency to protect itself against inroads from organizational rivals, not merely in the short-run struggle for funds, but especially in the competition for long-run status. The institutional leaders of the various armed services recognize that the way the mission of the service is formulated will reflect, and in part influence, the evolving balance of forces.

They themselves are under strong pressure to promote definitions of mission which have the best chance of enlarging the scope, or at least protecting the flanks, of their organizations. Hence, in formulating aims and jurisdictions, the statement of mission must be more than "clear"; it must take account of the pressures that will arise from within the agency to redefine its aims in ways that lend it increased security.

For example, an independent Air Force may naturally overvalue strategic rather than tactical weapons, methods, and intelligence, particularly in an early period of intense struggle for an assured status. An emphasis on strategic competence—that is, the ability to mount an offensive using weapons that will directly and independently affect the outcome of the battle—is congenial in the struggle for autonomy and prestige. The ground forces might seek control of tactical air units, but would not readily challenge the autonomy of a strategic air command and its squadrons.

Further, an emphasis on strategic competence justifies large independent staff agencies for planning, procurement, and training, as well as for research and development. And probably most important of all, such a stress connotes, to the Air Force leaders and to the public, a sense of power that cannot so easily come from a role that emphasizes tactical air support for land armies.[8] Similar considerations apply, of course, to other agencies. Organizational design is unrealistic when it fails to take account of such tendencies.

2. *External pressures.* In addition to internal concerns, "institutional commitments" also include such externally set goals as must be accepted if significant deprivations are to be avoided. These commitments arise wherever a specific "payoff" is externally demanded and can be enforced. An effective and self-conscious leader learns to test his environment, including the strength of higher authority and the seriousness of its demands, in order to discover just what the required payoff is. As every such leader knows intuitively, to find out what one is "really responsible for" requires an assessment of the needs and responsibilities of those who formally tell him what to do.

Leadership in the United States military establishment has been confronted with this problem in an acute form. It must accurately assess the demands that are made upon it, i.e., discover its true commitments. Under modern con-

---

[8] See James A. Huston, "Tactical Use of Air Power in World War II: The Army Experience," *Military Affairs,* XIV, No. 4 (Winter, 1950), p. 172, where the following statement by former Assistant Secretary of War John J. McCloy is quoted: "It is my firm belief that the Air Forces are not interested in this type of work, think it unsound, and are very much concerned lest it result in control of Air units by ground forces. Their interest, enthusiasm and energy is directed to different fields." The conditions that channel "interest, enthusiasm and energy" are closely related to institutional development and character-formation.

ditions, these cannot be reduced to the responsibility of preparing the defense of the U.S. against the eventuality of total war. American military power may also be called upon to act in limited and peripheral controversies. Consequently, planning in the military establishment must distinguish the preparation of deterrents to the initiation of a general conflict from the development of capabilities to intervene effectively in isolable conflicts. Acceptance of an institutional commitment to be prepared for limited warfare requires much more than verbal acquiescence. Those who design weapons systems, integrated with political and economic strategy, may have to recognize, for example, that limited warfare presumes relatively inefficient operation of military forces, because an isolated conflict necessarily means that "privileged sanctuaries" exist on both sides. A commitment is not truly accepted and understood unless its consequences are also understood.

An organization's "true commitments," however, are not unchanging. They must be reassessed continuously. An air arm struggling for recognition may have, as a corollary of its weakness, no effective external demand to satisfy beyond demonstrating the utility of its weapons. This will leave it free to concentrate overwhelming attention on the building and protection of an air force. But once it assumes a central role in the defense system, it loses this freedom, and its leadership will fail if this transition is not recognized. This may be compared with the "irresponsibility" of a minority political party which, when it wins a majority and forms a government, must accept the commitments of power and forsake its narrow role of opposition.

This problem of accommodating internal and external

demands is a source of much misunderstanding. It divides administrative analysts and responsible officials into hostile camps. The leader, sensitive to internal pressures and to the heavy price that must be paid for co-operation, is impatient with the analyst whose narrow logic of efficiency leads to proposals for change that are irresponsible from the standpoint of the institution. The analyst, for his part, is sensitive to the tendency of a leader to lapse into opportunism, to conceive his entire role as one of self-defense. For the present, it appears that the analyst bears the greater fault, since his theories of organization do not adequately account for the factors with which the responsible institutional leader must deal. Even where the importance of internal morale is recognized, this tends to be restricted to a concern for the well-being and adjustment of individuals rather than of interest-groups within the enterprise and of the latter as a whole.

The Retreat to Technology

A characteristic threat to the integration of purpose and commitment—hence to the adequate definition of institutional mission—is an excessive or premature technological orientation. This posture is marked by a concentration on ways and means. The ends of action are taken for granted, viewed as essentially unproblematic "givens" in organization-building and decision-making. The enterprise is conceived of as a tool whose goals are set externally. This may not raise difficulties, if tasks are narrowly and sharply defined, as in the case of a typist pool or machine records unit. At this extreme, the organization is totally absorbed in routine tasks and leadership is dispensable. However, as we move to areas where self-determination becomes increasingly important—where "initiative" must be exercised—the setting of goals loses its innocence. In particular, if a leadership acts as if it had no creative role in the formulation of ends, when in fact the situation demands such a role, it will fail, leaving a history of uncontrolled, opportunistic adaptation behind it.[9]

The retreat to technology is associated with the difficulty of integrating political and military strategy. When military commanders—or diplomats—attempt to define a sphere of "purely military" decisions,[10] this is congenial to the creation of secure boundaries within which known principles can be applied; and it abets the avoidance of responsibility

[9] In his study of the adult education program in Los Angeles, Clark found that the leaders of the program tended to abandon a creative role in setting goals. A diffuse ideology of "service" comes down to a program based upon customer preference. The adult school is conceived of as a tool whose goals are set externally, by "the public," leaving the school official only the simple technical task of "servicing the demand," whatever that may be. This opportunism may well leave the program inadequately prepared when new agencies with clearer missions invade this growing field of work. See B. R. Clark, *Adult Education in Transition: A Study of Institutional Insecurity* (Berkeley and Los Angeles: University of California Press, 1956), pp. 145 ff.

[10] Some of General Dwight D. Eisenhower's comments in *Crusade in Europe* (New York: Doubleday, 1948) are instructive. In discussing Churchill's Mediterranean Orientation, Eisenhower points to the former's "concern as a political leader for the future of the Balkans. For this concern I had great sympathy, but as a soldier I was particularly careful to exclude such considerations from my own recommendations" (p. 194). The word "soldier" as used here and in similar contexts obscures the distinction between low-echelon and high-echelon responsibilities. See also p. 80, on the decision to attack Casablanca: "As far as I can recall, this was the only instance in the war when any part of our proposed operational plans was changed by intervention of higher authority. We cheerfully accepted the decision because the governing considerations were political more than tactical, and political estimates are the function of governments not of soldiers." Note also the following comment by Dean Acheson, June 15, 1947, then Undersecretary of State, quoted in Robert Ingrim, "The Conversion to the Balance of Power," *The Review of Politics,* Vol. 14, No. 2 (April, 1952), p. 242: "In our military operations we pursued purely military objectives. The cross-channel invasion of Europe was directed solely toward the destruction of the German armies, not the occupation of territory."

for decisions that cut across these boundaries. More important, the idea that there is a division of labor—some people charged with political decisions, others with military ones —opens the way to the evasion of responsibility even within the more narrow fields. When either political or military decisions are especially difficult, dealing with vague and unpredictable elements, it is convenient to allow the decisions to be made on other grounds.

This problem is more aggravated than eased by the ritual acceptance of Clausewitz's classic apothegm: "War is a mere continuation of policy by other means." If this means that war is not an end in itself but is determined by and subordinated to political objects, we have an important emphasis leading to the ready acceptance by military commanders of political authority. But the same formula can lead to a sharp divorce of political and military areas of decision. The military commanders have, in this perspective, only to "accept" the priority of political objectives formulated by diplomats and politicians, while they themselves give all their attention to the "purely military" tools. This point of view accommodates Clausewitz to the traditional subordination of military to civilian authority in the United States—a subtle process that permits the American military planner to cite Clausewitz with approval and at the same time to neutralize his impact upon strategic planning.

This may be clarified if we take a closer look at Clausewitz:

The war of a community—of whole nations and particularly of civilized nations—always arises from a political condition and is called forth by a political motive. It is, therefore, a political act. Now if it were an act complete in itself and undisturbed, an absolute manifestation of violence, as we had to deduce it from its mere conception, it would, from the moment it was called forth by policy, step into the place of policy and, as something quite independent of it, set it aside and follow only its own laws, just as a mine, when it is going off, can no longer be guided into any other direction than that given it by previous adjustments.[11]

In other words, if military strategy were a technology, a system having its own laws, then these laws could "take over" once the political objectives were set.

This is how the thing has hitherto been regarded even in practice, whenever a lack of harmony between policy and the conduct of war has led to theoretical distinctions of this kind. But it is not so, and this idea is radically false. . . . War is, therefore, so to speak, a regular pulsation of violence, more or less vehement and consequently more or less quick in relaxing tensions and exhausting forces—in other words, more or less quickly leading to its goal. But it always lasts long enough to exert, in its course, an influence upon that goal, so that its direction can be changed in this way or that—in short, long enough to remain subject to the will of a guiding intelligence. Now if we reflect that war has its origin in a political object, we see that this first motive which called it into existence naturally remains the first and highest consideration to be regarded in its conduct. *But the political object is not on that account a despotic lawgiver: it must adapt itself to the nature of the means at its disposal and is often thereby completely changed, but it must always be the first thing to be considered. Policy, therefore, will permeate the whole action of war,* and exercise a continual in-

[11] Karl von Clausewitz, *On War* (New York: Modern Library, 1943), pp. 15–16.

fluence upon it, so far as the nature of the explosive forces in it allow.[12]

The significant idea here is the *interrelation* of political aims and military strategy, not simply the subordination of one to the other. Further:

Now, the first, the greatest and the most decisive act of the judgment which a statesman and commander performs is that of correctly recognizing in this respect the kind of war he is undertaking, of not taking it for, or wishing to make it, something which by the nature of the circumstances it cannot be. This is, therefore, the first and most comprehensive of all strategic questions.[13]

This decision, particularly under modern conditions, is the joint responsibility of military and political planners. It is easily blurred by general aims, such as "to achieve a stable peace" or "to defend the U.S." The design and procurement of weapons, the organization of commands, the training of troops—these and many other activities of a military establishment must rest on assumptions regarding the nature of wars to be fought. If these assumptions are not made in a conscious and controlled way, they will either be made irresponsibly by whatever group is powerful at the moment, or they will not be made, and detailed decisions will remain unguided by long-run objectives. In either case, there is a failure of institutional leadership.

The problem of politico-military integration is set by the close interdependence of means and ends. The unfolding

---

[12] *Ibid.*, p. 16. Italics supplied.
[13] *Ibid.*, p. 18.

of military power necessarily conditions political decisions regarding the use of that power. If the development of capabilities is not adequately controlled—and this will occur if purely military criteria are applied in the preparedness effort—then ends will be subordinated to means, for alternative strategies will be limited by available capabilities. This is only avoided by an integration achieved in depth, that is, when political considerations reach down to influence every important area of military planning—the design of weapons, the selection of targets, intelligence, training, etc. In effect, a new institution requiring a unified political and military leadership has arisen—the *security establishment*. The real problem of unification today is the creation of an organization that will strengthen this emerging institution and provide it with effective leadership.

The retreat to technology occurs whenever a group evades its real commitments by paring its responsibilities, withdrawing behind a cover of technological isolation from situations that generate anxiety.[14] This endangers the central task of goal-setting, particularly when there is need to accommodate a technical "logic" to political conditions and aims.

This withdrawal from institutional responsibility finds comfort in a positivist theory of administration.[15] A radical separation of fact and value—too often identified with the

[14] The bureaucratic penchant for expansion of responsibilities (and concomitant power) is often noted. But self-restriction also occurs, often with equally serious consequences. As in the case of personalities, we have a number of characteristic responses to threat. Just as we would like to know more about the conditions under which individuals resort to one or another of such responses (aggression, withdrawal, etc.), so should this be a goal in the study of organizations.

[15] See Herbert A. Simon, *Administrative Behavior* (New York: Macmillan, 1947), pp. 45 ff.

logical distinction between fact *statements* and preference *statements*—encourages the divorce of means and ends. On this view, values belong to an alien realm, outside the pale of scientific assessment:

No knowledge of administrative techniques, then, can relieve the administrator from the task of moral choice—choice as to organization goals and methods and choice as to his treatment of the other human beings in his organization. His code of ethics is as significant a part of his equipment as an administrator as is his knowledge of administrative behavior, and no amount of study of the "science" of administration will provide him with that code.[16]

This statement illustrates a characteristic strategy. The importance of values is affirmed, but the choice of goals and of character-defining methods is banished from the science of administration. "This emphasis on the factual does not mean that we discount the importance of values. It simply reflects our belief that the competent practitioner reaches his desired ends—whatever they may be—through a mastery of the phenomena he is dealing with and a clear, objective understanding of their behavior."[17] In other words, they say given your ends, whatever they may be, the study of administration will help you to achieve them. We offer you tools. Into the foundations of your choices we shall not inquire, for that would make us moralists rather than scientists. This recalls the separation of military and political decisions discussed above. There, too, the importance of

[16] H. A. Simon, D. W. Smithburg, and V. A. Thompson, *Public Administration* (New York: Knopf, 1950), p. 24.
[17] *Ibid.*, p. 20.

political ends could be affirmed while relegating them to a separate and inaccessible realm.

The difficulty in this position is not that it lacks ultimate philosophical justification. As so often happens, it is the polemical formulation that has the most impact. Like other forms of positivism, this position in administrative theory raises too bright a halo over linguistic purity. Pressing a complex world into easy dichotomies, it induces a *premature* abandonment of wide areas of experience to the world of the aesthetic, the metaphysical, the moral. Let us grant the premise that there is an *ultimately* irreducible nonrational (responsive) element in valuation, inaccessible to scientific appraisal. This cannot justify the judgment in a particular case that the anticipated irreducible element has actually been reached.

That there are wide areas of administration—as of military decision—that have a technical autonomy cannot be denied. But the real problem is: Shall this be *assumed* or is it open to investigation at every point? The effective leader continuously explores the specialized activities for which he is responsible to see whether the aims taken for granted are consistent with the evolving mission of the enterprise as a whole. The propagandist and the military commander are technicians. Each must take specific goals as given, if his technical skill is to be applied. But the institutional leader cannot permit any partial viewpoint to dominate decisions regarding the enterprise as a whole. This is well understood. Less obvious, however, is that this control will not be possible unless a true conception of the nature of the enterprise—its long-run aims as shaped by long-run commitments—is grasped and held. Leadership fails if it permits a retreat to the short run. And this retreat is facilitated by an uncontrolled reliance on technologies, for they overstress means and neglect ends.[18]

To summarize: Institutional aims cannot be taken as given, for they are conditioned by changing self-definitions, by alterations in the internal and external commitments of the enterprise. If the effect of this process is to be controlled rather than left to opportunistic adaptation, an awareness of it is essential. And we have maintained that an excessive or premature technological orientation inhibits this awareness.

Organization Roles

In the U.S. military establishment it has become common to speak of the "roles and missions" of the various armed services. This usage rests on an important insight. The mission of an organization cannot be adequately defined without also determining (*a*) its basic methods, the main tools or ways of acting with which it should be identified, and (*b*) its place among organizations that carry on related activities. These are key elements of an organization's role, and when set they go a long way toward fixing the limits within which a mission can be defined.

The idea of "role" has stimulated much interest among students of personality and social structure. Put rather generally, *a role is a way of behaving associated with a defined position in a social system*. Every society, and every group within society, assigns positions to members. These positions

[18] For a related point of view see Norton E. Long, "Public Policy and Administration: The Goals of Rationality and Responsibility," *Public Administration Review*, 14:22–31 (Winter, 1954); also Dwight Waldo, *The Study of Public Administration* (New York: Doubleday, 1955), Chap. 6.

carry expectations regarding the behavior of those who fill them. We learn how to be sons, teachers, clerks, neighbors, citizens. Some of these roles are accepted consciously and formally, others unconsciously and responsively; some are peripheral, others central to our self-conceptions. Especially relevant here is that role-*taking* connotes an adaptive process, a mode of unconscious self-structuring. It is this significance of role-taking—as against the formal and external assignment of roles—that can help us here.

These informal, emergent roles are reasonably familiar on the level of individual behavior. As we observe a group of men in conference, for example, we may note that one is a "spark plug" or "idea man" who assumes responsibility for initiating discussions; another may be the perennial arbitrator, stepping in with a soothing formula or a compromise when dissension endangers the unity of the group; still another may act as the representative of some outside interest. These roles are often independent of formally assigned positions or tasks, and are likely to be closely related to the personality structure of the individuals involved. Thus the characteristic ways of behaving are often adaptive, not consciously controlled. On the other hand, although this is rare, a group may be designed with a view to creating an optimum combination of just such roles.

Role-taking is in effect a decision by the individual—not always consciously arrived at—regarding how he ought to work. And this involves an estimate of his own place among others, including the demands made upon him and his own capabilities. This self-assessment searches out the demands and limitations which determine what means may be used, hence also the free choice of ends. A man comes to understand the roles he can play as he tests the alternatives open to him, given his own personality and the social system of which he is a part. Of course, as his place in the system changes—or as he moves to a new system—a reassessment of commitments is in order. It is probable that confusion regarding role behavior, due to inadequate self-assessment, is a major source of personal difficulty. The same logic appears to hold in organizational experience.

In his history of the Air Transport Command, Oliver La Farge points to the differing self-conceptions of the Air Service Command and the Ferrying Command:

Air Service Command was a sort of Air Force Quartermaster and Ordnance Corps; handling supplies, maintenance, and repairs peculiar to the Air Forces. Each of the overseas Air Forces contained its own Air Service Command, of which the central, domestic organization was the parent. Understandably, A.S.C. was inclined to give heed particularly to the requests of its overseas opposite numbers. The Ferrying Command, on the other hand, would often have a different appreciation of relative urgencies, and might well substitute for some of the cargoes flown to its departure points by A.S.C. for rush delivery, others, received by mail, and requested by other agencies—including supplies needed for the maintenance of its own activities. The result was haphazard and inefficient.

It is my own impression, fairly well grounded, I think, that A.S.C. tended strongly to the view that the Air Forces' air transportation was intended primarily for Air Force use, while increasingly *as the Ferrying Command developed its philosophy and realized its own potentialities, it moved away from this concept towards the concept of itself as an agency for the service of the whole war effort.* These differences of philosophy had historical cause: from the very beginning the Ferrying Command served international clients in its ferrying, and its pre-war transport lines were for the use of much higher levels of government than just the Air Corps. Air Service Command's history was just the opposite.[19]

References to an organization's "philosophy," as above, very often signify that a particular way of perceiving itself has evolved. If this were not an adaptive product, reflecting an intuitive assessment of potentialities and commitments, there would be no point in such phraseology. It would suffice to indicate the formal goals and methods as prescribed by higher authority. Of course, such a philosophy, if well-established, can become accepted and even formalized in due course. Before that time, this self-conception is treated as a unique characteristic of the agency, to be learned only in close association with it. It is especially important to note the consequences for decision-making, in this case affecting the assignment of priorities to shipments.

Administrative history is replete with similar illustrations of developing organizational roles. Cline points out that as combat operations were increasingly mounted from overseas rather than from the U.S., as skill in the readying and transportation of troops and materiel developed, and as the overseas headquarters staff grew in importance, the Operations Division acted "as monitor much more often than agent of the execution of the Chief of Staff's decisions as to Army operations."[20] This shift in role reflected the chang-

[19] Oliver La Farge, *The Eagle in the Egg* (Boston: Houghton, Mifflin, 1949), p. 56. Italics supplied.

[20] Ray S. Cline, *Washington Command Post: The Operations Division* (Washington, D.C.: Office of the Chief of Military History, 1951), p. 210. It is interesting that the index (p. 411) refers to this as the "mature monitoring role" of the OPD's Theater Group.

ing capabilities of other organization units and the need for OPD to adapt itself to the changes. Millett's study of the Army Service Forces inevitably deals with the ASF's struggle to work out a role vis-à-vis the Army Ground Forces and the Army Air Forces, an effort conditioned by the ASF's own internal diversity, the basic drive of the AAF to become a separate service, and the often obscure connections between strategy and supply.[21]

An agency's general *purpose* may be to promote improved soil conservation practices, but its *role* will depend on whether it decides to do this by educational means alone, or by more aggressive methods, such as offering direct aid and establishing local "districts" with powers of control. The New Deal "action" agencies in the Department of Agriculture adopted a different role in their relation to farmers and farm organizations than had been acceptable to older agencies, and this role was intimately related to the missions that the new agencies could formulate and pursue.

Among educators today a problem of organizational role arises from the growing diversity of institutions of higher education. The public junior colleges seem to face this problem in an acute way. The junior college originally offered the first two years of college work, and viewed itself as having a preparatory function junior to the university and the four-year college. An evolution away from that accepted role seems to have gone through two stages: first, an emphasis upon terminal two-year programs as the particularly unique activity of the junior college, and secondly, the more recent tendency to define the school as a "community"

[21] John D. Millett, *The Organization and Role of the Army Service Forces* (Washington, D.C.: Office of the Chief of Military History, 1954).

college, with responsibilities for adult education as well as preparatory and terminal curricula. Whatever the reasons for this trend, it is evident that the working out of an institutional role will require an assessment of the junior colleges' own potentialities and a testing of related institutions. The relative weakness of adult education agencies undoubtedly offers the junior college administrators an opportunity to move into that area.[22]

An institutional role cannot be won merely by wishing for it or by verbalizing it clearly. It must be founded in the realistic ability of the organization to do the job. The distinctive competence of the enterprise is the vital factor. In this connection the relation between the Army Service Forces and G-4 of the War Department General Staff in World War II is revealing. The reorganization of the War Department in 1942 contemplated that G-4 would be the chief supply planning agency and that ASF would work out detailed programs and plans. But according to Millett, "In practice the 'top supply planner' of the War Department was not the Assistant Chief of Staff, G-4, but the commanding general of the Army Service Forces."[23]

This division of theory and practice had a very practical basis:

OPD [Operations Division] consistently agreed in principle that G-4 ought to establish Army-wide supply policies that would correlate logistic activities throughout the three major commands [ASF, AGF, AAF] and the overseas theaters. In practice the handful of officers in G-4 Division could offer comparatively little assistance to the mammoth Services of Supply [ASF] organiza-

[22] See Clark, *op cit.*, pp. 130 ff.
[23] Millett, *op. cit.*, p. 138.

tion or to the well-staffed OPD sections. Consequently G-4 tended to be squeezed out of an important part in logistic problems. Services of Supply proceeded to make its own policies in the course of performing day-to-day tasks delegated to it, and OPD often predetermined logistic policy by the nature of the demands it made in the interests of supporting specific combat operations.[24]

In effect, the ASF headquarters went far to displace G-4, which was then reduced to a weak and highly anomalous position in the General Staff. Whatever the formal provisions, the 1942 reorganization left G-4 without the strength to enforce the ASF's theoretical subordination to G-4's broad policy-making role. The ASF's leader, General Brehon Somervell, came to speak with increased authority as the war progressed. This was not so much the result of the formal powers of his office; rather, it emerged as the dependence of others upon the capabilities of his organization became increasingly clear.

Thus roles are shaped by capability, including the extent to which one organization is dependent upon another and must heed (or may ignore) the pressures it exerts. This is sufficiently obvious when roles are *assigned* in the course of routinely establishing well-defined organizations. A task is set forth and, as a matter of course, the key methods of working are also indicated, as is the relation of the new group to other parts of the larger enterprise. Insofar as possible, mission and role are prescribed in advance. When this can be done, institutional leadership is of little significance and technical skill can determine the selection of

[24] Cline, *op. cit.*, pp. 114 ff.

personnel. When, however, we must rely on "experience" to help define the nature of an agency, the working out of roles becomes important. Leadership—in the sense of a hand at the helm to steer a course through uncharted waters—is then *required*.

FOUR

The Institutional Embodiment of Purpose

Beyond the definition of mission and role lies the task of building purpose into the social structure of the enterprise, or, to repeat a phrase used earlier, of transforming a neutral body of men into a committed polity. In this way, policy attains depth. Rooted in and adapted to the daily experiences of living persons, policy is saved from attenuation and distortion as lines of communication are extended.

The phases of leadership as here conceived add up to a total, indivisible responsibility. There is thus no sharp division between the tasks of defining mission and embodying purpose. Each entails a self-assessment, an appreciation of internal pressures and external demands. This self-knowledge leads to the formulation of truly guiding aims and methods. It identifies opportunities as well as limitations, indicating how far leadership can or must go in changing the nature and direction of the organization. A leader will just as surely fail if he too readily yields to the limitations of his organization as if he ignores those limits. The problem is always to explore and test apparent restrictions, to see which must be accepted as inevitable, as areas of true recalcitrance, and which may be so altered as to create the institutional conditions for achieving the goals retained.

Policy and Social Structure

When we discuss large communities and great issues, there is ready agreement that policy is closely dependent on sustaining social conditions. There will be quick assent to the proposition that a democratic constitution is strong or weak according to the culture and social organization upon which it rests. A strong constitutional system is built into the underlying social structure. The latter includes the balance of power among contending interests as well as the values transmitted by family and school. But when we leave this broad arena, the basic principle that policy needs social support is easily lost.

Perhaps the difficulty of making the transition from society as a whole to smaller entities stems from our inadequate understanding of the elements of social structure. In the larger society, these elements attain gross and obvious form; but the internal social structure of specialized groupings is often hidden, or cast into unfamiliar forms, or overshadowed by the normal emphasis on avowed aims. It may be helpful, therefore, to review briefly some of those aspects of social structure that affect the maintenance and change of policy decisions.

1. *Assigned roles.* The division of labor, with its multi-

plication of more or less fixed positions, is perhaps the most obvious way of connecting policy and social structure. The assignment of formal roles sets out the tasks, powers, and expected procedures of the participants, including the lines of communication among them, according to some officially approved pattern. This is the technical organization, the rationally designed instrument, the legal system. It is not the only source of order within the group or enterprise or society, but it can often be the most important.

According to the theory developed in previous chapters, leadership declines in importance as the formal structure approaches complete determination of behavior. Management engineering is then fully adequate to the task. On the other hand, it should not be supposed that the formal system is always readily observed and understood. The officially approved patterns are not necessarily codified or even written down, nor are they always fully comprehended by the participants. There may or may not be an organization chart. Sometimes the official relations are so simple and well understood that there is no need to write them down. Or the relations may be so complex that a chart of the whole system would be too complicated to be helpful. And most important, many patterns receive official approval (or are denied it) only when they are challenged and must be submitted to the controlling officials for review. This is a problem with which lawyers are familiar, for they know how difficult it is to determine what is the law. As in the case of the law, the question is what patterns will be openly recognized and enforced as part of official policy. In any complex organization, to find this out is itself no simple task.

An assigned position or role may carry inherent difficulties that endanger the aims of policy. A classic case is that of the foreman in many industrial situations. His job requires that he represent management's interest; on the other hand, if he is to do that job effectively, he must somehow establish rapport with the men he supervises, who form their own groups and have their own interests. It is difficult to do both of these things at once, yet both are required. As a result, there is a built-in tension in the foreman's role, a tension that probably is inherent in any role that combines the exercise of authority with a need for face-to-face, empathic communication. Therefore, organizational design, even when dealing with apparently simple aspects of the division of labor, must be based on an accurate understanding of the social structure created in the course of assigning formal roles.

2. *Internal interest-groups.* Interest-groups take many forms within large organizations. They range from the small informal group of workers seeking protection from potentially arbitrary rules to the large department able to summon its own loyalties. Some such groups will be weak, others strong. Some will muster support only from within the enterprise, others will find external allies. Some interest-groups follow the lines of the formal structure, transforming technical units into unities of persons; others cut across the officially approved lines of communication. But from the standpoint of the leader all have this basic significance: *they represent sources of energy,* self-stimulated, not wholly controllable by official authority. They may subvert the enterprise or lend it life and strength. It is the task of leadership, in embodying purpose, to fit the aims of the organization to the spontaneous

interests of the groups within it, and conversely to bind parochial group egotism to larger loyalties and aspirations.

There are a number of important ways in which interest-groups may serve the ends of policy. The most obvious is the defense of a value by an organization unit that is psychologically as well as formally committed to it. If we inspect any large organization, we soon discover that at least some of its constituent units are the guardians of particular standards or aims. The personnel department defends standards of employee selection and training; accounting has its commitments to standards of reporting and fiscal control; sales defends lines of communication to buyers; production is committed to a schedule of output. All of these units are expected to defend the values entrusted to them. Top management has the authority (and may have the power) ultimately to dispose of the resulting conflicts; but it must have confidence that each constituent unit is maximizing the potentialities and defending the integrity of its special province. The transformation of technical units into interest-groups, largely through personal identification, strengthens these commitments.[1]

Thus particular values or policies find a *social base* in the group structure of the enterprise. But more general policy also needs a social base, a source of more than formal support, a center from which influence may radiate, a training ground for loyal and self-conscious adherents. Where leadership undertakes the task of truly directing the organization into desired channels, it must search for internal

[1] The general problem of internal interest-groups in administration is well treated in H. A. Simon, D. W. Smithburg, and V. A. Thompson, *Public Administration* (New York: Knopf, 1950).

sources of political support. This may take the form of creating new groups committed to new policies; or of using existing constituent units to serve as such a base. This strategy attempts to order the interest structure of the enterprise—especially the relative power of contending factions—and thus to control the conditions that affect the evolution and viability of policy.

3. *Social stratification.* The usual administrative organization includes a system of ranking. This has many uses, including fixing authority, dividing the work effectively, and supplementing formal incentives. The effects of such a system go beyond these technical functions, however. The life experiences of men at different levels in the organization differ, and these variations affect (1) how individuals in similar social positions view the world and themselves, and (2) the stake they have in the enterprise. As the ranking system shapes the general social behavior of the men who hold the ranks, social stratification emerges.

Organizations are both aided and hindered by this transformation of technical rankings into social strata. On the one hand, the development of appropriate attitudes lends support to the hierarchical system: men who have feelings of deference toward their superiors will more readily accept commands. On the other hand, the generation of special interests and attitudes by the status system brings rigidities into the organization and tends to break the unity of the enterprise.

Many of the problems created by social stratification are readily handled at the level of human relations diagnosis and treatment. Thus we know that communication among organization members is filtered as it moves up and down the line. Unpleasant information is withheld from superiors; subordinates frequently misinterpret offhand comments by their chiefs. Problems of misunderstanding and false perception, insofar as they spring from interpersonal relations, may be dealt with by management engineers who have learned their social psychology. Such problems arise continuously in any organization and do not necessarily require the attention of leadership, at least after sensitivity to human relations has been built into the organization's methods of supervision.

On the other hand, the gap between higher and lower levels in the enterprise may go beyond individual dissatisfaction or misunderstanding, to raise *political* questions affecting the basic distribution of power. For this reason, the problems of trade-union power cannot be handled by routine management *expertise* until after the fundamental issues of recognition and prerogative are settled, if they ever are.

4. *Beliefs.* The social structure of an organization also includes the relevant shared beliefs of the participants. It obviously matters a great deal whether management is perceived as benevolent or hostile. Belief systems may arise internally, as products of social stratification and the formation of interest-groups. They also reflect the social backgrounds of the personnel, who may have brought distinctive outlooks with them when recruited. As in any polity, the existence of set beliefs creates problems for the leader who undertakes to move in new directions.

A leader must know how to use law to neutralize belief by splitting it from behavior; and to employ law as a creative agency restructuring environments to foster desired understandings. The effort of the military to abandon racial segregation has involved both of these techniques. When this problem arises in administration, assuming secure control by the directing group, we see a blending of the human relations and political perspectives. The ultimate aim is political, and some of the devices (e.g., use of law) are political, but much may also be done by changing the conditions that influence interpersonal experience.

It is characteristic of authoritarian situations that political problems become readily transformed into administrative ones. Thus public opinion within the administrative organization tends to be viewed as something to be handled from the top, as a problem of organization design, training, and selective recruitment. However, political problems persist as long as conflict over policy can express itself through subordinate leaders who are too strong to be handled by administrative fiat. Only when such potential opposition has been leveled and the possibilities of its arising anew foreclosed, do we approach the pure type of authoritarian system. So long as that state has not been reached—and this is scarcely the case even in military organizations—leaders are faced with the need to assess the political capabilities of those holding undesired views, particularly whether they can form effective power blocs within the enterprise. It is often necessary to adapt the technical organization to this aspect of the social structure in order to redistribute or isolate recalcitrant elements. At the same time, this "pluralism" may be perceived as a constructive source of creative effort and a secure leadership may allow it considerable free rein.

5. *Participation.* The social structure of an organization is not mapped until we understand the different kinds and

degrees of commitment that members have to the enterprise. "Membership" does not mean the same thing to all who belong to an organization. Thus individuals differ widely in the importance they assign to their own membership and to the organization itself. It will often (but not always) be found that leaders place a higher value on the organization than do nonleaders. Since the former usually have a greater personal investment in the organization, this is hardly surprising. Morale is closely related to the possibility of increasing participation as a way of developing personal commitment to the organization. The difficulty is, however, that the division of labor usually provides but few opportunities for significant participation by the members.

Participation also affects communication. Members playing different roles, and involved in varying degrees, will differ in their ability to understand the reasons behind many decisions. Many members will have only partial views of the organization, and only a limited understanding of its objectives and principles. And because of weak or narrowly defined participation, their experience within the organization may offer little opportunity for greater comprehension. This makes it difficult to channel information easily, and especially, to hold the organization to its basic goals and values. Many organizations discover that they must adapt communication to the varying social situations of the participants. They also find that under conditions of low participation it is necessary to multiply controls, always guarding against misunderstanding of information and directives. The connection between participation and communication is of central importance in contemporary studies of organizational effectiveness.

In addition to its effect on personal stake or commitment, and on communication, differential participation affects the distribution of power within the organization. This is perhaps most evident in voluntary associations, where the highly restricted participation of members often amounts to virtual abdication; or, on the other hand, greater involvement may sustain internal political factions.

In administrative organizations participation also affects the distribution of power in a number of ways. Varying degrees of interest may affect the willingness of even high officials to expend the energy necessary to influence decisions. Some staff members may actually represent outside interests, and this will be the most significant meaning of their participation. And there may be important unintended effects on the power structure when efforts are made to increase participation of subordinates as a way of improving morale or communication; the groups set up may not be content to continue as mere devices of management.

6. *Dependency.* An executive may become the prisoner of a staff group on which he is dependent for information and specialized skills. Or the "staff" organization may be relatively weaker than the "line" because members of the staff units are dependent on the line officials for success in their day-to-day work as well as in their careers. Similarly, the dependence of rank-and-file members on the special capabilities of experienced leaders is an important basis for the tendency to self-perpetuation of leaders in many voluntary associations.

These situations suggest the value of understanding who needs whom. Of course, much of this is explicitly set out in the assignment of formal roles, which is why "reorganization" is often fraught with both terror and opportunity. Dependency patterns are also *indirect* products of the division of labor. The technical allocation of positions carries with it special opportunities for access to communication, for direct contribution to the most vital work of the enterprise, for personal advancement, for contact with outside groups. These opportunities affect the dependence of different parts of the organization on the goodwill of other parts as well as their relative ability to influence the evolution of policy. This phenomenon has received little explicit attention in the study of social structure.

* * *

These six elements of social structure, taken together, form a complex network of relations among persons and groups. This network acts as a filter through which policy is communicated; and it represents a system of accommodation among potentially conflicting parts. As a result, policy may be nullified in the filtering process; and any imbalance may lead to active measures for self-protection or aggrandizement by constituent units. To become the master of his organization, the leader must know how to deal with the social structure in all its dimensions.

When we say that policy is built into the social structure of an organization, we mean that official aims and methods are *spontaneously protected or advanced*. The aspirations of individuals and groups are so stimulated and controlled, and so ordered in their mutual relations, as to produce the desired balance of forces. This is, of course, the explicit aim of formal role assignment, but that assignment is inadequate by itself to fulfill the aim. In order to provide support for a policy, it may be necessary to alter the social structure. This occurs when "new blood" is brought in and made effective by changes in old lines of communication and dependency. Or it may be concluded that in the given circumstances the policy is not a viable one. In either case, a clear picture of the social structure of the enterprise, as a basis for making essentially political decisions, will be required.

The relation between social structure and policy may be approached in a piecemeal way, to discover the specific institutional conditions that support specific policies. For instance, certain patterns of belief and perception are suitable to an aggressive propaganda policy; others tend to nullify it. This may help us in the design of recruitment and training procedures, as well as in deciding what kinds of tasks may be brought together in the same agency. Or, to take an even more difficult problem, we may attempt to discover a pattern of participation by agency representatives on co-ordinating committees and staffs that will mitigate the tendency of such representatives merely to defend the interests of their agencies. The comparative study of similar problems in varying situations would undoubtedly lead to results of practical value.

In the long run, however, effective diagnosis depends on the discovery of general relations between types of policy orientation and kinds of social support. In other words, are there any clues to the *chararacteristic* troubles that arise in typical situations? This assumes that organizations do find themselves in "typical situations" and that these situations impose more or less uniform limitations upon the policy-maker, or offer him characteristic opportunities.

A Historical Perspective

In the search for more general connections between policy and social structure, something may be gained from the study of organization histories. Thus, in a review of group studies in social psychology, Daniel Katz called attention to some of the characteristics of organizations that may be associated with growth patterns:

What is still very much needed for social psychology in general, as well as for a knowledge of leadership, is a set of descriptive concepts for the attributes of organizations which will go well beyond the old formal-informal distinction. For example, we need to direct attention to such elementary aspects of organizations as growth patterns. A rapidly developing organization which has certain goals to achieve under emergency time-pressures presents an entirely different time pattern from a stable organization which may have passed the peak of its power. In the former case, the leadership pattern may emphasize initiative, creativity, daring and, to some extent, a rejection of traditional pathways to goals and even a reformulation of organizational goals. The organization may be one in which there is tremendous upward mobility and high motivation. In the latter case of the older, even declining, institution, the pattern may be one of conformity to tradition, an emphasis upon conventional pathways to conventional goals and even a change from the goal of the organization to the goal of efficiency as such. It is only necessary to maintain motivation at a minimum and efforts are bent toward stability rather than toward maximum productivity.[2]

[2] Daniel Katz, "Social Psychology and Group Processes" in C. P. Stone and D. W. Taylor (eds.), *Annual Review of Psychology*, Vol. II (Stanford, Calif.: Annual Reviews, Inc., 1951), p. 144.

These remarks suggest the need to place the interpretation of organizational behavior in historical perspective. Apparently similar events or practices should not be compared directly, but only as their relation to the organization's stage of development is determined. The design of forms and procedures will then be guided by this interpretation. Administrative issues will be decided only after a diagnosis that takes account of the historical context.

The language of evolution or life-cycle can be misleading when applied to organizations, but at least a natural-history approach can call attention to the developmental problems that arise in organizational experience. In doing this, we must distinguish problems posed by the task at hand, which do not call for organizational changes, from problems that are set for an organization by the stage of growth in which it finds itself. Some of these are quite obvious, as when we anticipate the need for more regularized budgeting procedures as size increases. Less obvious are problems that emerge as changes occur in the roles and needs of the participants and of the organization as a whole. Although such changes may be consciously planned and directed, they are characteristically unplanned and responsive. Taken as a total experience, each such history is of course unique. Nevertheless, to the extent that similar situations summon like responses from similar groups, we may expect to find organizational evolutionary patterns. The hope is that this uniformity, once discovered, may provide tools for more adequate description and more perceptive diagnosis.

Certain types of problems seem to characterize phases of an organization's life-history. As these problems emerge, the organization is confronted with critical policy decisions. Examples of these developmental problems are:

1. *The selection of a social base.* Among the critical decisions facing leadership, closely related to the definition of mission, is the selection of a clientele, market, target, allies, or other segment of the environment to which operations will be oriented. Personnel recruitment, public relations, and many other areas of decision will be affected by this key choice of an external "social base." The early phase of an institution's life is marked by a scrutiny of its own capabilities, and of its environment, to discover where its resources are and on whom it is dependent. The achievement of stability is influenced by this appraisal; and the future evolution of the institution is largely conditioned by the commitments generated in this basic decision. Of course, the "decision" is not always consciously made; and often the outcome is forced upon the organization by compelling circumstances which leave little freedom of choice.

When a merchant adapts his enterprise to a particular market, say for luxury goods; when a political organization bases itself on some special social force, say the labor movement or business interests; when a government agency adapts itself to the influential groups it must please in order to stay alive—there is created an effective and controlling environment of decision. As these commitments evolve, the organization loses its purity as an abstractly or ideally envisioned entity; it assumes a definite role in a living community; it becomes institutionalized. The *design* of that role, insofar as freedom to do so exists, is very largely a matter of choosing the social base upon which the organization will rest. Often this outcome is not designed but simply emerges in an unplanned way, as a precipitant of many short-run decisions.

2. *Building the institutional core.* Another developmental problem is that of creating an initial homogeneous staff. The members of this core group reflect the basic policies of the organization in their own outlooks. They can, when matured in this role, perform the essential task of indoctrinating newcomers along desired lines. They can provide some assurance that decision-making will conform, in spirit as well as letter, to policies that may have to be formulated abstractly or vaguely. The development of derivative policies and detailed applications of general rules will thus be guided by a shared general perspective. This is especially important, of course, where the assessment of tasks and results cannot be settled by routine formulae. As always, the "openness" of decision-making calls for leadership, in this case to build a social structure that will induce a spontaneous regularity of response. Where this regularity may be imposed formally, as a clear-cut technical matter, leadership is more readily dispensable.

The creation of an institutional core is partly a matter of selective recruiting, and to this extent overlaps with the task of selecting a social base. By choosing key personnel from a particular social group, the earlier conditioning of the individuals can become a valuable resource for the new organization. Conversely, of course, just such conditioning is in question when a particular source of personnel is *rejected*. But core-building involves more than selective recruiting. Indoctrination and the sharing of key experiences

—especially internal conflicts and other crises—will help to create a unified group and give the organization a special identity.

The importance of core-building for institutional development is quite familiar. The recruitment of key personnel for the new CIO Steel Workers Organizing Committee from the United Mine Workers Union decisively influenced the later evolution of the steelworkers' union, particularly in ensuring tight control from the top; the dependence of the new "action agencies" in the U.S. Department of Agriculture on a pool of agricultural personnel brought up in another tradition required special emphasis on "orientation," i.e., self-definition, in the new agencies; the emergence of communism from a socialist background entailed a very large effort to overcome earlier conditioning and create a new institutional core. Even in business, where self-definition may seem less important than in political and other community enterprises, there is a need to build a self-conscious group that fully understands "the kind of company this is."

While core-formation may be a conscious and designed process, it also develops naturally, as an indirect result of day-to-day interaction. Hence the general problem of leadership is *control* of core-formation, whether to build one congenial to desired policy or to restrain one that creates unwanted rigidities in organization and policy. This problem is developmental. It is associated with a special phase in the organization's life-history, and must be dealt with in some way if control over the long-run evolution of policy is to be maintained.

3. *Formalization.* A very familiar phase in the life-history of organizations is the formalization of procedure. The or-

ganization reduces its dependence on the personal attributes of the participants by making supervision more routine and by externalizing discipline and incentive. Formalization limits the open-endedness of organizations and thereby reduces the number of leadership decisions required.

While this process is well known, it is worth noting here that the transition from personal supervision to managerial control is developmental and brings with it characteristic growing pains, including shifts in top personnel. Formalization should be understood as an emergent problem, for in diagnosis we must ask whether a given instance of formalization is *premature,* as well as whether necessary adaptations to the new stage have been made. Premature formalization, sometimes reflecting an overemphasis on the quick achievement of clarity in communication and command channels, may seal off leadership during the early stages of organization building, when it is most needed. As a result, leadership decisions—such as those affecting the institutional core and the social base—may be left to uncontrolled adaptation.

A historical sensitivity will aid the planner to revamp organizational structure in the light of developmental changes that have created new risks and opportunities. These advantages will be illustrated in the following comments on (1) some characteristic personnel crises in organizational evolution, and (2) the relation of decentralization to social integration.

Personnel Crises and Growth Stages

Developmental changes are most sharply reflected in personnel turnover. This does not mean just any turnover, such as routine attrition and replacement, but that involving a shift from one type of person to another. As new problems emerge, individuals whose ways of thinking and responding served the organization well in an early stage may be ill-fitted for the new tasks. Characteristically, this is not so much a matter of technical knowledge as of attitudes and habits. These shape an individual's outlook and orientation to the job, resulting in a distinctive pattern of emphasis and judgment. The more firmly set the personal pattern—a condition that may be highly desirable during creative periods of organization development—the less adaptable is the individual.

A good example of personnel crisis associated with developmental change is found in the early history of many unions and in particular of the United Automobile Workers. This union was founded in 1935, in a situation of severe economic distress. Militance was the keynote during its early years. The problem of leadership was largely one of conducting a struggle for power and recognition, in which techniques of mobilization necessarily played a large role. The men who came to the fore reflected this emphasis on militancy. Successful office-seekers in the locals were those who could be counted on to deal roughly with management. Such men met the needs of a union more concerned with hewing out a place for itself, and surviving, than with responsible management of a stable organization.

After the union achieved its initial aims, the older methods of direct strike action, associated with a class-struggle outlook, became inappropriate and sometimes even harmful. Work stoppages were costly for both labor and management. While they might be thought indispensable as demonstrations of power by a group struggling for recognition, they could not be satisfactory as a permanent way of dealing with management. As this became clear, new leadership—locally and nationally—was indicated. While earlier shop stewards and local presidents were chosen for their strength in facing up to management, now it was necessary to choose men at the local level who could keep out of trouble and avoid unnecessary shutdowns. There began a movement away from militance, toward more astute negotiating techniques. To implement this change, a widespread turnover of personnel was required.[3]

Similar problems arise in industrial management. A characteristic crisis is the shift from a production orientation to an emphasis on sales and public relations. The Ford Motor Company, among others in the auto industry, went through a crisis of this sort. The organization that produced the famous "Model T" was dedicated to the goal of producing more cars per day at an ever lower cost per car. In this it was highly successful. But the organization that made this achievement possible failed to recognize or respond to changes in the market. Consumer preference was shifting to comfort, styling, and performance. By 1926, when sales were off disastrously, Ford permitted his company to engage in a national advertising campaign. He accepted this technique grudgingly, only under the pressure of a major crisis.

But much more than advertising was needed to permit sales an adequate role in the organization. Design and engineering had to be influenced as well. Finally, in 1927, production of the Model T was stopped, and Ford undertook

[3] Based on an unpublished analysis by Edward Boehm. For the experience in the steel industry, see Clinton S. Golden and Harold J. Ruttenberg, *Dynamics of Industrial Democracy* (New York: Harper, 1942), pp. 59 ff.

the monumental task of retooling for a completely new automobile and rebuilding factory interiors so that it could be manufactured. It was now clear that the very techniques that brought about the great production achievement of the Model T were stumbling blocks when the need was speedy and efficient changeover. Huge, single-purpose machines had been built into production lines where more flexible machines were needed to keep up with periodic model changes. When the policy that "the customer could have any color he wanted as long as it was black" gave way to color styling, the old finishing process became completely obsolete. "Nearly every piece of the company's monolithic equipment, laid out on the assumption that the Model T would linger on forever, had to be torn down and rebuilt. The staggering changeover necessitated the replacement of some 15,000 machine tools, the total rebuilding of another 25,000, as well as the redesigning and rearrangement of $5,000,000 worth of dies and fixtures." [4]

Conversion to the Model A took eighteen months and cost $100,000,000. Yet even this did not bring about the changes in orientation, with attendant upward revisions in the status of sales and public relations activities, that were required. Only after World War II was a reorganization in depth completed. The Ford enterprise paid a heavy price for a policy, valuable in the early state of development, that was not abandoned in good time. Given a deep initial commitment, so often required by pioneering ventures, such adaptations are likely to require correspondingly severe shifts in personnel.

[4] Keith Sward, *The Legend of Henry Ford* (New York: Rinehart, 1948), p. 199.

An important caution is necessary at this point. Such terms as "early" and "late" can be misleading, if they are taken too literally, as referring to chronological periods in a *given* organization. In fact, of course, we must see an organization in its historical context, as an institution. When, for example, the production problems of an industry have been largely solved, it is not to be expected that a new firm will go through a stage of "production orientation." It begins at the level already reached by the industry (or branch of it) as a whole. This means that developmental analysis is most relevant where there is "openness," where the organization enters new paths. Every organization does this to some extent, and has some developmental problems, but it is safe to say that these problems will be most acute among ground-breaking enterprises or where there are few sure guides to decision and action.

It seems evident that the proper assignment of personnel and the diagnosis of administrative troubles will gain from a better understanding of the relation between personnel orientations and organization life-history. Consider, for example, the following administrative problem: In the case of a large research organization, what sort of men should be chosen as chiefs of the various research divisions? Should they be subject-matter specialists or administrators? This decision presumes an assessment of the stage of development in which the organization finds itself. If basic policy has not been worked out or not yet effectively communicated, if key staff members have not been chosen, there may well be a need for the research-oriented, creative person, whose job will be to give direction to the division and to build that orientation into its personnel structure and operating procedures. When these tasks have been accomplished, it may be in order for a person whose speciality is administrative skill to take over the reins. The selection of key personnel requires an understanding of the shift in problems that occurs as the organization moves from one stage of development to another. And for best results the participants should be able to recognize the phase through which they are passing.

The connection between personnel crisis and developmental stages recalls the suggestive images used by Machiavelli and Pareto to designate leadership types. In the latter's discussion of the "circulation of elites" we are offered the hypothesis that innovator types (the "Foxes") are needed to devise new programs and techniques. To be effective, these "Foxes" must be associated with more conservative, forceful elements having strong institutional loyalties and perseverance. As the new system or institution gains strength, and has something to defend, the "Foxes" become more expendable; and the "Lions" take over complete control, trimming innovations to meet the needs of survival. But this in turn may limit adaptation to new conditions. The institutional problem is to keep a proper balance of the social types needed at each stage. This theory might well be salvaged and reformulated in more workaday terms for use in the study of specific institutions, including administrative structures, rather than of whole societies and historical epochs.

Decentralization and Social Integration

In the design of decision-making procedures, much attention is devoted to the maintenance of policy without overly concentrated or multiplied controls. Various patterns of administrative decentralization have been developed to achieve this balance. Here too, however, diagnosis and prescription should heed the life-cycle conditions that affect the application of administrative principles. Precepts regarding the value of administrative decentralization will be more adequately formulated and more intelligently applied if they take account of organizational evolution.

The need for centralization declines as the homogeneity of personnel increases. A unified outlook, binding all levels of administration, will permit decentralization without damage to policy. When top leadership cannot depend on adherence to its viewpoint, formal controls are required, if only to take measures that will increase homogeneity. On the other hand, when the premises of official policy are well understood and widely accepted, centralization is more readily dispensable. Hence we shall expect that a relatively high degree of centralization will be required in the early stages of institutional development. Later, when homogeneity has been achieved, decentralization will be feasible without undue loss of control.

A study of administrative behavior in the U.S. Forest Service showed how this informal control could be substituted for more formal centralization:

But to interpret dispersal of structure and function as the absence of central control would be to fly in the face of the facts. For what is to be said, then, of an organization which carefully instills in the minds of its members an identity of outlook, a sameness of objectives, a sense of mutual obligation and of common identification and common values? It is clear that the organization would enjoy a unity, indeed, almost a conformity, of action as marked as that of any group in which the members must take all matters to a central point for decision. There would be as noticeable an absence of internal conflict as in any organization in which all possibly controversial matters are settled in a single office. In a word, though one type of organization may manipulate the thinking and values of its members while the other directly controls their behavior by orders, both types succeed in obtaining the kind of administrative decisions and behavior they desire; one just as certainly as the other molds the actions of its members. It is meaningful, therefore, to call one centralized and the other decentralized only in the sense that they utilize different techniques to secure identical results.[5]

Of course, "identical" is not meant literally, since the social integration envisioned may well yield more flexible and efficient types of decision-making. (It may also result in excessive conformity and rigidity.) The point is simply that conformity and thus control may be won through other than formal devices. And a certain amount of social homogeneity is required if subordinate personnel are to be allowed wide discretion in the application of policies to special circumstances.

Decentralization requires a preparatory period of training, in which leadership has the opportunity to influence deeply the ideas that guide decision-making at lower levels. This influence may take the form of indoctrination, including the informal promotion of an official philosophy or even formal schooling. Educational measures are especially important where circumstances impose barriers to close contact. More useful is the collaborative development of plans and policies by as many levels of the organization as possible,

[5] Herbert Kaufman, "Field Man in Administration" (Unpublished doctoral dissertation, Columbia University, 1950), pp. 225 f.

so that a unified view, or at least understanding of the controlling viewpoint, will be achieved. This entails the participation of top leadership in low-echelon decisions and the participation of subordinate staff personnel in high-level planning.

If the chief aim of this participation is understood—the creation of a unified staff—then these procedures may later be changed, in the direction of greater clarity of responsibility and command, without excessive strain. The normal process will be one of withdrawal of top leadership from decision-making delegated to lower echelons, and a lessening of participation by subordinate personnel in policy planning. Once the task of unification is accomplished—to the extent required by the nature of the enterprise—the narrower techniques of administrative management can be brought into play. In particular, extensive delegation of responsibility may be worked out on the assumption that the prerequisite social organization is in being.

Perhaps the best-known example of decentralization in American industry is found in General Motors.[6] Yet historically the period of decentralization was preceded by a decade of tight control. Centralization was required in order to reorient the organization after the DuPont interests took over the company. The significance of this experience for administrative analysis is (1) that decentralization would have been an unfeasible policy during the stage of reorientation; and (2) that the period of tight control probably created precisely those social conditions essential to a later policy of decentralization.

Participation is a way of deepening communication and

[6] See Peter F. Drucker, *Concept of the Corporation* (New York: John Day, 1946), pp. 41 ff.

developing group cohesion. (This is sometimes associated with democratic doctrine, but need not be so understood.) Yet a given level of communication and cohesion may be adequate to the circumstances at hand. Hence maximal participation is not always required. It should be prescribed only when there is a problem of cohesion, when cohesion cannot be taken for granted and must be reinforced. Among the general conditions generating such problems is the newness of organizations. We expect, therefore, that leadership will attend to the problem of cohesion before techniques of administration that presume its solution are instituted. At least it will be understood that this problem must be solved before the full promise of these administrative methods can be fulfilled.

An interesting example of progressively lessening need for centralized co-ordination has been observed in the California prison system.[7] In that system there are Reception-Guidance centers which have the responsibility, based on "treatment" principles, for designating the particular prison to which the inmate should be assigned. This procedure runs up against another problem of the system as a whole, the need to have some reasonable balance of populations within the prisons. It was felt in the beginning that the Guidance Center personnel should not have the task of adapting their treatment-based assignment decisions to the demands of operating the system; that they should concentrate strictly on the inmate and his needs, letting other officials worry about adjusting the recommendations. A headquarters job was created—the Supervisor of Classifica-

[7] As reported in unpublished notes by Sheldon L. Messinger, who is currently engaged on an institutional study of the California Department of Corrections.

tion and Parole—with the responsibility of adjusting transfer recommendations to system demands. The device also reflected the policy of putting in charge of the Guidance Center a professional treatment specialist who would not, at least in the early period, be familiar with the operation of the prison system. There was also the wish to keep whoever did the adjusting close to headquarters, so that he could be constantly apprised of changes in the population needs of the prisons.

The continued need for this type of headquarters coordination is now questioned, however. Certain basic policies are now more widely disseminated and accepted. The need to have professionally self-conscious clinical personnel as heads of the Guidance Centers is less urgently felt, because the clinical program is now well established and no longer requires aggressive defense. The two Guidance Center chiefs can now be (and are) primarily administrators. Moreover, the present heads have in the past held subordinate professional posts in the Guidance Centers and have also served in the headquarters Bureau of Classification. Finally, the technique of population balancing is generally known and is no longer experienced as a threat by the professional personnel. All this leads to the feeling that the work of the Supervisor of Classification has become more routine and less important.

A high administrator of the system said in 1954:

"In general, I feel that the position of Associate Warden, Reception-Guidance Center [head of the Guidance Center] should be strengthened administratively to eliminate the present situation of being a 'middle man.' By this, I mean that he is currently forced by administrative rules to be an apologist for his staff when their recommendations, which he presumably has endorsed, are rejected or changed by the representatives of the Director's staff and conversely, to his own staff when rationalizing for them the rejection of recommendations which he has presumably approved. I feel that administratively the dividing of this responsibility for review of the output of the Reception-Guidance Centers is a serious administrative defect. . . . Further, it must be pointed out that both Associate Wardens formerly worked as representatives of the Bureau of Classification and therefore are quite aware of transfer policy and the technique for equalizing and meeting institutional population quotas." [8]

If this administrative procedure is defective, it is so not as an abstractly incorrect rule of administration but because it is inappropriate to the new stage of institutional development.

Thus a historical (perhaps even an evolutionary) perspective can tell us something about the conditions under which such administrative methods as decentralization may be applied. The lesson is that in appraising organizations we cannot draw conclusions regarding administrative practices unless we can place those practices in a developmental context. As we learn more about the social conditions that characterize various growth stages, we should be able to formulate principles capable of guiding the application of general precepts to specific situations.

In concluding this section, it may be well to recall the orientation that prompted an emphasis on organizational evolution. First, we have been interested in exploring the *natural* processes that condition organizational experience. Hence a concern for the products of adaptive, responsive

[8] Quoted *ibid.*

behavior, among which are social homogeneity and cohesion. Second, we are examining the area of *critical* experience, which calls for leadership rather than routine management. The study of growth stages, especially as they bear on the restructuring of role and need, seems to cast some light on critical phases. Third, the developmental patterns noted here have a common element in that they reflect changes in *commitment,* in those relations to men and ideas that are not readily altered. Changes in commitment—to markets or clienteles, to constituencies, to allies, to an institutional core, to ingrained habits of thought and modes of response—create organizational crises. The resolution of these crises markedly affects the range of competence of the enterprise as well as the survival of its distinctive aims and methods.

Precarious Values and the Defense of Integrity

Although every effective policy requires sustaining social conditions, the urgency of this need varies greatly. It is most important when aims are not well defined, when external direction is not easily imposed or easily maintained, when fluid situations require constant adaptation, and when goals or values are vulnerable to corruption. This open-endedness, we have argued earlier, generates the key problems of institutional leadership. Among these is the defense of institutional integrity—the persistence of an organization's distinctive values, competence, and role.

The integrity of an institution may be threatened, regardless of its own inner strength, if sufficiently great force is applied to it. But in diagnosis we are mainly concerned with points of special inner weakness. From that standpoint we may say that institutional integrity is characteristically vulnerable *when values are tenuous or insecure.* This variation in the strength of values has received little scientific attention.[9] Yet it commands much energy and concern in practical experience. In the course of building an organization, and establishing its separate units, group responsibility is fixed. But these "custodians of policy" will not be equally capable of sustaining their distinctive aims and standards. We need to know something about the social conditions that affect this competence.

The ability to sustain integrity is dependent on a number of general conditions, including the adequacy with which goals have been defined. Here we shall consider a special problem, the relation between precarious values and professional or elite autonomy. Our primary aim is to illustrate the potential contribution of institutional analysis to administrative theory. Therefore it may be helpful if, before dealing with administration proper, we first consider some other applications of the general idea. To do this, let us examine three ideas and how they are related.

Elite. For present purposes, this term refers to any group that is responsible for the protection of a social value. Often this responsibility is accepted consciously, but that is not essential. There would be no great harm in substituting the term "profession" or "professional group" for "elite," so long as the definition is kept in mind. Both terms have been used to designate men who carry out this basic social function.

[9] For an attempt to specify the meaning of "precarious values," based on the orientation developed here, see B. R. Clark, "Organizational Adaptation and Precarious Values," *American Sociological Review,* Vol. 21, No. 3 (June, 1956), pp. 328 f.

Social values are objects of desire that are capable of sustaining group identity. This includes any set of goals or standards that can form the basis of shared perspectives and group feeling.

Autonomy is a condition of independence sufficient to permit a group to work out and maintain a distinctive identity.

These definitions are hardly final or unambiguous, but they will permit us to make some progress. The basic relation to be considered may be formulated as follows: *The maintenance of social values depends on the autonomy of elites.* Let us turn to the bearing of this proposition on (1) the general problem of institutional integrity, as it is familiar to the historian of culture; (2) certain aspects of political organization, as revealed in the history of Communism; and (3) certain technical problems of administrative management.

1. *Elite autonomy and cultural viability.* In modern society, social institutions are exposed to many demands to provide short-run benefits for large numbers. Educational and political agencies have been sharply affected by this process, and they tend to adapt themselves to the mass by permitting participation on the basis of low standards of knowledge and conduct. This adaptation makes it increasingly difficult for professional groups or elites to maintain their own standards, hence ultimately their special identity and function. And they tend to lose their "exclusiveness"—that insulation from day-to-day pressures which permits new ideas and skills to mature.

It appears that what is critically necessary for the functioning of elites is enough autonomy to allow the maturation and protection of values. The achievement of this autonomy is a central task of professional associations, "little magazines," specialized schools, and a host of other devices for self-insulation used by groups in society that wish to protect and promote a particular set of values. Private universities with large endowments are better insulated from day-to-day pressures than are many public institutions, sustaining the autonomy of their professors and scientists. Literary elites are hard-pressed from the standpoint of autonomy because of the high cost of publishing and the commitment of that industry to the mass market. Hence literary groups may seek the shelter offered by private colleges able to subsidize esoteric journals. In our culture, the legal and medical professions are well insulated, others much less so. Those who are concerned for the protection of political, educational, aesthetic, and religious values, must find ways of providing the conditions needed to sustain the autonomy of culture-bearing elites.

The point summarized here is quite familiar to the historian of culture. But the basic relation between value maintenance and elite autonomy may cast some light on rather different and more unfamiliar situations.

2. *Political isolation and the combat party.* In an earlier work referred to previously, the author attempted to analyze the organizational aspects of Communist strategy and to understand the inner dynamics of the "combat" party. Here is a characteristic elite phenomenon. The Bolsheviks attempt to build a leadership corps of "professional revolutionaries" that maintains a long-run dedication to the aims of Communism while engaged in the struggle for immediate power objectives. Any elite group, to maintain itself as such, must

take special measures to protect its integrity. Among the most common of these measures are: (1) selective recruiting; (2) specialized training, as in the elite school; and (3) withdrawal from the everyday pursuits of mankind, especially from exposed competition in the marketplace. Each of these devices strengthens the isolation of the elite, its capacity to shape its own identity free of external pressures. All of these devices, among others, have played an important part in Bolshevik political and organizational experience. For the purpose of this discussion, a single illustration will suffice.[10]

An important phase of Bolshevik political history took place during a period of "ultra-left isolation" from about 1924 to 1935. During these years the Communist parties throughout the world followed a policy of extreme (but mostly verbal) aggression against democratic and socialist forces. The latter were presented as "social fascists," against whom all means, including violence, were in order. This was a period of "dual" trade-unionism, in which the Communists disdained to work within the legitimate—"yellow" —labor movement but created their own "red" trade-unions. The latter usually included only Communist party members and their periphery, but they did lay the basis for later effective penetration of the mass unions.

The general effect of this ultra-left activity was organizational isolation. At first glance, this seems to have been self-defeating, and the later reversal might be understood as a corrective measure. The Communists did indeed isolate themselves from the main body of the workers, hence from any significant influence in society. Nevertheless, *this long period of isolation served to consolidate the power of the Rus-*

[10] Selznick, *The Organizational Weapon*, pp. 126 ff.

sian party over the International, to test and train the party cadres, and to intensify reliance on conspiratorial methods. Out of this period of ultra-left phrases, revolutionary adventures, splits, purges, and intensive indoctrination, there emerged a powerful political movement. This is not to say that the Communist leaders designed it so. But the modern Communist movement is a product of its history; it owes elements of strength, as well as of weakness, to the apparently irrational period of "social fascism" and "united front from below."

Specifically, this character-forming period readied the organization for a new period of propagandistic deception and organizational maneuver. After 1935, organizational isolation was definitively—and permanently—rejected. Open Communist propaganda was increasingly retired to the background, and the party turned to slogans of "unity," "peace," and similar generalities that might offer access to wider sections of the population. The "red" unions were abandoned and the party entered the legitimate trade-unions. The old aggression against "bourgeois" politicians was relaxed, and the party could support a Franklin Roosevelt when that was expedient.

On the organizational front the new turn permitted a wide range of targets, a multiplicity of new devices and maneuvers, unrestricted by the need continuously to repeat revolutionary phraseology. It opened up a whole new arena for political intervention from which the Communists have not withdrawn despite subsequent major shifts in the party line. The Seventh Congress of the Comintern, in 1935, initiated a permanent effort to break through long-standing isolation by the free use of deceptive symbols and organizational stratagems. In effect the conclusion was drawn that the day for worrying about the Communist integrity of the parties was past; the basic weapon had been forged; the time for wielding it effectively had arrived. Insistence on correct ideological formulae was to be exchanged for acceptance of more flexible slogans, and organizational practices were to be adapted to the conditions of the arena.

The period of ultra-left propaganda and organizational isolation was an *internally-oriented* period, dedicated to preparing a weapon that would maintain its integrity when it was thrown into active political combat. It was this period of sharp break with the looser, more relaxed socialist traditions; of heavy emphasis on party discipline, on political orthodoxy, on conspiracy, and on intensive indoctrination that made possible the maintenance of the hard core of the party despite severe shifts in political line (as at the time of the Stalin-Hitler pact), and despite the heavy pressures on party members to become adapted to trade-unionist and reformist perspectives. Communist members could become *deployable agents* in other organizations—always serving the interests of the party—only as they accepted the authority of the party leadership. To create an organization able to exert such authority was a task that could not be accomplished without strenuous effort. Most of the early history of the Communist movement was devoted to that task of building "revolutionary cadres."

The Communist combat party, by assuming an ultra-left propaganda posture, preserved its autonomy as an elite, isolating itself from the pressures of the political arena *until it was ready to resist those pressures.* Put another way, the Bolsheviks wished to maintain an institution embodying a precarious value: a party competent to deploy members as disciplined agents. A period of organizational isolation, fostered by ultra-left propaganda, helped to contribute the sustaining social conditions. This only repeats, in a particular context, the generalization noted above, that the maintenance of values depends on the autonomy of elites. We have drawn here on a general institutional theory to help make sense of a particular historical development. The better developed such a general theory is, the more inferences can be drawn regarding the phenomena under analysis.

3. *Administrative autonomy and precarious values.* One of the perennial problems confronting the architect of organizations is administrative autonomy. When should an activity be thought of as distinctive enough to be allowed a relatively independent organizational existence? Should political intelligence personnel be assigned to geographic desks in the State Department, or should they have their own organization? Should education in a trade-union be bracketed administratively with public relations? Should psychological warfare operations be attached to G-2?

Applying the theory of professional or elite autonomy dicussed above, we may recast the problem in the following way:

(1) When an organizational unit is set up, especially if it is large enough to have its own administrative staff, an elite is created in the sense that some men now become professionally responsible for the protection of a social value. Probably this elite function is the source of most organizational rivalry.

(2) It follows from our general theory that isolation is necessary during periods of incubation and maturation, but

may be modified when this character-forming task has been accomplished. Moreover, the more readily subject to outside pressure a given value is, the more necessary is this isolation. (Roughly, this means that the more technical a function is, the more dispensable is organizational isolation. In highly technical fields, a large degree of *social* isolation is won simply by the use of esoteric techniques and language, and by the evident importance of professional criteria as to appropriate methods of work.)

(3) This provides us with a principle that can help in making decisions about administrative autonomy. We appraise the given value (be it intelligence, health, education, psychological warfare, or customer service) and consider (*a*) whether the elite function of value-protection is required, and (*b*) whether special safeguards against outside pressures are needed. This may lead to the conclusion, for example, that a new staff unit ought to be attached directly to a top-command echelon—not permanently, but during a period when its basic perspectives are being laid down, its distinctive mission being evolved. Or such a unit might be attached to one *quite different* in function (but institutionally strong) for the express purpose of offering a haven to an organization charged with defending and developing a precarious value. Strong groups with similar responsibilities, who might feel threatened by the new unit, would thus be restrained from attacking it too directly.

An approach to autonomy in these terms is a radical departure from the attempt to build organizations according to the logical association of functions. That principle—which will of course always be relevant—is often violated in practice, and for good reason. It must be violated whenever values are unequal in strength. Organization planning is unrealistic when it fails to take account of the differential capacity of subordinate units to defend the integrity of their functions. The theory of elite autonomy permits us to deal with this problem systematically and openly. This is important because many decisions that do in fact face up to this issue must now be justified obliquely, and be half-hidden, since there is no accepted administrative principle allowing organizations to be treated differently according to the strength of their respective values.

Let us apply this idea to the classic headquarters-field problem. Given a headquarters organization and a field organization, to whom shall subject-matter specialists (say in recreation, medicine, or personnel selection) be responsible? To the technical staff chief at headquarters or to the head of the local field organization? The dilemma is that the headquarters staff will be concerned over values (whether good accounting procedure or good medical practice), but the field executive will be under pressure to get an immediate job done while perhaps taking insufficient account of the long-run consequences of his decisions. One answer has been "dual supervision," in which certain officers are thought of as "administratively" responsible to one superior while "technically" responsible to another.[11] This recognizes the special role of technical staff personnel in developing and defending values.

But "dual supervision" really presumes an optimum situation, in which a strong value-oriented elite (the technical

[11] See A. W. MacMahon, J. D. Millett, and Gladys Ogden, *The Administration of Federal Work Relief* (Chicago: Public Administration Service, 1941), Chap. 11; also J. D. Millett, "Field Organization and Staff Supervision," *New Horizons in Public Administration,* University of Alabama Press, 1945.

staff) has had enough autonomy to lay down professional criteria that are accepted by the line officials. When, as in medicine and engineering, values have been effectively matured, dual supervision is relatively easy, for the boundaries within which the technical and administrative personnel may operate are reasonably clear-cut and are tacitly or even formally recognized as part of the code of proper behavior. Even in such fields, however, where the boundaries are unclear, as in the development of criteria for certifying military personnel fit for duty, it is to be expected that the professional group will be vulnerable to external pressure.

When we deal with *precarious* values—say an information and education program, or a political intelligence operation—special attention to the problem of elite autonomy is required. In such cases, we may accept a much closer relation between headquarters staff and field personnel than would otherwise be justified, because we recognize the need for intensive communication during character-forming periods. Such periods also require special measures to resist potentially corrupting external pressures, and this means a more intense professional self-consciousness. Suppose a government agency establishes a new labor relations policy, championed by the headquarters staff, but of necessity using line executives (say on construction jobs) who are not fully in sympathy with this policy. In the early days of the agency, we may expect a centralization of the labor relations program, perhaps manifested in a rule permitting workers to register complaints directly at headquarters and in the establishment of field labor relations specialists who conceive of themselves as self-conscious outposts of headquarters in an alien environment. This centralization permits the autonomous maturation of values; later, when the desired policies have been well established, a greater degree of decentralization will be in order.

In general, headquarters staffs perform elite functions. They tend to be highly self-conscious about the values for which they have assumed responsibility. That is why co-operation among field representatives is often easier to attain than co-operation among headquarters staffs. And it is the headquarters staff that puts pressure on its field representatives to avoid co-operation that may prejudice distinctive identity. The appropriate response to this phenomenon is neither to deplore it generally nor to accept it as inevitable, but to investigate the actual circumstances to determine how much elite autonomy is in fact needed, given the strength of the value in question.

The theory of elite autonomy, thus applied, helps make explicit what is really at stake in much confused conflict and oblique debate. It leads us away from rigid rules of administrative organization, yet it helps to identify the key elements that need to be controlled and in terms of which guiding principles can be set forth.

* * *

Few aspects of organization are so important, yet so badly neglected by students of the subject, as this problem of institutional integrity. No one knows how much in resources and strategic capability is sacrificed by the U.S. military establishment (and other great enterprises) as a result of organizational rivalry. The educated guesses would run very high. Yet this rivalry is no simple result of personal egotism; it is closely related to the legitimate effort of leaders to defend the values with which they have been entrusted. The military services have faced this problem continuously, and have tried at various times to define the administrative conditions of professional integrity. The Air Force fought for decades to be recognized as an agency that ○ needed a distinctive identity in order to do its job effectively. This identity, it was held, would need support in the following "clearly demonstrated principles":

(1) Freedom through "independent experimentation and research" to develop new forms of aircraft; (2) the power to procure for itself new types of planes; (3) freedom to select and train the special personnel to operate airplanes and to plan air tactics; (4) the power to create an air staff to plan air strategy; and (5) the power to "insure the permanence of the technique" thus created through an adequate permanent force of regular officers.[12]

Similarly, during the controversy over unification, a naval leader attempted to set out an administrative principle that would help protect the integrity of the services. He called for recognition of two phases in decision-making regarding major weapons: development and procurement. In the first phase, each service should be autonomous in deciding what weapons should be carried through to the prototype stage, without veto power by other services. Decisions on large-scale procurement, however, justify a greater degree of external co-ordination and control.[13]

And here is a defense of Marine Corps aviation:

[12] John D. Millett, "The War Department in World War II," *American Political Science Review*, XL (1946), p. 870.
[13] Statement of Arthur W. Radford, Admiral, U.S. Navy, *Hearings*, U.S. House Committee on Armed Services, 81st Congress, 1st sess. (1949), p. 48.

I will probably be asked: Why a Marine aviation at all? Why can't naval aviation or Air Force squadrons support Marine landing forces? In answer, I would invite your attention to the peculiar qualifications of Marine aviators. Unique among military fliers, each Marine pilot is required to serve two years as a Marine infantry officer before he may even apply for aviation duty. Thereafter, throughout his career, he must attend the same professional schools as does his ground contemporary; he frequently finds himself a member of a combined staff where his daily work requires intimate familiarity with the tactics of all elements of the Marine Corps. In other words, he knows what the commander on the ground needs and he knows how to deliver it. What is equally important, he knows what a deployed battalion looks like from the air; the troops of that battalion have no hesitancy in asking him to drop bombs or shoot rockets in the closest proximity to their front lines.[14]

Whatever the merits of the claims and counterclaims implicit in these statements, they do indicate the practical importance of identifying the conditions that sustain the integrity of an enterprise. This applies, of course, not only to the great agencies mentioned here, but to all organizations and constituent units that are in some degree custodians of a policy. These statements also suggest that the defense of integrity is not a matter of sheer organizational survival; it is rather the policy, the mission, the special capability—in a word, the identity of the group that is at stake.

As we have suggested, the basic answer society has evolved for the protection of institutional integrity is professionalism. While some very general aspects of this phenom-

[14] Statement of General Vernon E. Megee, *ibid.*, p. 198.

enon have been known since Plato's time, very little attention has been given it as *operating within specific organizations* rather than in society at large. In the case of organizations that initiate ideas, where creativity and independence are at a premium, the role of internal and external professional associations can be crucial, buttressing the independence of key personnel. If a man is to take risks, he needs social supports. Yet the role of professionalism will vary in different types of organizations, depending on the balance required between those men whose primary commitment is to a specific organization and those whose sense of responsibility is broader. These matters are as yet hardly touched by students of the sociology of professions.

FIVE

Conclusion

The main task of this essay has been to explore the meaning of institutional leadership, in the hope of contributing to our understanding of large-scale organization. We have not offered recipes for the solution of immediate problems. Rather, we have sought to encourage reflection and self-knowledge, to provide some new guides to the diagnosis of administrative troubles, and to suggest that the posture of statesmanship may well be appropriate for many executives who now have a narrower view and a more limited aspiration.

This final chapter summarizes the main ideas developed above, with some added notes on responsibility and creativity in leadership.

Beyond Efficiency

It is easy to agree to the abstract proposition that the function of the executive is to find a happy joinder of means and ends. It is harder to take that idea seriously. There is a strong tendency not only in administrative life but in all social action to divorce means and ends by overemphasizing one or the other. The cult of efficiency in administrative theory and practice is a modern way of overstressing means and neglecting ends. This it does in two ways. First, by fixing attention on maintaining a smooth-running machine, it slights the more basic and more difficult problem of defining and safeguarding the ends of an enterprise. Second, the cult of efficiency tends to stress techniques of organization that are essentially neutral, and therefore available for any goals, rather than methods peculiarly adapted to a distinctive type of organization or stage of development.

Efficiency as an operating ideal presumes that goals are settled and that the main resources and methods for achieving them are available. The problem is then one of joining available means to known ends. This order of decision-making we have called *routine,* distinguishing it from the realm of *critical* decision. The latter, because it involves choices that affect the basic character of the enterprise, is the true province of leadership as distinct from administrative management. Such choices are of course often made unconsciously, without awareness of their larger significance, but then the enterprise evolves more or less blindly. Leadership provides guidance to minimize this blindness.

In many situations, including those most important to the ultimate well-being of the enterprise, goals may not have been defined. Moreover, even when they are defined, the necessary means may have still to be created. Creating the means is, furthermore, not a narrow technical matter; it involves molding the social character of the organization. Leadership goes beyond efficiency (1) when it sets the basic mission of the organization and (2) when it creates a social organism capable of fulfilling that mission. A company's decision to add a new product may be routine if the new is but an extension of the old. It is a critical decision, however, when it calls for a re-examination of the firm's mission and role, e.g., whether to remain primarily a producer of a raw commodity or to become a manufacturer of consumer goods. The latter choice will inevitably affect the outlook of management, the structure and control of the company, and the balance of forces in the industry.

Not only the setting of goals by top leadership but many other kinds of decisions at all administrative levels can be part of critical experience. Anything may enter the area of critical experience providing it affects the ability of the organization to uphold its distinctive aims and values. If an atmosphere congenial to creative research is required, the methods of assigning work, policing diligence, or judging output must be governed by that aim. This often produces tension between those executives most sensitive to the special needs of the enterprise and those who seek to apply more general and more neutral techniques of efficiency.

In going beyond efficiency, leadership also transcends "human engineering," at least as that is usually understood. Efficiency may require improved techniques of communication and supervision, but these techniques are largely indifferent to the aims they serve. The human relations specialist like his predecessor, the efficiency expert, is characteristically unmoved by program, by the content of what is to be done. His inspiration does not derive from the aim of creating a particular kind of auto firm or hospital or school. Rather his imagination is stirred by the processes of group interaction and the vision of a harmonious team, whatever its end may be.

This does not mean that communication and other forms of human interaction are unimportant to leadership. They do become vitally important when they are given content, when they serve the aim of fashioning a distinctive way of thinking or acting and thus help establish the human foundations for achieving a particular set of goals. Indeed, the *attainment* of efficiency, in the sense of transforming a basically inefficient organization into one that runs according to modern standards, may itself be a leadership goal. But here the task is a creative one, a matter of reshaping fundamental perspectives and relationships. It should not be confused with the routine administrative management of an organization already fully committed to the premises of rational accounting and discipline.

Beyond Organization

The design and maintenance of organizations is often a straightforward engineering proposition. When the goals of the organization are clear-cut, and when most choices can be made on the basis of known and objective technical criteria, the engineer rather than the leader is called for. His work may include human engineering in order to smooth personal relations, improve morale, or reduce absenteeism. But his problem remains one of adapting known quantities through known techniques to predetermined ends.

From the engineering perspective, the organization is made up of standardized building blocks. These elements, and the ways of putting them together, are the stock-in-trade of the organization engineer. His ultimate ideal is complete rationality, and this assumes that each member of the organization, and each constituent unit, can be made to adhere faithfully to an assigned, engineered role. Furthermore, the role assigned does not stem so much from the peculiar nature of *this* enterprise; rather, the roles are increasingly generalized and similar to parallel roles in other organizations. Only thus can the organization engineer take advantage of the growth of general knowledge concerning the conditions of efficient administrative management.

The limits of organization engineering become apparent when we must create a structure *uniquely adapted to the mission and role of the enterprise*. This adaptation goes beyond a tailored combination of uniform elements; it is an adaptation in depth, affecting the nature of the parts themselves. This is really a very familiar process, brought home to us most clearly when we recognize that certain firms or agencies are stamped by distinctive ways of making decisions or by peculiar commitments to aims, methods, or clienteles. In this way the organization as a technical instrument takes on values. As a vehicle of group integrity it becomes in some degree an end in itself. This process of becoming infused with value is part of what we mean by institutionalization. As this occurs, *organization management* becomes *institutional leadership*. The latter's main responsibility is not so much technical administrative management as the maintenance of institutional integrity.

The integrity of an enterprise goes beyond efficiency, beyond organization forms and procedures, even beyond group cohesion. Integrity combines organization and policy. It is the unity that emerges when a particular orientation becomes so firmly a part of group life that it colors and directs a wide variety of attitudes, decisions, and forms of organization, and does so at many levels of experience. The building of integrity is part of what we have called the "institutional embodiment of purpose" and its protection is a major function of leadership.

The protection of integrity is more than an aesthetic or expressive exercise, more than an attempt to preserve a comforting, familiar environment. It is a practical concern of the first importance because the defense of integrity is also a defense of the organization's *distinctive competence*. As institutionalization progresses the enterprise takes on a special character, and this means that it becomes peculiarly competent (or incompetent) to do a particular kind of work. This is especially important when much depends on the creation of an appropriate atmosphere, as in the case of efforts to hold tight transportation schedules or maintain high standards of quality. A considerable part of high-level salesmanship is an effort to show the firm's distinctive capability to produce a certain product or perform a special service. This is important in government too, where competing agencies having similar formal assignments work hard to develop and display their distinctive competencies.

The terms "institution," "organization character," and "distinctive competence" all refer to the same basic process —the transformation of an engineered, technical arrangement of building blocks into a social organism. This transition goes on unconsciously and inevitably wherever leeway for evolution and adaptation is allowed by the system of technical controls; and at least some such leeway exists in all but the most narrowly circumscribed organizations. Leadership has the job of guiding the transition from organization to institution so that the ultimate result effectively embodies desired aims and standards.

Occasionally we encounter a self-conscious attempt to create an institution. The history of the *New York Times,* for example, suggests such an effort. Ideals of objectivity and public instruction have deeply affected many aspects of the organization, including the nature of the staff, the pace of work, the relations to advertisers, and its role among other newspapers. Of course, it is relatively easy to see a newspaper as an institution because it so apparently touches familiar ideals. Whether it truly embodies those ideals is a question that appeals to all as relevant and sensible. But we have argued that the formation of institutions is a far more widespread phenomenon and is a process that must be understood if the critical experience of leadership is to be grasped.

Institutional analysis asks the question: What is the bearing of an existing or proposed procedure on the distinctive role and character of the enterprise? Very often, of course, organization practices are institutionally neutral, just as many body functions are independent of the personality structure. But the question must be put. Thus recent efforts to establish statistical and administrative control units for the judiciary look to improvements in the division of labor among judges, and to similar matters, for the achievement of a more "orderly flow of litigation." The proponents of greater efficiency reaffirm their adherence to the principle of judicial independence, and they believe this principle is not affected by improved administrative controls; they seek to "serve, not supervise." In this case it seems altogether likely that a wide measure of reform in judicial administration is possible without seriously undermining the judge's traditional image of his own role and sense of independence. Nevertheless, the experience of other institutions suggests that the managerial trend can have far-reaching effects, and the question of whether a set of proposed administrative reforms endangers the maintenance of desired values is always legitimate and necessary.

The lesson is this: Those who deal with the more obvious ideals—such as education, science, creativity, or freedom— should more fully recognize the dependence of these ideals on congenial though often mundane administrative arrangements. On the other hand, those who deal with more restricted values, such as the maintenance of a particular industrial competence, should be aware that these values too involve ideals of excellence, ideals that must be built into the social structure of the enterprise and become part of its basic character. In either case, a too ready acceptance of neutral techniques of efficiency, whatever their other merits, will contribute little to this institutional development and may even retard it.

The study of institutions is in some ways comparable to the clinical study of personality. It requires a genetic and developmental approach, an emphasis on historical origins and growth stages. There is a need to see the enterprise as a whole and to see how it is transformed as new ways of dealing with a changing environment evolve. As in the case of personality, effective diagnosis depends upon locating the special problems that go along with a particular character-structure; and we can understand character better when we see it as the product of self-preserving efforts to deal with inner impulses and external demands. In both personality and institutions "self-preservation" means more than bare organic or material survival. Self-preservation has to do with the maintenance of basic identity, with the integrity of a personal or institutional "self."

In approaching these problems, there is necessarily a close connection between clinical diagnosis of particular cases and the development of sound general knowledge. Our problem is to discover the characteristic ways in which *types* of institutions respond to *types* of circumstances. The significant classifications may well depart from common-sense distinctions among enterprises according to whether they perform economic, political, religious, or military functions. We may find that more general characteristics, such as professionalized managerial control, competence to make full use of creative talents, or dependence on volunteer personnel, are more helpful in classifying organizations and in understanding the types of problems they face and the solutions that may be available. Students of personality have had similar objectives and have made greater, although still very crude, efforts to get away from common-sense rubrics. Yet, despite theoretical difficulties, real progress has been made, and clinical success in diagnosis and therapy lends confidence to the larger scientific quest.

Responsible Leadership

As the organization becomes an institution new problems are set for the men who run it. Among these is the need for institutional responsibility, which accounts for much of what we mean by statesmanship.

From a personal standpoint, responsible leadership is a

blend of commitment, understanding, and determination. These elements bring together the selfhood of the leader and the identity of the institution. This is partly a matter of self-*conception,* for whatever his special background, and however important it may have been in the decision that gave him his office, the responsible leader in a mature institution must transcend his specialism. Self-*knowledge* becomes an understanding not only of the leader's own weaknesses and potentialities but of those qualities in the enterprise itself. And the assumption of command is a self-*summoning* process, yielding the will to know and the will to act in accordance with the requirements of institutional survival and fulfillment.

From a policy standpoint, and that is our primary concern, most of the characteristics of the responsible leader can be summarized under two headings: the avoidance of opportunism and the avoidance of utopianism.

Opportunism is the pursuit of immediate, short-run advantages in a way inadequately controlled by considerations of principle and ultimate consequence. To take advantage of opportunities is to show that one is alive, but institutions no less than persons must look to the long-run effects of present advantage. In speaking of the "long run" we have in mind not time as such but how change affects personal or institutional identity. Such effects are not usually immediately apparent, and therefore we emphasize the lapse of time. But changes in character or identity may occur quite rapidly.

Leadership is irresponsible when it fails to set goals and therefore lets the institution drift. The absence of controlling aims forces decisions to be made in response to immediate pressures. Of course, many large enterprises do drift, yet they survive. The penalties are not always swift, and very often bare survival is possible even though the fullest potentialities of the enterprise are not realized and significant changes in identity do occur.

The setting of institutional *goals* cannot be divorced from the enunciation of governing *principles*. Goal-setting, if it is institutionally meaningful, is framed in the language of character or identity, that is, it tells us what we should "do" in order to become what we want to "be." A decision to produce a new product or enter a new market, though it may set goals, is nevertheless irresponsible if it is not based on an understanding of the company's past and potential character. If the new venture, on analysis, requires a change in distinctive competence, then *that* becomes the new goal. Such a goal is bound up with principles because attaining and conserving a distinctive competence depends on an understanding of what standards are required and how to maintain them. If a grain processing firm moves into the chemical industry, it must learn how to build into its new division the competence to keep pace with rapid technological changes on pain of falling behind in the struggle against obsolescent products and techniques. Because the technique of attaining this is seldom based on explicitly formulated principles, it would be prudent to staff the new division, *especially* at the top, with men drawn from the chemical industry rather than with men drawn from the parent firm and representing its tradition and orientations.

When an enterprise is permitted to drift, making short-run, partial adaptations, the greatest danger lies in uncontrolled effects on organization character. If ultimately there is a complete change, with a new character emerging, those who formed and sustained the organization at the beginning may find that they no longer fit the organization. There is also the likelihood that character will not really be transformed: it will be *attenuated and confused.* Attenuation means that the sought-for distinctive competence becomes vague and abstract, unable to influence deeply the work of staff and operating divisions. This occurs when the formulation of institutional goals is an afterthought, a way of rationalizing activities actually resulting from opportunistic lines of decision. A confused organization character is marked by an unordered and disharmonious mixture of capabilities. The practical result is that the organization cannot perform any task effectively, and this weakens its ability to survive in the face of strong competition.

In addition to sheer drift stemming from the failure to set institutional goals, opportunism also reflects an excessive response to outside pressures. To be sure, leaders must take account of the environment, adapting to its limitations as well as to its opportunities, but we must beware of institutional surrender made in the name of organizational survival. There is a difference between a university president who *takes account* of a state legislature or strong pressure groups and one who permits these forces to determine university policy. The leader's job is to *test* the environment to find out which demands can become truly effective threats, to *change* the environment by finding allies and other sources of external support, and to *gird* his organization by creating the means and the will to withstand attacks.

Here, too, we come back to the problem of maintaining

institutional integrity. The ultimate cost of opportunistic adaptation goes beyond capitulation on specific issues. A more serious result is that outside elements may enter the organization and dominate parts of it. When this happens the organization is no longer truly independent, no longer making specific compromises as necessity dictates while retaining its unity and distinctive identity. Rather, it has given over a piece of itself to alien forces, making it possible for them to exercise broader influence on policy. The transformation of compromise or even defeat into partial organizational surrender can sometimes be a conscious measure of last resort, but it also occurs without full awareness on the part of the participants. In our study of the Tennessee Valley Authority, referred to above, just such a phenomenon was observed. A political compromise with local and national agricultural interests was implemented by permitting part of the TVA as an organization to be controlled by those forces, with extensive and unanticipated effects on the role and character of the agency. The avoidance of opportunism is not the avoidance of all compromise; it is the avoidance of compromise that undermines institutional integrity.

Opportunism also displays itself in a narrow self-centeredness, in an effort to exploit other groups for immediate, short-run advantages. If a firm offers a product or service to other firms, expectations of dependability are created, especially in the matter of continuing supply. If supplies are abruptly discontinued, activities that depended upon them will suffer. Hence a firm's reputation for dependability and concern for others becomes a matter of great importance wherever continuing relationships are envisioned. To act as if only a set of impersonal transactions were involved, with no responsibility beyond the strict terms of a contract, creates anxiety in the buyer, threatens to damage *his* reputation for dependability, and in the end weakens both parties.

The responsible leader recognizes the need for stable relations with the community of which his organization is a part, although he must test the environment to see how real that requirement is. A large and enduring enterprise will probably have to contribute to the maintenance of community stability, at least within its own field of action. In industry, this may take the form of participation in trade associations and other devices for self-regulation. The marginal firm, on the other hand, can afford to be irresponsible in dealing with the community because it is less dependent on stable relations with other firms or with a special clientele or labor force. Such firms have also less need of responsibility to themselves as institutions, for they have fewer hostages to fortune. Generally, responsibility to the enterprise and to the community go hand in hand, each increasing as the transition from organization to institution becomes more complete.

If opportunism goes too far in accepting the dictates of a "reality principle," utopianism hopes to avoid hard choices by a flight to abstractions. This too results in irresponsibility, in escape from the true functions of leadership.

In Chapter Three we outlined some of the sources of utopianism. One of these is the *overgeneralization of purpose*. Thus "to make a profit" is widely accepted as a statement of business purpose, but this is too general to permit responsible decision-making. Here again, the more marginal the business, that is, the greater its reliance upon quick returns, easy liquidation, and highly flexible tactics, the less need there is for an institutionally responsible and more specific formulation of purpose. Indeed, the very generality of the purpose is congenial to the opportunism of these groups. But when institutional continuity and identity are at stake, a definition of mission is required that will take account of the organization's distinctive character, including present and prospective capabilities, as well as the requirements of playing a desired role in a particular industrial or commercial context.

Utopian wishful-thinking enters when men who purport to be institutional leaders attempt to rely on overgeneralized purposes to guide their decisions. But when guides are unrealistic, yet decisions must be made, more realistic *but uncontrolled* criteria will somehow fill the gap. Immediate exigencies will dominate the actual choices that are made. In this way, the polarities of utopianism and opportunism involve each other.

Another manifestation of utopianism is the hope that the solution of technical problems will solve institutional problems. We have discussed the "retreat to technology" as a way of avoiding responsibility for the multiple ends that must be satisfied if the institution as a whole is to be successful. To be "just a soldier," "just an engineer," or even "just a businessman" is inconsistent with the demands of statesmanship. It is utopian and irresponsible to suppose that a narrow technical logic can be relied on by men who make decisions that, though they originate in technical problems, have larger consequences for the ultimate evolution of the enterprise and its position in the world.

This brand of utopianism is associated with adventurism, a willingness to commit the organization as a whole on the basis of a partial assessment of the situation derived from a particular technological perspective, such as that of the propagandist in foreign affairs or the engineer or designer in industry. Here again the utopian as technologist becomes the victim of opportunism.

Responsible leadership steers a course between utopianism and opportunism. Its responsibility consists in accepting the obligation of giving direction instead of merely ministering to organizational equilibrium; in adapting aspiration to the character of the organization, bearing in mind that what the organization has been will affect what it can be and do; and in transcending bare organizational survival by seeing that specialized decisions do not weaken or confuse the distinctive identity of the enterprise.

Creative Leadership

To the essentially conservative posture of the responsible leader we must add a concern for change and reconstruction. This creative role has two aspects. First, there is what we have called the "institutional embodiment of purpose." Second, creativity is exercised by strategic and tactical planning, that is, analyzing the environment to determine how best to use the existing resources and capabilities of the organization. This essay has not treated the problem of externally oriented strategies. On the other hand, what can be done to establish policy internally depends upon the changing relation between the organization and its environment.

The inbuilding of purpose is a challenge to creativity because it involves transforming men and groups from neutral, technical units into participants who have a peculiar stamp, sensitivity, and commitment. This is ultimately an educational process. It has been well said that the effective leader must know the meaning and master the techniques of the educator. As in the larger community, education is more than narrow technical training; though it does not shrink from indoctrination, it also teaches men to think for themselves. The leader as educator requires an ability to interpret the role and character of the enterprise, to perceive and develop models for thought and behavior, and to find modes of communication that will inculcate general rather than merely partial perspectives.

The main practical import of this effort is that *policy will gain spontaneous and reasoned support.* Desired ends and means are sustained and furthered, not through continuous command, but as a free expression of truly accepted principles. This presumes that at least the core participants combine loyalty to the enterprise with a sensitive awareness of the principles by which it is guided. Loyalty by itself is not enough, just as blind patriotism is insufficient. There must also be an ability to sense when a course of action threatens institutional integrity.

To be sure, this ideal of rational, free-willed consent is virtually impossible to achieve in organizations that have narrow, practical aims and whose main problem is the disciplined harnessing of human energy to achieve those aims. But such organizations, just because of this narrowness, are but meagerly institutionalized and have correspondingly little need for executive statesmanship. The creativity we speak of here is particularly necessary—and peculiarly possible—where, as discussed earlier, the transition from organization to institution is in process or has occurred.

To create an institution we rely on many techniques for infusing day-to-day behavior with long-run meaning and purpose. One of the most important of these techniques is the elaboration of socially integrating myths. These are efforts to state, in the language of uplift and idealism, what is distinctive about the aims and methods of the enterprise. Successful institutions are usually able to fill in the formula, "What we are proud of around here is. . . ." Sometimes, a fairly explicit institutional philosophy is worked out; more often, a sense of mission is communicated in more indirect but no less significant ways. The assignment of high prestige to certain activities will itself help to create a myth, especially if buttressed by occasional explicit statements. The specific ways of projecting a myth are as various as communication itself. For creative leadership, it is not the communication of a myth that counts; rather, creativity depends on having the will and the insight to see the necessity of the myth, to discover a successful formulation, and above all to create the organizational conditions that will sustain the ideals expressed.

Successful myths are never merely cynical or manipulative, even though they may be put forward self-consciously to further the chances of stability or survival. If a state university develops a concept of "service to the community" as its central ideal, as against more remote academic aspirations, this may have its origins in a sense of insecurity, but it will not be innocent in application. To be effective, the projected myth cannot be restricted to holiday speeches or to testimony before legislative committees. It will inevitably color many aspects of university policy, affecting standards of admission, orientations of research, and the scope of the curriculum. The compulsion to embody the myth in practice has a dual source, reflecting inner needs and outer demands. Externally, those who can enforce demands upon the institution will not be content with empty verbal statements. They will expect conformity and the myth itself will provide a powerful lever to that end.

The executive acts out the myth for reasons of self-expression, but also for quite practical administrative reasons. He requires *some* integrating aid to the making of many diverse day-to-day decisions, and the myth helps to fulfill that need. Sharp discrepancies between theory and practice threaten his own authority in the eyes of subordinates; conformity to the myth will lessen "trouble" with outside groups. Not least important, he can hope that the myth will contribute to a unified sense of mission and thereby to the harmony of the whole. If the administrator is primarily dedicated to maintaining a smooth-running machine, and only weakly committed to substantive aims, these advantages will seem particularly appealing.

In the end, however, whatever their source, myths are institution builders. Making the myth effective willy-nilly entrenches particular objectives and capabilities, although these may not be the ones that initially inspired the sponsors of the enterprise. Myth-making may have roots in a sensed need to improve efficiency and morale; but its main office is to help create an integrated social organism.

The art of the creative leader is the art of institution-building, the reworking of human and technological materials to fashion an organism that embodies new and enduring values. The opportunity to do this depends on a considerable sensitivity to the politics of internal change. This is more than a struggle for power among contending groups and leaders. It is equally a matter of avoiding recalcitrance and releasing energies. Thus winning consent to new directions depends on how secure the participants feel. When many routine problems of technical and human organization remain to be solved, when the minimum conditions for holding the organization together are only precariously met, it is difficult to expend energy on long-range planning and even harder to risk experimental programs. When the organization is in good shape from an engineering standpoint it is easier to put ideals into practice. Old activities can be abandoned without excessive strain if, for example, the costs of relatively inefficient but morale-saving transfer and termination can be absorbed. Security is bartered for consent. Since this bargain is seldom sensed as truly urgent, a default of leadership is the more common experience.

On the same theme, security can be granted, thereby releasing energies for creative change, by examining established procedures to distinguish those important to a sense of security from those essential to the aims of the enterprise. Change should focus on the latter; stability can be assured to practices that do not really matter so far as objectives are concerned but which do satisfy the need to be free from threatening change. Many useless industrial conflicts have been fought to protect prerogative and deny security, with but little effect on the ultimate competence of the firm.

If one of the great functions of administration is the exertion of cohesive force in the direction of institutional security, another great function is the creation of conditions that will make possible in the future what is excluded in the present. This requires a strategy of change that looks to the attainment of new capabilities more nearly fulfilling the truly felt needs and aspirations of the institution. The executive becomes a statesman as he makes the transition from administrative management to institutional leadership.

Index

Index

Formalization, premature, 107
Forrestal, J., 49–50
Fromm, E., 33

Gar Wood Industries, 53–54
Golden, C. S., 109
Gruenther, A. M., 49

Human relations, 4, 136–137
Huston, J. A., 72

Ideologies, administrative, 14
  and institutionalization, 151–
  152
  and organization roles, 85
Ingrim, R., 75
Institution
  contrasted to organization,
  5–6
  and internal life of organizations, 7 ff.
  and social setting, 6
Institutionalization, 16, 139
  as value-infusion, 17
  see also Organization character
Integrity, institutional, 63
  and precarious values, 119–
  133
Intelligence, military, 10–11
Interest-groups, 15, 58–59, 63–
  64, 74, 93–95

Jacobs, P., 52
Jenkins, W. O., 22

Katz, D., 102
Kaufman, H., 114

La Farge, O., 84, 85
Leadership, 22 ff.
  creative, 75, 149–154
  default of, 25–27, 81–82
  dispensability of, 24–25, 41,
  74–75
  institutional, 28, 37; functions of, 62–64; and integrity, 138–139
  personal, 27–28, 37
  and responsibility, 62, 74,
  75 n., 142–149
  and routine qualities, 36
Learned, E. P., 38
Lepawsky, A., 56
Long, N. E., 82

McCloy, J. J., 50, 72
Machiavelli, N., 112
MacMahon, A. W., 128
Marine Corps, 19, 131–132
Messinger, S. L., 116
Millett, J. D., 86, 87, 128
Millis, W., 50˙

Roles, of organizations, 82–89
assigned, 91–93
and competence, 87–88
and self-conceptions, 84–85
Ruttenberg, H. J., 109

Sears, Roebuck and Co., 54–55
Self-images, and institution-alization, 17–18
Self-maintenance of organi-zations, and institution-alization, 20–21
Selznick, P., 42, 45, 54, 123
Simon, H. A., 79, 80, 94
Smithburg, D. W., 80, 94
Social composition of organi-zations
and critical decision, 57
and distinctive competence, 46–47
Social structure of adminis-trative organizations, 15–16
elements of, 91–101
and historical phases, 102–107
and precarious values, 119–133
Speier, H., 68, 69, 70
State, Department of, 51–52

Statesmanship, 4–5
and definition of mission, 70 n.
and institutional leadership, 37
Stein, H., 13
Stogdill, R. M., 22
Stone, C. P., 102
Strategy, military
and capability, 11–12, 71–73, 78–79
and political aims, 75–79
Survival of institutions, and distinctive identity, 63
Sward, K., 110

Taylor, D. W., 102
Technological orientation
and dispensability of lead-ership, 74–75
and political-military strat-egy, 75–79
retreat to, 74–82
Tennessee Valley Authority, 42–45
Thompson, V. A., 80, 94
Trade-unions, 21

Ulrich, D. N., 38
Unification of U.S. military agencies, 10–12, 19

United Automobile Workers
Union, 108–109
Universities, 16, 70

Values, 57 n., 60, 151–152
and efficiency, 141
and elite autonomy, 121–133
and institutional survival,
63

Values—(*Continued*)
and institutionalization, 17–
22
precarious, 119–133

Waldo, D., 56, 82
War aims, formulation of, 68–
70
Wars, types of, 73, 78

THE
CARPENTER'S
APPRENTICE

The Spiritual Biography
of Jimmy Carter

THE
CARPENTER'S
APPRENTICE

*The Spiritual Biography
of Jimmy Carter*

DAN ARIAIL
CHERYL HECKLER-FELTZ

ZondervanPublishingHouse
Grand Rapids, Michigan

A Division of HarperCollins*Publishers*

The Carpenter's Apprentice
Copyright © 1996 by Cheryl Heckler-Feltz and Daniel G. Ariail

Requests for information should be addressed to:

ZondervanPublishingHouse
Grand Rapids, Michigan 49530

Library of Congress Cataloging-in-Publication Data

Ariail, Dan, 1938
   The carpenter's apprentice: the spiritual biography of Jimmy Carter / Dan
Ariail and Cheryl Heckler-Feltz.
       p.   cm.
   ISBN: 0-310-20012-1 (hardcover: alk. paper)
   1. Carter, Jimmy, 1924- . 2. Carter, Rosalynn. 3. Baptists—Georgia—Plains—
Biography. 4. Presidents—United States—Biography. 5. Christian life. I. Heckler-
Feltz, Cheryl. II Title.
BX6495.C35A75 1996
286'.1'092—dc 20   96-11203
[B]   CIP

This edition printed on acid-free paper and meets the American National Standards
Institute Z39.48 standard.

Sources and credits, including permissions, for citations in this book are provided
in the "Sources" on pages 174-76.

Published in association with Sealy M. Yates, Literary Agent, Orange, CA.

Edited by Lyn Cryderman and James E. Ruark
Interior design by Sue Vandenberg Koppenol

Printed in the United States of America

---

96 97 98 99 00 01 02 03 / ❖ DH/ 10 9 8 7 6 5 4 3 2 1

To Nelle, beloved wife and best friend
—Dan

To Glenn, the patient one
—Cheryl

q 86

Contents

Jimmy Carter in his home workshop.

FOREWORD

Linda and Millard Fuller
Founders, Habitat for Humanity International

Jimmy Carter is a truly great human being and a devoted servant of God. His intelligence, compassion, humility, determination, and faith are well-known. More than anyone we know, Jimmy fully utilizes his talents, skills, energy, and resources to make the most of his life as well as to improve the lives of others all over the world.

Jimmy and his wife, Rosalynn, have the distinction of being the most famous volunteers in our work with Habitat for Humanity. Since 1984, they have been faithful and incredibly effective in their partnership with us, working one full week every year on a Habitat site and helping out in numerous other ways. They have ridden all night on a bus with other Habitat volunteers, built houses in the pouring rain, slept on the ground in tents in Mexico and on an Indian reservation, and shared tears of joy with new homeowners.

At Habitat for Humanity worksites, the Carters do not simply show up for a few television interviews and then quit. In fact, they attempt to limit direct media contact because they prefer staying focused on building. Press conferences at the beginning and end of each building blitz are a must because there is such a strong fascination with a former president and first lady wearing blue jeans and building a house with a poor family they previously had not known. But otherwise, they just pour themselves into getting the houses built.

The Carters set a difficult work pace matched only by a few of the other volunteers. We have seen them jog to a construction site early in the morning and then work a twelve-to-fourteen-hour day. We have even seen Jimmy down on his hands and knees, laying tile at one o'clock in the morning so that his Habitat blitz house would be finished on time.

It has been a high honor and a wonderful privilege to know and work with Jimmy and Rosalynn Carter over the years. They have blessed us personally, and the ministry of Habitat for Humanity, beyond words to express.

Soon after the Carters became involved with Habitat for Humanity, Jimmy talked with us about joining Maranatha Baptist Church. It was an easy decision to make, due to the warm fellowship there as well as the added privilege of attending his Sunday school class.

Jimmy's commitment to teaching the class is strong. He has at times traveled late into the night on Saturday in order to be in Plains for Sunday school and church. He is always prepared and lively even though he may have just returned from dealing with a major crisis thousands of miles away.

Jimmy's knowledge and understanding of the Bible are exceptional. He is a very serious student of the Bible. Most of the time he reads the passage of Scripture for the lesson himself "to save time," as he usually says, ant then he asks questions throughout the lesson to get participation from the class. His teaching is relevant and challenging, emphasizing forgiveness, justice, love, and faith. He closes with his own prayer spoken in an easy and sincere way.

As you read this book, you will gain deeper insight into Jimmy Carter's strong spiritual nature and his dogged determination to make his life count for the cause of Christ in the world. Whether he is swinging a hammer, resolving a conflict, monitoring elections in a distant land, stamping out human rights abuses, lending a helping hand to a neighbor, or teaching Sunday school, it is obvious that Jimmy Carter takes great joy in being a servant of God, a true apprentice of the Carpenter.

INTRODUCTION

Dan Ariail

For fourteen years I have had the privilege of serving as pastor to the Maranatha Baptist Church of Plains, Georgia. This congregation includes in its membership Jimmy and Rosalynn Carter, two people whom I formerly had admired from afar and whom I have subsequently come to love dearly and respect greatly. My serving as pastor to a former president of the United States has allowed me an unusual degree of intimacy and understanding regarding these two very special people.

In the beautiful poem "The Creation," from *God's Trombones*, James Weldon Johnson describes the scene as God brings the universe into being and then begins work on humanity:

This Great God,
Like a mammy bending over her baby,
Kneeled down in the dust
Toiling over a lump of clay
Till he shaped it in his own image.

As God the Father created the world, so Jesus worked as a carpenter (Mark 6:3), fashioning with his hands yokes for oxen, household furnishings, and other useful items for the citizens of Nazareth. Jesus took pieces of wood and created things that people needed.

Like Jesus, the thirty-ninth president of the United States is a carpenter. Jimmy Carter often takes a break from work in his home office and goes out to his woodworking shop. He has made beds, chairs, stools, and cabinets—and even carved a chess set. For his church he has made four splendid walnut offering plates turned on his own lathe, tables for the nursery and front vestibule, several bookcases, a large cabinet with rollers, and several shelves in various classrooms. To avoid unsightly holes in what he makes, he uses glue and craftsmanship and, sometimes,

11

wooden pegs. He is a student of the grain, texture, and qualities of various cuts and varieties of wood.

Having been president of the United States has not caused Jimmy Carter to cease being a learner—hence the term "apprentice" in the title of this book. Seemingly devoid of the hubris that is common in prominent and successful people, Jimmy is always willing to listen to the other side, never automatically assuming that he has all the answers. He long ago determined to fashion his life along principles laid down by Christ.

The story in this book is told in my voice. While this was done for the sake of unity and readability, the book is a collaboration accomplished in large measure by Cheryl Heckler-Feltz. She was the first to articulate the idea of writing the book, and she did most of the interviews and research work, incorporating my memories of the past fourteen years into the text in a logical form. After she had prepared a preliminary manuscript, I reviewed it and recast it into my own writing style. This project has been both a pleasure and a great learning experience for me and, I hope, for Cheryl also.

This book makes extensive use of quotations from Jimmy and Rosalynn Carter, some of which have earlier appeared in print. The reason is that much of what I wanted to communicate had already been expressed by them and far more succinctly than I could say it. The sources for each chapter are given at the end of the book.

William Hazlitt is quoted as saying, "Though familiarity may not breed contempt, it takes off the edge of admiration." Not true! While the Carters are quite human, I have found no basis for disparagement in either of them. My prayer is that through this book you will come not only to admire the Carters more but also appreciate the Christian faith that undergirds their lives.

INTRODUCTION

Cheryl Heckler-Feltz

Student.

Teacher.

Like most of us, these roles are a greater part of my life than I sometimes understand or appreciate. I move from one to the other so quickly that I don't really think about it, and I suspect this is true for many people.

I throw myself into research about the life of Rosalynn Carter, and I am the student. My ten-year-old daughter comes to me with new material and her favorite skirt pattern, and I become the teacher.

In seminary I began to develop an understanding of these dual roles because my professors emphasized that inevitable link between education and communication, and they taught me to ask questions like, "What is the difference between what this pastor thinks he's teaching and what he's really teaching?" (For instance, you can't shout "Guh-od loves you!" in a harsh, arrogant voice and expect to teach anything but harsh arrogance.)

This training also serves me well in my work as a religion writer and essayist by providing some effective tools in identifying the essence of one's spirituality.

Years ago, I entered Jimmy Carter's Sunday school classroom—like everyone else—as a student. It began a unique spiritual adventure that eventually produced this book. I had many delightful travel companions, and it seems fitting to identify for readers some of what I learned from those individuals.

- Dan and Nelle Ariail and their family taught me that the link between faith and hospitality isn't just Southern—it's spiritual.
- Through my meetings with him, through extensive research and interviews with historians and his associates, I learned most profoundly from Jimmy Carter that nothing is more important in life than how we define ourselves.

13

- From Rosalynn Carter I discovered that we women have a powerful and historic legacy in our ability to influence the spiritual development of a child, a family, a community, a nation. Rosalynn has Christ's teachings in her heart, fire in her soul, and iron in her spine.
- Because this project sometimes challenged any claim to a normal routine within the Feltz house, it gave my family great opportunities of learning. From my husband, Glenn, the lesson was strength; from my son, Brady, it was always humor; and from Leah, exuberance.
- From my literary agents, Tom Thompson and Sealy and Susan Yates, I learned that while "teamwork" always feels like a worn-out cheer at sporting events, it is a powerful experience in the real world of publishing.
- Patrick Vance, my editor at the New York Times Syndicate, was my strongest guide and mentor regarding the quality of the book's research and original content. Much of the material here was also written as columns for the syndicate, and my best writing reflects his influence.
- My closest, coolest buds—Peggy, Marv, Jill, and The Very Proper Miss Janet—always represent lessons of loyalty and intimate friendship. They didn't write one word or edit one phrase, but their fingerprints are everywhere in my life, and this book is no different.

It is not possible for me to identify what lessons I have taught to the people I have encountered on this journey—or the benefit of my lessons. For instance, there is one little girl in Plains, Georgia, who learned that I can spit watermelon seeds with the best of them, but I'm not certain that point has much value. (We do have a lovely friendship, though.)

I can say that as you begin this book, you may find benefit in considering the plan Dan and I used while writing it: Set aside what you think you know about Jimmy and Rosalynn Carter—and what you know you feel about them—and approach this as if meeting them for the first time.

THE
CARPENTER'S
APPRENTICE
The Spiritual Biography
of Jimmy Carter

Tent City of the Tijuana Habitat Project at Matamoros, Mexico

A Night in Tijuana

*Despite their critics, I've always suspected
Jimmy and Rosalynn Carter go to bed at
night and rest well with the Lord.*

MARTIN E. MARTY

Calm and quiet have finally settled on the "tent city"
pitched in Colonia Matamoros, a dusty hillside shantytown just
east of the Otay Mesa border crossing in the El Florido district
of Tijuana, Mexico. It is the end of a very long day and an even
longer week for the 1,200 volunteers who came from the United
States, Canada, Europe, Australia, and Papua New Guinea with
Moses-like determination to lead 100 families out of the bondage
of shacks and cardboard huts into a promising new community
of decent, two-bedroom homes for their families.

This day, like all the others here, had begun with a wake-
up call from a bullhorn: "It's five A.M. and time to get going."

In this locale—which offers no running water and will
never be included in the Top Ten list of places you must see
when visiting Mexico—"getting going" has a distinctive flair:
cramped, two-person tents; hot, dry, ten-hour workdays; a bar-
racks-style mess hall; portable toilets; and five-gallon, black
vinyl shower bags hanging over makeshift shower stalls of
black plastic sheets stretched over two-by-fours.

But now it is dark. Only the remarkably energetic are
counting stars. Rest is well-deserved but also comes uneasily
in such a strange environment.

At least the night sounds are comforting: a gentle wind, faint laughter a couple of rows away, and the steady, predictable footsteps of Secret Service agents outside the neighbor's tent.

Images of today's events float across the minds of the volunteers on the verge of sleep: school children, clean and tidy, leaving the shacks and walking to catch their bus; homebuilders working side by side with the new homeowners and overcoming the language barrier with hand signals and smiles. In the evening, in total darkness, lies the most heartwarming image of all: a hundred new homeowners carrying lighted candles and making their way from the shantytown along a short road to their new homes and new community. The symbolism was not lost on anyone, and many scrambled for handkerchiefs.

Sleep tarries. Then softly, from the next tent, comes a man's voice with a southern cadence: "*En el principio era al Verbo* [In the beginning was the Word], *y el Verbo era con Dios* [and the Word was with God], *y el Verbo era Dios* [and the Word was God]."

Jimmy Carter is reading to his wife a chapter of the Bible in Spanish by the dim glow of a flashlight. Every night for twenty years they have followed this bedtime routine. First Jimmy reads, then Rosalynn, from a Book that has guided both of them through the highs and lows of their remarkable lives. Their nightly Scripture reading helps them maintain their daily devotional studies and practice Spanish at the same time.

Jimmy Carter, who once presided over the world's most powerful nation, tonight sleeps in a blue-gray tent, like the rest of the Habitat for Humanity volunteers. The only noticeable difference between this tent and the many others is the spray of red plastic flowers that Rosalynn has tied to the tent frame—flowers given to her by admirers in Mexico.

"*Y le dijo: De cierto, de cierto os digo: De aquí adelante veréis el cielo abierto, y los angeles de Dios que suben y descienden sobre el Hijo del Hombre*" [He then added, "I tell you the truth, you shall see heaven open, and the angels of God ascending and descending on the Son of Man"].

Jimmy finishes the chapter and turns off the flashlight. Volunteers in surrounding tents who have heard his reading close their eyes, perhaps thinking of one last Scripture verse: "The LORD replied, 'My Presence will go with you, and I will give you rest.'"

Like other former presidents, Jimmy Carter has physical trappings of that exalted office: the Carter Center in Atlanta, twenty-four-hour security protection from the Secret Service, and guest appearances at formal state functions. Yet, in a way unlike his colleagues in that elite group of living former presidents, Carter has distinguished himself in his service to the least fortunate of this planet's citizens.

Despite the constant publicity, despite all the other perquisites of celebrity life, and despite the controversy that inevitably surrounds those who are dedicated to social reform and peacemaking, the attention of Rosalynn and Jimmy Carter remains centered on some specific and profound convictions.

Like Moses, who had claim to royalty but identified himself with the anguish of the Hebrew slaves, Jimmy Carter has had the power of a king but still has the heart of a servant.

The Carters at Jimmy's boyhood home in
Archery

CHILDHOOD IN ARCHERY

*The hot Southern sun was a gift in my child-
hood. Between early April and the end of
October we never wore shoes, and seldom
wore a shirt except for church or school.*
                                    WHY NOT THE BEST?

Jimmy Carter grew up in one of the most nurturing environments of any of our country's commanders-in-chief: a stable family, a close-knit community with social events almost
exclusively surrounding the church and school, an educator
determined to take him to the other side of excellence, a genuinely positive view of the world around him, and a remarkable
determination to explore the world beyond Plains.

But there were also opposing worlds to confront and
reconcile.

THE FARM IN ARCHERY

James Earl Carter was born in the Wise Hospital in Plains,
Georgia, on October 1, 1924—the first American president to
be born in a hospital. This was the same year that Calvin
Coolidge won the presidency, the Ford Motor Company made
its ten-millionth automobile, and bandleader Paul Whiteman
premiered George Gershwin's "Rhapsody in Blue." Ironically,
1924 was also the year the world bid farewell to another Southern president, Woodrow Wilson, who died peacefully in his
sleep on February 3.

Farm life in the little community of Archery was as elemental to Jimmy's youth as fire is to Earth. I find it ironic that tourists wanting to understand better the life of the thirty-ninth president spend most of their time in Plains visiting the local stores and attending our church. When they venture out nearly three miles to the southwest to see Jimmy's boyhood home, either it is an afterthought or they have taken the van tour offered by a local businessman. Only rarely does a person come to town saying, "I want to go to Archery and see the boyhood farm."

In his earliest years, Jimmy didn't really feel a part of Plains. The unique and extremely tight-knit community of Archery was composed of twenty-five African-American families and two white families, one of which was the Earl and Lillian Carter home.

Unquestionably, the most prestigious person in Archery was Bishop William Johnson of the African Methodist Episcopal Church, a man charged with overseeing pastors and churches in at least five states. He was the most respected member of the community, the best educated, the most widely traveled, and the probably the richest. "He lived about a half mile west of where I lived," Jimmy told me. "We looked on him with respect, friendship, admiration, brotherhood, and love."

My own father was a county agricultural agent, and we also lived on a farm out in the country. Although we ourselves were not often engaged in farming, so many of my early childhood experiences parallel those of Jimmy Carter that I had a strange feeling of déjà vu when I reading his book of poems, *Always a Reckoning*. Much of the material there closely matches my own experience. I, too, had a close friend who was black. I drew water from a well. I learned to milk a cow—though I was never a fool about it. And the "bathroom" was a washtub on the kitchen floor, and the toilet was connected to the house by a path. While some may long for "the good old days," I will take paved roads, indoor plumbing, and penicillin over that life as I remember it.

Jimmy and I have had many conversations about farm life, but my favorite description about his family's farm comes from his autobiography, *Why Not the Best?*

> We lived in a wooden clapboard house alongside the dirt road which led from Savannah to Columbus, Georgia, a house cool in the summer and cold in the winter. It was heated by fireplaces within two double chimneys, and by the wood stove in the kitchen. There was no source of heat in the northeast corner room where I slept, but hot bricks and a down comforter helped to ease the initial pain of a cold bed in the winter. For years we used an outdoor privy in the back yard and a hand pump for water. Later, another shallow well was dug under our back porch and a hand pump was installed there, and eventually we had a windmill and running water in our home.

Jimmy goes on to explain that the yard was covered, not with grass but with sand. There were several good reasons for this: Power lawn mowers were not available, open spaces made the presence of snakes easily visible, and bare clay is terribly messy in wet weather. A common saying was: "Anybody with grass in their yard is just too lazy to dig it up!"

A sanded yard required constant maintenance. The sand would wash away and have to be replaced regularly from streams in the vicinity. It also had to be raked and swept often to keep it tidy. It was constantly being tracked by the geese, ducks, guineas, and dogs that had the run of the place rather than being kept in pens.

People reared in cities can hardly imagine not running to the supermarket as needed for a dozen eggs. On the farm, however, gathering eggs often involved a game of hide-and-seek. Hens laid their eggs whenever and wherever they chose—even in the forks of tree limbs now and then. But the fresh eggs and ready availability of chickens meant delicious baking smells and the regular appearance of Southern fried chicken—a delicacy never duplicated by the fast-food chains regardless of their extravagant claims; they never even come close!

WILL THE REAL BILLY CARTER PLEASE STAND UP?

Early in my ministry at Plains, I shared the public's perception of Billy Carter portrayed by the media: a hard-drinking man with little ambition who was given to making odd decisions such as consorting with Muammar al-Qaddafi of Libya. I was intrigued and surprised when Jimmy once remarked, "Billy is a very intelligent man and a much better businessman than I." Only years later, when Billy and Sybil moved back to Plains and became my cherished friends, did I begin to understand what he meant.

I cringe when I read in a book or article a statement such as "How could the same family have produced a president of the United States and Billy Carter?" This question reveals profound lack of insight into who Billy was.

Understanding this complex man requires a look both at him and at the history of Plains. During the presidential campaign of 1976 and afterward, over a hundred reporters from national and international new services were camped out under the water tank in Plains, each facing the challenge to file a story every day. Billy was still drinking, and he loved both their company and being in the limelight—so he provided antics, which they happily printed. His language and antics were both funny and mildly embarrassing to the presidential candidate, but just the sort of things the media love.

The Billy I knew was quite different. Hardly a churchman, he was nevertheless a committed Christian with a heart of gold. Jimmy's book of poems shows their father as a man who was generous to a fault—but always behind the scenes. So it was with Billy. He had managed the family peanut business wisely and well during the campaign; then, when Jimmy was elected, it was put into a blind trust to avoid any conflict of interest. It was under the trust administration that the business lost over a million dollars, not under Billy Carter's leadership.

When Billy and Sybil moved back to Plains, he and I hit it off as friends from the start. We were near the same age and size, so close that when Billy died, he left me his wardrobe—and it fit. We even looked enough alike that several times I was asked to give my autograph to folks who were certain I was Billy Carter.

Billy moved his membership to Maranatha by asking me to read a note at the Wednesday night prayer service. He knew there would be no visitors and that this would not be caught up in the media.

Indeed, he steadfastly maintained his public image as a buffoon and forbade the rest of us to blow his cover. "Don't you tell on me," he would say when reporters were around. Not even in his book *Billy* did he reveal much below the public surface. But he was a faithful and valued member of our church and had been sober for more than nine years at the time of his death.

Water came from a well and arrived in the house, not in pipes but in buckets. A hand-cranked windlass at the well-house wound the rope that raised a water bucket from the cool depths below. Wells were also used to keep butter cool on hot summer days when no refrigeration was available.

Harvest season meant that field workers and farm owners alike got up well before daylight—around four in the morning, God forbid!—awakened by the clanging of the farm bell, which also served as a signal for all to converge at the house in the event of fire or other emergency. Illuminated by kerosene lanterns, the workers and young Jimmy would get the mules from the barn and load the wagons with the implements and supplies required for the working day, which would last from dawn until dark—or "from can 'til can't."

Jimmy recalls:

> Then we would unhook the mules from the wagon harness, hook up the plows, and wait for it to be light enough to cultivate without plowing up the crops.
>
> When I was a small boy, I carried water in buckets to the men from the nearby spring, and filled up the seed planters and fertilizer distributors, or ran errands. Later, I was proud to plow by myself. . . .
>
> Our farm work was heavy all year round. My daddy saw to that with his widely diversified farm industries. My school work always came first, but farm children could expect the teachers to give few time-consuming homework assignments. . . . Some of these jobs were enjoyable; some were pure drudgery. But there was always an ability to look back and see specifically what had been

25

accomplished during the day's work. We always took advantage of opportunities to explore the woods, fields, and swamps, to fish and hunt, to harvest fruits and vegetables, from the garden and orchards, and to harvest wild fruits and nuts during their seasons.

Unlike today's huge farms dedicated to a single crop or product, the Carter farm produced watermelons, peanuts, pecans, cotton, sweet potatoes, cane syrup, honey, wool, goose feathers, milk, meat from hogs and cattle, blackberries, fruits and vegetables, timber products, and processed items made from those raw materials. The wool from their sheep was exchanged for manufactured blankets. The featherbeds, pillows, and comforters made from goose down—which was plucked every six months from the breasts of the flock—remained with the family or were given as gifts or sold to certain special people. "Plains Maid" syrup from the farm was a familiar brand name to shoppers at stores in the surrounding area. Earl Carter also sold milk, cream, and butter to the grocery stores and peddled chocolate milk at five cents a bottle to stores and filling stations.

EARL'S INFLUENCE

Jimmy says that in his earliest years, life centered almost exclusively around family and farm. Both were headed by Earl Carter, a formidable patriarch, difficult taskmaster, and thoroughly successful businessman who was thirty years old when his firstborn entered the world. Earl stood five-feet-eight-inches tall, weighed about 175 pounds and, according to Jimmy, was an excellent athlete who pitched for the local men's softball team and beat everyone at tennis.

Hardly a sport associated with farmers in the 1920s, tennis was a part of Jimmy's childhood because Earl insisted on installing a tennis court only a stone's throw away from the blacksmith shop. Even before there was electricity on the Carter farm, there was tennis.

Earl finished the tenth grade at Riverside Academy in Gainesville, Georgia (not far from where I grew up), up above

Atlanta. Thus, he attained the most advanced education of any Carter man since the family moved to Georgia in the 1770s. Following his educational experience at Roverside, Earl returned to his family in Sumter County.

Jimmy grew up on a 360-acre spread that included five tenant families. Earl bestowed on Jimmy all the privileges and expectations associated with a "landowner's oldest son." He nicknamed Jimmy "Hot Shot," expected the best work from him, and typically included him in the "men only" activities such as overnight hunting and fishing trips. Eventually, Earl Carter opened a small office in Plains, where he bought peanuts from other farmers on a contract basis for a nearby peanut oil mill, and where he eventually began to sell fertilizer, seed, and other supplies to neighboring farmers—as Jimmy would do twenty years later.

Jimmy once told me, "As a boy, I was close to my father in a totally admiring and subservient way. My father never told me what to do. He would say, 'Hot, would you like to pick cotton this afternoon?' and I would say, 'Yessir, Daddy.'

"That was the way he ordered me around, but I never dreamed of rejecting what I thought my daddy wanted. He was so kind. A lot of times Daddy would go on a fishing trip with other men, and by the time I turned ten he insisted on taking me along. I was kind of a privileged character."

For his part, Jimmy seemed to wear the mantle of high expectation with ease—walking the three miles of railroad track into Plains regularly by age five to sell bags of boiled peanuts, announcing by first grade that he wanted to attend the U.S. Naval Academy, and even reading Tolstoy's *War and Peace* by age twelve.

His childhood friend, Mary Wright Minion, recalls that Jimmy always was special. "Jimmy and I grew up together. My mother and his mother worked together. Me and his sister Ruth were close. We made mud pies and cakes as girls, and when I was older, I would keep Billy while his mother worked. Jimmy always seemed more sincere than others. He seemed more patient. He seemed more religious, and he always seemed concerned about those less fortunate than him."

Like Jimmy today, Earl Carter was a deacon and a Sunday school teacher, and he made certain that his young children attended church weekly. The first Bible verse Jimmy learned as a child was "God is love" (1 John 4:8). He accepted Christ and was baptized in the Plains Baptist Church at age eleven.

The arrival of electricity in rural Sumter County in 1939 radically changed fourteen-year-old Jimmy's world because it brought "modern conveniences" to the farm and brought his father into politics.

> My father was a natural leader in our community and with the advent of Rural Electrification Program, when I was about 13 years old, my father became one of the first directors of our local REA organization. He then began to learn the importance of political involvement on a state and national basis to protect the program that meant so much in changing our farm life-style. He served for many years as a member of the county school board, and one year before his death, he was elected to the state legislature.

It was a wrenching experience for both Jimmy and Rosalynn when in 1953 they received news that Earl Carter was dying from pancreatic cancer. Having left behind them the rural village of their youth, they were embarked on an exciting career with the United States Navy, with Jimmy in command of one of the first nuclear submarines. The young couple moved back to Plains and into an apartment in the local housing project so that Jimmy could take over the administration of the family peanut warehouse business.

As he assumed the reins of the warehouse and became reacquainted with the folk of Plains, Jimmy discovered a side to Earl Carter that he had not known. People in Plains went out of their way from the moment of Earl's death to tell Jimmy just what his father had done for the community. He would hear from this or that person how Earl had given the person's family help in time of need, about Earl's furnishing graduation dresses or suits for youngsters whose family would have otherwise been embarrassed. Much of this had been concealed from Jimmy's mother, Lillian. It was upon learning of the quiet good deeds of his father and Earl's consistent service to others that Jimmy began to reassess just where his life was headed and what the call of Jesus Christ was for his future.

Jimmy Carter is a man of strong intellect, capable of seizing an opportunity, calling on inner strength, and outworking his competitors. In that regard, he is his father's son, and as a youth Jimmy showed very early that he knew how to extract a profit in even small business ventures. As a young man returning to Plains, however, he soon set higher standards for himself than even his father had.

But he learned from both parents how to demonstrate compassion and camaraderie within his community. There is as much of Miss Lillian in Jimmy Carter as there is of Earl.

LILLIAN'S INFLUENCE

People not reared in the American South are sometimes mystified that most Plains townspeople called Jimmy's mother "Miss Lillian." The term "Miss So-and-so" is a Southern title of respect and deference, even of endearment, and it is usually reserved for older ladies. It has nothing whatever to do with marital status. Mrs. Lillian Gordy Carter was known to one and all around Plains as "Miss Lillian," and that is how most of us addressed her.

I first met Miss Lillian, briefly, on a visit to Plains during the 1976 presidential campaign. She was sitting in a rocking chair on the loading platform of the depot campaign headquarters, and my friend Pauline Lewis of Perry introduced her to my wife, Nelle, and me. Because of arthritis and her having shaken hands with many thousands of people, she extended a ballpoint pen for me to shake.

The next time we met was after I had arrived in Plains as the pastor at Maranatha Church. Jimmy suggested that I call on his mother, who was quite ill with cancer. Local accounts of this formidable lady had led me to expect almost anything, and

I approached this visit with a far greater sense of awe and trepidation than meeting Jimmy and Rosalynn themselves.

I need not have feared. Miss Lillian and I had a very pleasant and easy conversation, partly because of my interest in her many travels and activities, which she seemed glad to share. We talked about the campaign and some of her exploits during the Carter presidency. Then she said, "Of course, you know how proud I am of Jimmy, but Billy is my heart." It was only years later that I understood. This was not a case of maternal partiality but a frank admission that Billy Carter was far more of a man than I had been led to believe by the media. I came to understand fully what she meant: Jimmy was her pride and Billy was her joy.

Even though Earl was undoubtedly the head of the Carter family, I strongly suspect that his wife, Lillian, was, as the saying goes, the neck. She attained unusual independence for a woman in rural Georgia in the first half of this century. "Mother did live her own life, though she was very close to Daddy," Jimmy once told me. "She nursed and had an income, and she gathered all our pecans on the farm. That was also her source of income. She used the money to buy all of [her daughters] Gloria's and Ruth's dresses."

While Earl loaded up the children each Sunday for church, Lillian—who, like Rosalynn, was born a Methodist—was often working. "She didn't go to church all that regularly because back then she was a registered nurse, and nurses worked twelve hours a day or twenty hours a day and got paid either four dollars or six dollars," Jimmy said.

Working sometimes at the Wise Hospital and sometimes in patients' homes, Lillian ignored both skin color and income level as she treated diphtheria, polio, strep infections, and even cancer. Often she was gone hours or even days at a time, depending on the nature of the illness and the progress of the disease. When Rosalynn as young teenager was losing her father to cancer, Lillian helped the family tremendously. In fact, Rosalynn was spending the night with Ruth at the Carter home when Lillian awakened her to tell her of her father's death. "She served as a community doctor for our neighbors and for us, and was extremely compassionate toward all those who were afflicted with any sort of illness," Jimmy said.

Lillian's compassion was demonstrated in her actions but not always in her attitude or words. She was practical and strong-willed and wielded a razorlike tongue on occasion. Like the other members of the Carter family, her personality seemed paradoxical.

One of my favorite stories about Miss Lillian involves the time when a reporter sat in her living room during the 1976 campaign and issued a challenge to Jimmy's well-publicized claim, "I'll never lie to you."

"Come on, now, Miss Lillian," the reporter goaded her. "Do you mean to tell me this man doesn't lie?"

"Well, Jimmy might tell a white lie now and then," she responded.

"See, that's a lie," he abruptly responded, thinking he had trapped her.

"No, that was a white lie," she said. "There's a difference."

"Okay, so what *is* the difference?"

"Well, do you remember when you came to my front door a few minutes ago and I said I was happy to see you and that you are welcomed here? That, young man, was a white lie, because I'm merely tolerating you."

The thing about Miss Lillian is that she was much more concerned that she be respected than liked.

EARLY EDUCATION

Miss Julia Coleman was both, in abundance. I deeply regret that I came to Plains too late to get acquainted with this special lady. Long before the era of the bookmobile, Miss Julia would encourage students to read, read, read. About her, Jimmy wrote:

> My life was heavily influenced by our school super-intendent, Miss Julia Coleman, who encouraged me to learn about music, art, and especially literature.

31

> Miss Julia . . . encouraged all of her students to seek cultural knowledge beyond the requirements of a normal rural school classroom. We were highly competitive in debating, an essay contest called "Ready Writing," music appreciation, one-act play productions, spelling bees, and other cultural activities.
>
> Every student in the classroom was required to debate, to memorize and recite long poems and chapters from the Bible, and to participate in spelling contests. Each of us had to learn the rudiments of music and play some musical instrument—if it were only a ukulele, harmonica, or even a small piccolo. . . . As a school boy who lived in an isolated farm community, my exposure to classical literature, art, and music was insured by this superlative teacher. She prescribed my reading list and gave me a silver star for every five books and a gold star for ten book reports.

Actually, it was Miss Lillian who first instilled in young Jimmy a love of reading. Also, he relates, "When I was four years old my godmother—also a nurse like my mother, though apparently not a great reader—gave me a set of the complete works of Guy de Maupassant. It was, of course, many years later before I read through this set of volumes."

But it was Miss Julia who exerted the most profound influence educationally, not only on Jimmy but on all the young students in the Plains community. It was common knowledge that Miss Julia often issued the challenge to her students that any one of them might become president of the United States someday.

Yet her own future president was thinking more at that time about the navy. Early on, he set a goal of entering the U.S. Naval Academy. He wrote in *Why Not the Best?*

> Even as a grammar school child, I read books about the Navy and Annapolis. I wrote to ask for the entrance requirements, not revealing my age, and I almost memorized the little catalogue when it came. Then I planned my studies and choice of library books accordingly. I had ridiculous and secret fears that I would not meet the requirements.

Jimmy also demonstrated from his earliest days—especially in the classroom—the inner resources, optimism, and genuine belief that one life can make a tremendous difference in the world. His determination to improve the lives of those around him is reflected in this little-known essay he wrote when he was twelve:

There are certain habits of thinking which have a good effect upon health. If you think in the right way, you'll develop:

1) The habit of expecting to accomplish what you attempt.

2) The habit of expecting to like other people and to have them like you.

3) The habit of deciding quickly what you want to do, and doing it.

4) The habit of "sticking to it."

5) The habit of welcoming fearlessly all wholesome ideas and experiences.

6) A person who wants to build good mental habits should avoid the idle daydream, should give up worry and anger, hatred and envy, should neither fear nor be ashamed of anything that is honest or purposeful.

But always in Jimmy's education there was the presence of Miss Julia. Ever mindful of his indebtedness to his special teacher, the thirty-ninth president began his inauguration speech by quoting her on the need for adhering to unchanging principles in changing times. It was a credo Miss Julia would have applauded in her star pupil had she been there that day.

Billy Carter and Dan Ariail at a gala
at the Carter Center in Atlanta
(see p. 24)

THE MAN, THE PARADOX

In the speech-writing office we used to say it was no coincidence that the man's initials are "J.C."

HENDRICK HERTZBERG

The international community had suspected for months that Kim Il-Sung, the elderly, iron-fisted president of North Korea, was violating his country's commitment to the United Nations-sponsored Non-Proliferation Treaty prohibiting the construction of atomic bombs. When Kim refused to allow the warranted inspections, the U.N. Security Council met with United States officials to discuss economic sanctions—which North Korean culture interprets as an act of war.

Jimmy Carter informed the White House that he had a standing invitation to visit North Korea and felt he could intervene to dissipate the growing tension. This was no reckless, ill-informed proposal. Those who have known Jimmy a long time are well aware that when he believes in something, nothing will stop him from acting on that belief. He will stubbornly absorb stacks of information about the people and situation he is about to encounter, push aside critics' harsh attacks, and focus his whole attention on the task—even down to minuscule details—in search of small victories as well as big ones.

President Clinton agreed that Jimmy should go. So Jimmy and Rosalynn traveled to Pyongyang, the capital city of North Korea, in June 1994.

After just two days in the country, Jimmy strode to a podium in the presence of Kim Il-Sung and the media to announce the dictator's willingness to open the disputed sites and even to meet for the first time with President Kim Young Sam of South Korea—marking the first breakthrough in a forty-year rivalry. As if that wasn't dramatic enough, Jimmy continued by announcing that the United States would place in abeyance its agenda within the United Nations to seek sanctions against North Korea—a comment that drew emotional reactions from every corner of the world.

Leaders in China, Japan, and South Korea were relieved. *Perhaps he will prevent bloodshed.*

North Koreans were thrilled. *He treats us with respect. He's listening. He has honored our leader.*

The media were confused. *How could he achieve so much in two days?*

The White House, which had not yet agreed to withhold the sanctions, was stunned. *Is he speaking for us?*

The U.S. State Department was furious. *We cannot have freelance diplomats interfering with our policies.*

The hawks were howling. *This gullible hayseed has become Kim Il-Sung's hand-picked stooge.*

And many Americans took a look at the former president as if for the very first time. *Who is this man we thought we knew?*

Jimmy Carter, whose popularity in the White House buckled under the weight of long lines at gas pumps, runaway inflation, and Iranian hostages, at this moment reemerged in the national consciousness. Many knew he had built homes for the poor and monitored democratic elections throughout the world, and a few were aware of his role in helping to eradicate deadly diseases in the Third World.

But at this miraculous and controversial moment, Americans observed the focus and determination of one man who was certain he could pull two countries back from the edge of war, a man who was willing to face down the U.S. State Department, if necessary, to make that happen.

"I could see that an international confrontation was becoming inevitable unless there was some way to communicate with the only person in North Korea who could make a decision to change the course of events," Jimmy told me. "I don't think it would have been possible for North Korea to accept an international branding. The sanctions threatened were insignificant themselves, but *branding* them would have been the precipitation of war."

"JUST DO IT!"

There was still more happening during those two days in North Korea that the public did not learn immediately. During the time that they spent with Kim and his wife, Jimmy and Rosalynn heard a fair amount of North Korean propaganda, insisted on toasting to human rights at a formal dinner in Jimmy's honor, and politely masked their surprise when Kim's wife described in considerable detail her adventures in boar hunting.

At one point during their mission, the Carters boarded the dictator's yacht and headed down the historic Taedong River, setting sail with Kim, his wife, and an entourage of translators, North Korean cabinet officials, and photographers.

Jimmy wanted something else from his host, and the timing seemed right. He turned to Kim Il-Sung and said, "One thing you could do that would be very much appreciated by the American people would be to allow us to go into our cemeteries here and recover the remains of our war dead."

There were several smaller victories for the Carters as well. More than 3 million people died in the Korean conflict from 1950 to 1953, including 40,000 Americans—5,000 of whom were buried in North Korea. He was aware that the U.S. government had reliable maps showing the exact locations of the cemeteries. He knew because, unlike American soldiers killed in Vietnam, who were buried by the enemy, GIs killed in North Korea were buried by American comrades while the area was occupied by the Allied forces.

Kim balked at Jimmy's suggestion. With a dismissive gesture, he responded, "Well, we'll talk about it later."

NO OBSCURE MINORITY

Rabbi A. James Rudin says of Jimmy Carter, "He will certainly be remembered historically within the Jewish community and the general community as one of the first presidents in this century who was born again and used the term openly. Other presidents said religion was important to them, but demonstrated it differently. Eisenhower, for instance, didn't join a church until he entered the White House. FDR was an Episcopalian, and Richard Nixon, a Quaker, brought church services into the White House, but Jimmy Carter was clearly one of the first presidents who articulated the language and position of an evangelical from his openness in interviews right down to his teaching Sunday school. All of that had a dramatic impact and in some ways a bewildering impact on the general American public.

"One of my jobs at that time [the presidential campaign in 1976] was to interpret for the Jewish community what this language meant, and I told them that despite the commonly held belief that Jimmy Carter represented an obscure minority, he did, in fact, actually represent millions and millions of Americans."

"But I don't want to talk about it later. I want to talk about it now," Jimmy said.

"Well, we'll have some early discussions about it when we meet with your country."

Jimmy held firm. "No. I don't want to talk about it later. I'd like to talk about it now."

The dictator and his top officials began to argue in their native language, and Jimmy watched as the dictator's wife suddenly interrupted the dispute. Speaking firmly to her husband, she blurted a single command: "Just do it!"

And with that, Jimmy extracted one more victory. "When we left the country," he said, "they were already preparing to get backhoes and excavating equipment and teams ready to go in and recover the remains."

Back in Plains the day after he returned from Pyongyang, Jimmy assisted me at the funeral of one of our church members and concluded the ceremony by presenting an American flag to the widow. It was a graveside service for a man who had few local friends and whose relatives all came from another state. Jimmy had been assigned as their deacon at Maranatha Baptist Church, and he was there along with his pastor to comfort the bereaved family.

OPINIONS AND PARADOXES

Such contrasts—whether bargaining for soldiers' remains lying in a North Korean cemetery or comforting a bereaved friend in a Plains cemetery—point up the paradoxes that surround Jimmy.

There seem to be as many opinions about Jimmy Carter as there are peanuts in the Carter family's warehouse. How he is perceived can depend on whether you are a news anchor or the person watching the six o'clock news, whether you live in a developing country or in the United States, whether you are over forty or part of the college generation.

Each of us carries a range of titles. The biblical David was a brave boy, a brilliant musician, a bold king, a scheming murderer, and an unfaithful adulterer. How is that for a range? I am a husband, father, pastor, and grandfather, but also a writer, musician, swimmer, photographer, and afficionado of things Australian. Jimmy Carter is a staunch Southern Baptist in the moderate camp, a Democrat, a church deacon, an international peace negotiator, a man with a comfortable relationship with African-Americans, and a former president of the United States. I have heard each of these titles hailed with great admiration, but I have also heard them decried in derision and disgust.

When Jimmy, a Southern former governor, announced his candidacy for the presidency at the National Press Club in Washington in December 1974, few outside Georgia knew what to call him. Probably most Americans would have yawned had they paid any attention at all. Instead of quitting in discouragement, he remained on the campaign trail for almost a full year until polls indicated that the average American recognized his name. Even then the media's toothy, hayseed caricature of a smiling peanut continued to illustrate the worn-out question, "Jimmy who?"

However, Jimmy struck a chord with the average American, who perceived him as a decent, moral person capable of reclaiming the national political spirit that had been crushed amid civil rights violence, turmoil over the Vietnam conflict, and the Watergate scandal from the mid-sixties to the mid-seventies.

Attitudes change with the times. While an older generation of Americans soundly rejected the Carter administration by choosing not to reelect him in 1980, America's youth hold no grudges and have discovered their own ties to the thirty-ninth president. Jimmy is warmly received on college campuses, often by students telling of their work with Habitat, their interest in service, their hopes of making a difference in their communities.

Jimmy won over this generation with his idealism and dedication to improving living standards around the world and with his book *Talking Peace*, which he wrote specifically for high school- and college-age young people. When he describes the victory against guinea worm or river blindness, when he proclaims his goal of seeing all the children of the world immunized by the age of two, students roar with exuberant applause.

From people over forty, however, Jimmy inevitably draws a range of responses. Even the popular expression "He's the best former president ever"—an epithet Jimmy detests—has to be interpreted on a continuum. At one end is the person who means, "He was a lousy president, but at least he got his act together in retirement." At the other end is the response, "It was tragic that he didn't get to serve another term. We really needed him, but I am grateful he kept going even after leaving Washington."

Some American political cartoonists and writers continue to portray him as a naive Southern "homeboy" who is just too unsophisticated to comprehend life's real issues. Rosalynn's quick and soft-spoken response is, "Who cares about being sophisticated all the time when there is so much work to be done? Good heavens!"

I read one dreadful book by an obscure White House staffer during Jimmy's presidency who recited the theme "I adore him. We once met in person." By contrast, I have read the work of columnists who cynically threw out an attitude of "Yeah, but what have you done for me lately?"—literally within hours of Jimmy's achievements in the Camp David Accords in 1978 and his successful negotiations in Haiti in 1994. To her credit, another writer noted wryly, "He brings us back from the brink of war in North Korea and Haiti, and some columnists criticize the color of his shirts during the negotiations."

THE FORGOTTEN COMPONENT

Sometimes the press today gives him a kinder treatment than he received during his term in the White House. Considering that the Carter Center gets more than seventy requests each week from journalists throughout the world, reporters seem eager to endorse Jimmy's agenda at the Center, to support his work with Habitat for Humanity International, his continual search for peace, and even his lesser-known comments endorsing the separation of church and state, and his warnings against religious extremism in America.

Yet, writers and reporters still often overlook completely one important component of Jimmy's life. Certainly his childhood in Archery, his black playmates, his avid reading, his nurturing home, and his exceptional teacher all contributed to the making of a remarkably literate and compassionate person. But it is his strong religious faith that has directed Jimmy's life most profoundly. Spirituality is the steel foundation on which his entire life is constructed. It is not simply one small room in the mansion of life.

From the beginning of his presidential campaign, Jimmy made no secret of his religious faith, and this fact became well-known around the world. For example, one time, after they were in the White House, the Carters appeared at a formal reception in Europe, and another head of state approached to greet them with the words, "I'm a Christian, too." But at home, in the United

States, Jimmy's spirituality was—and still is—frequently maligned, misunderstood, or minimized in significance.

Martin E. Marty, senior editor of *Christian Century* magazine and distinguished professor at the Divinity School at the University of Chicago, tells a story that illustrates the fourth estate's original response to Jimmy during his presidential campaign.

> In March of 1976 I was visiting an evangelical theological seminary when a reporter from a national news magazine called me there and said, "Okay, so what's the scoop with this phony?"
>
> I said, "What phony?"
>
> She said, "This Carter from Georgia who claims to be born again."
>
> "I don't think he's a phony," I said. "Why do you suggest that?"
>
> "Because I asked around here in the newsroom," she said. "No one in our office is born again. No one even knows anyone who is born again."
>
> "Listen," I said. "I'm hundreds of miles from you and standing on the campus of one of the largest evangelical seminaries in the United States. Everyone here is born again. All their friends are born again—or will be if these folks have their way."

Ironically, even the emerging religious right, which might have been expected to embrace an evangelical Baptist, would have little to do with Jimmy Carter.

Almost from day one of his administration, Jimmy Carter was being attacked and criticized rather than supported by the extreme conservatives. "The religious right gave up on him quickly," Martin Marty said. "Somehow, in their eyes, decisions like the Panama [Canal] treaty deal made him 'unborn again.'" Many pastors openly vilified him for having favored the Equal Rights Amendment and almost rabidly attacked his emphasis on human rights as evidence of his being motivated by a deep-seated secular humanism rather than the guiding Christian faith and principles by which he lived."

Rabbi James A. Rudin, director of interreligious affairs for the American Jewish Committee in New York, said, "Here was a Southern, born-again Sunday school teacher who had done well-publicized missionary work and who, by all rights, should have appealed perfectly to the religious right but instead was attacked by that very group. I would suspect the Moral Majority was in its beginnings at that time." Regarding the campaign of 1980, Rudin added, "When you think about the people we associate with the religious right, I'm sure their votes overwhelmingly went to Ronald Reagan. I think that hurt Jimmy Carter. The one group of people who should have been part of his constituency went to his opponent."

Yes, paradoxes do seem to dog the public perceptions of Jimmy Carter.

Mashuq and Sue Askerzada (see p. 51)

4

CHOOSING CHRIST

For the first time I saw that I was the Pharisee.
JIMMY CARTER,
WHY NOT THE BEST?

As Jimmy Carter's term in the White House was coming to an end, one of his staff members made a remark, picked up by the press, to the effect that while he had worked for the president for four years, he did not feel he really knew the man. I feel that I really do know very well what makes Jimmy Carter tick. Granted that in this life we can never fully know any other person, not even our spouses or children, it is sufficient if we are comfortable with our expectations of that person and not fearful of unpleasant surprises. That characterizes my relationship with Jimmy.

The key to understanding Jimmy Carter is understanding Jimmy Carter's Christian faith. It makes all kinds of questions and misperceptions disappear, perhaps two in particular.

The first has to do with my role as his pastor. I am often asked whether I find it a formidable thing to serve as the pastor of a former president of the United States. I can honestly say I do not; I serve not so much as the pastor of a former president—presumably someone with a towering ego—as the pastor of an often self-effacing man who is a committed Christian, one whom I can trust and from whom I know fairly well what to expect. We do not always agree on every issue, but we will search together to find the most Christlike answer to the question at hand. He has always treated me with respect.

KEEPING SPIRITUALLY FIT

During the 1976 campaign a reporter asked Jimmy, "How do you keep yourself fit in the frenzy of a campaign? Mentally fit? Spiritually fit?"

Jimmy gave this response: "I can't say there is an overt self-initiated effort that is successful. It's a part of my nature, a part of my character; it's a part of my religious faith; it's a sense of equanimity.

"At night the last thing I do, every night, is to have a brief period of worship. I've never failed, since we began the campaign in January, to read a full chapter in the Bible every night in Spanish. This has been a good habit to maintain.

"And, almost like breathing, during the day I have moments of maybe silent prayer and meditation, not often in a structured way, but asking God for wisdom or sound judgment or compatibility with people who depend upon me or whatever would be appropriate under the circumstances."

The second has to do with public perceptions of Jimmy, particularly in the media. There has been an almost universal reading of Jimmy Carter's faith as being a department of his life, an addendum with little relationship to the rest of him. But I have discovered that you can never adequately grasp Jimmy Carter himself unless you see his Christian faith, along with its standards and principles, as being the framework on which all the rest is built, the stackpole that holds up the whole thing. For Jimmy, being "born again" embraces Jesus' words in John 3:3–21—the account of Nicodemus the Pharisee, who was told that he must experience a whole new beginning of life, a new life from the Spirit rather than mere flesh, a new life that comes only through Jesus Christ.

A NEW AWARENESS

A spiritual reevaluation and change in Jimmy followed his unsuccessful bid to become governor of Georgia in the election of 1966. His sister, the late Ruth Carter Stapleton, described that experience this way:

> He was a 'church Christian.' Jimmy was having a series of awarenesses of some lacks in his life, maybe motivation, a sense of direction. It was a time of self-analysis. He had already had two or three religious experiences. But he was wondering whether he was doing enough, caring enough for mankind. Then he moved into a new dimension, a deeper commitment of his political life before. After that, Christ came first because his ambitions were very fervent at the time. So it was a whole new phase of life that he was moving into. It was to serve Christ in his work.

Jimmy himself reflected on the experience in 1976, during the North Carolina primary campaign. He has always tried to express his faith in clear, plain terms in public, and a press conference on March 19 offered one of the first opportunities to talk about it at length during his run for the presidency.

> In 1967, I realized my own relationship with God was a very superficial one. . . . I was very proud of my status in the church. . . . I began to realize that my Christian life, which I had always professed to be preeminent, had really been a secondary interest in my life, and I formed a very close, personal intimate relationship with God through Christ. . . . It was not a profound stroke, a miracle, a voice of God from heaven. It was not anything of that kind. It wasn't anything mysterious. It was the same kind of experience that many have who become Christians in a deeply personal way and it has given me a deep feeling of equanimity and peace.

Jimmy said he realized in 1967 that he had visited 140 families for the church in the fourteen years he had been home from the navy. Yet, as he puts it, he "reached 300,000 people for politics in his unsuccessful bid for governor but only 140 visits for God. I recognized for the first time that I had lacked something very precious—a complete commitment to Christ, a presence of the Holy Spirit in my life in a more profound and personal

47

way. And since then I have had an inner peace and inner conviction and assurance that transformed my life for the better."

Again, in an interview on May 6, 1976, in an interview with Bill Moyers on the Public Broadcasting Service, Jimmy said,

I never had really committed myself totally to God. My Christian beliefs were superficial. They were based primarily on pride, and I'd never done much for other people. I was always thinking about myself, and I changed somewhat for the better. I formed a much more intimate relationship with Christ. And, since then, I have had just about like a new life.

I found it easy to pray without a special extra effort; it became part of my consciousness, and I felt a sense of peace and security that I had never felt before. I felt that Christ was a constant part of my daily life and recognized much more clearly my own failures, fallibilities, and sinfulness. I didn't feel embarrassed when I prayed about them. I was able to face them in a lot more relaxed and perhaps more courageous way, and without reticence. I felt that when I asked God for forgiveness it was there.

The intimacy with which I have accepted Christ in my own heart and the realization of the presence of the Holy Spirit, of my own need and how my need can be filled by Christ, the fact that I'm not better than other people but just have received the special blessing of God because He loves me through Jesus Christ, those personal realizations came much more forcefully to me later on in my life.

When Jimmy did win the governorship four years later, he felt more spiritually prepared for the task. In that same North Carolina primary, he explained to reporters:

I spent more time on my knees the four years I was governor in the seclusion of a little private room off the governor's office than I did in all the rest of my life put together because I felt so heavily on my shoulders the decisions I made might very well affect many, many people.

A CONSTANT THEME

Jimmy Carter is the most fascinating religious paradox I have ever encountered in six years of seminary study and thirty-five years of ministry. Even though the media and others may have been asking of the presidential candidate "Who *is* Jimmy Carter?" the local residents of Plains and the visitors to his Sunday school class have no doubt.

In class, they discover quickly the guiding principles of his faith, because they are common themes as he teaches. Theologically, for the past thirty years Jimmy has exemplified a faith based on three primary beliefs:

1. Jesus Christ is my personal Savior. I will serve him and maintain a pure relationship with him;
2. Scripture is my primary source for gaining clarity to God's will for my life;
3. The best way to serve God is by serving others, especially through the church.

These beliefs, in turn, find practical expression in other principles, as Jimmy related in a class he taught at First Baptist in Washington on January 29, 1978.

"A lot of people identify our present age as the age of anxiety. We measure what we have so that we can have more in a physical sense. It creates in us a sense of inadequacy, a feeling that I failed by human standards and human measure. We forget about the fact that God's standards for a Christian are quite different. In this lesson are spelled out five standards by which we can measure ourselves. It's the test of a Christian.

"1. A Christian must demonstrate obedience to God's commandments.

"2. The presence of the Holy Spirit. There's not a Christian here who has not felt in a tangible way, a fruitful way—perhaps even a miraculous way—the presence of the Holy Spirit. It takes hold of our heart. In times when trial and tribulations and testing of God's will come down, you've got to have some help.

"3. A growing understanding—with the accent on growing—which means that all through life there's got to be searching for a deeper relationship with Christ through the Holy Spirit, a deeper relationship with our fellow human beings. If we ever reach that plateau—'I have measured up to God's requirements. My life is a success. I'm an adequate Christian'—that's when we lose something precious. We need to dig more deeply and grow in the understanding of God.

"4. Our life must be consistent with Christ's life. We read in the New Testament what Christ actually did, what his life was about. The thrust of our lives, the philosophy under which we live, ought to be consistent with the life of Christ.

"5. An inner peace. It's not something you can will, as such. You can't say, 'Tomorrow I'm going to have inner peace in my heart.' It slips away from us. It's not something guaranteed to each of us. It comes in the first four points—if we subjugate our lives to God, if we open our hearts to the Holy Spirit, if our life is consistent with the purposes or example of Christ, in our relationship with God and others, then we will have inner peace."

In fact, his Sunday school teaching week by week is peppered with statements that reflect these principles and commitments:

- We are meant to measure all elements of our lives against the standards of Jesus.
- Stagnant spirituality is more than unfortunate: Anything in our lives that deters us from connecting with the purity of Christ's message and teachings should be identified and addressed directly.
- As individuals we must remain bold in looking past what is societal success and seek instead the higher standards as reflected in the life of Jesus Christ.
- Ultimately, there is no difference between the Gospel of Jesus and a social gospel today that leads naturally to the service of others. We must emulate the One we hold as Savior by serving others and remaining dedicated to the least among us through equality, justice, and human rights.

Those of us who live near him see these beliefs revealed in common activities—visiting the sick, repairing a roof for a widow, or helping a grade school boy or girl with a civics project.

Families moving to Plains experience Jimmy's genuine interest in welcoming and helping new neighbors.

When a young couple, Mashuq and Sue Askerzada, moved into Plains from Columbus, Georgia, several years ago, Jimmy stopped by to get acquainted and invite them to church. He then asked several times during his visit how he could best serve their family.

"We couldn't think of a thing we needed except to know where the landfill was to take our trash," Sue said. "So that's what we asked: 'Where's the landfill?' He explained very carefully how to find it. We felt he was genuinely interested in us and our coming into a new community. Later we had some of Mashuq's family to visit from Afghanistan, and he and Rosalynn graciously came to our home for a meal with them. President Carter also helped to cut through red tape to get Mashuq's mother a visa so she could visit here."

A PUBLIC CHRISTIAN

For me, as his pastor, friend, and neighbor, I encounter no paradox greater than this: In the United States there is a commonly held belief that somehow Jimmy Carter is a very different man now from when he lived in the governor's mansion or the White House, or that the public Jimmy Carter and the private person are markedly different. It simply is not true.

Bert Lance, the Director of the Office of Management and Budget in Jimmy Carter's Whie House, said recently:

> I think Jimmy Carter in 1966 was just who he is today. He was somebody who was concerned. He was somebody who cared about the people. He was somebody who was willing to try to make a difference in the way things were done.

Leonard Sweet, dean and a professor of church history at Drew University Theological School in Madison, New Jersey, wrote:

Jimmy Carter is a public Christian. Above all else, Jimmy Carter is just being who he is. I don't think he has a duplicitous bone in his body. It's O.K. to be a private Christian in America, but he doesn't know how to be a private Christian. Religion for him goes right to the streets, and he successfully relates his Sunday faith to his Monday world. The greatest irony to me is that we live in a culture which is just so interested in spiritual things and respects people who articulate and live out of an authentic spiritual core, yet our culture seems completely unable to understand Carter. I think if Carter were Zen or something other than Christian, he would have a tremendous following.

The conflicting perspectives about Jimmy Carter are likely to endure as long as he remains a public figure in the United States and abroad. But I believe there is no paradox in his spirituality. He is a guidepost, pointing first to Jesus Christ and then to the community as a place for service. He is a man who reads one chapter from the Bible every night—taking turns reading in Spanish with Rosalynn. He adheres to the biblical admonition "Pray without ceasing" by offering his petitions early and often through the day. Perhaps most profoundly: Jimmy Carter is a talented Christian educator who beautifully translates his Sunday faith into a Monday world.

Jimmy Carter is genuinely at peace with his decisions and seemingly at peace with his critics.

I think Rosalynn says it best:

He really believes and trusts in God to guide him in what God needs and wants him to do, and he doesn't worry much about criticism. I think he just believes so strongly that what he's doing is what's right and best—and what God wants him to do—that nothing bothers him much. I mean, I have never seen him not be able to go to bed at night and go sound asleep, even the whole time we were in the White House or anytime ever.

ON PRAYER

- "I never asked God to let me be president. I never asked God to let me win a single nomination. I don't pray to God to let me win an election. I ask God to let me do what's right. And to let me do what's best—that my life be meaningful—in an optimum way, and if I win or lose, I believe I can accept the decision with composure and without regrets, without animosities or hatreds or deep disappointment even."—Interview with Bill Moyers, 1976

- "You'd be amazed how many times we stand in a receiving line at the White House or go down a crowd of people at an airport—or when I walked across the front of this room tonight—and people say, 'We pray for you' or 'Every month, our church has a special prayer service for you.' And I say, 'Look, make it every week—or every day—because I really need it.'"—To campaign volunteers, Atlanta, January 20, 1978

- "We don't have to pray in public; we don't have to drop our money in the collection plate with a great clatter so everybody sees us; we don't have to push the fact that we love our neighbors. Genuine love can overcome human temptation for self-recognition."—Sunday school class of First Baptist Church of Washington, D.C., January 29, 1978

- "Yes, I pray many times during the day: when I'm approaching a new encounter with people, or when someone asks me for a special thought or consideration, or when I hear about someone who is afflicted or who is troubled, or when I have made a mistake and I want to avoid that mistake again, or when I'm faced with a responsibility that might affect others' lives. I pray as a routine thing."—Interview by National Religious Broadcasters, October 14, 1976

- "The Bible says, 'Pray without ceasing' (1 Thess. 5:17). I don't quite do that. It used to be I would pray maybe once or twice a day, or when I got in trouble! Now it's a much more routine and continuing thing for me. In moments of tension or quietness I have a habit of turning to God in a brief prayer, not just in a time of crisis or difficulty, but in a much more natural way. It means a lot to me."—Interview with the Reverend Pat Robertson during the 1976 campaign

(From left in front) Millard Fuller, co-founder of Habitat for Humanity; Andrew Young, former Ambassador to the United Nations; and President Carter at the Atlanta Carter Habitat Project. The young man in back is unidentified.

PRACTICING WHAT HE PREACHES

Soon we realized there were more than twenty blacks involved at all levels of his campaign. It was also clear to us that Carter hadn't even thought about it in those terms but that he was practicing what the others were only preaching.

ANDREW YOUNG

Whether he is walking the corridors of power as governor and president or simply fishing at a waterhole down in Sumter County, Jimmy has always felt at home with ordinary citizens and has never lost touch with them. The stories of Eloy Cruz and Mary Prince are two noteworthy examples; Jimmy's lifelong attitude toward and dealings with African-Americans is another.

ELOY CRUZ

Because he had learned Spanish in the navy, Jimmy Carter was asked by the Brotherhood Commission of the Southern Baptist Convention to join in a missions venture in New England among Spanish-speaking immigrants, many of whom had not yet been assimilated into their new country. He served as assistant to a Cuban pastor from Brooklyn named Eloy Cruz—whom Jimmy describes as "chunky, short, broad-shouldered, brown-skinned, the finest Christian I have known personally."

Jimmy speaks often in his Sunday school class about his experiences with Pastor Cruz.

"We would go to homes where they were poor, alienated, withdrawn, sometimes filled with animosity, and I listened to the simple message Eloy took to them. First of all, they were all sinners—and so are we, equally so. Second, he said, in spite of our sins God loves us. Third, he said that God sent his only Son, Jesus Christ, to take the punishment for our sins. And if you believe that, then you can be forgiven of your sins and have eternal life.

"Eloy Cruz explained theology to them. They don't know the meaning of the word, and I didn't know much about it either. He said, 'You only have to have two loves in your lives. One is a love for God. The other is a love for the person who happens to be in front of you at any particular moment.' That's a very difficult thing to do. It's easy to love your next-door neighbor who drives by your house in a Chrysler or Cadillac every Sunday morning on the way to church. It's easy to say you love black ladies in distant Africa or Asia. But to transfer your love repeatedly during the day, every day, to the person who happens to be with you at any moment is a great challenge to us all.

"I have seen lives changed and in the process, and I've developed, I think, a strong desire to reassess constantly who I am and what I believe and what I do.

"Because of Eloy, we felt the Holy Spirit among us. As we witnessed that week, forty-six people, I think, accepted Christ as their Savior. They formed a new church, and it is still there. We visited about a hundred homes during the week, and all I contributed was—because of my halting Spanish—I could read from the Bible.

"In one particular case, we went to a home—I'll never forget—that had about four or five chairs around a small, cheap breakfast table. Eight or ten children looked out the door when we were coming. The man had a bottle of beer in his hand. Eloy picked the eleventh chapter of John to read. Jesus was confronted with the impending death of one of his friends, Lazarus. Jesus went to visit Lazarus and found that he had already died. When Eloy Cruz read that, at Jesus' command, Lazarus had come forth from the tomb, the children broke into cheers, applauded, shouted, screamed, and jumped up and down.

"I've never seen anything so dramatic. But that's the way this story is. The knowledge that Christ has dominion over death also affects us. It's one of the crucial elements of Christian belief, that life does not terminate at the time of this physical death, that Christ has power or authority, demonstrably, in earthly terms, to prove that is true."

Jimmy was not through talking about the New England experience.

"The last day I was with Eloy Cruz, we went by to see a young man whose wife had died. He was much better educated than the other Spanish-speaking people we had seen; he was a certified public accountant. His wife, who was only nineteen years old, had gone to a dentist to have a tooth extracted, and because of a mistake she bled to death. They had a little baby. The young man was so wrought up about his wife's death, he tried to kill the little baby. He was kind of an outcast in the community. He had gone to a room in an apartment, and he wouldn't speak to anyone. Eloy Cruz found out about it and went to see him.

"The text of his talk was Revelation 3:20, 'Behold, I stand at the door and knock: if anyone hear my voice, and open the door, I will come in and sup with him, and he with me.' Eloy Cruz told the young man that in spite of his sorrow and in spite of his loneliness, Christ was available with all his love and all his protection and all his guidance and all his forgiveness for that young man who had tried to kill his own child.

"It was such a moving experience for me that when we came out of the apartment onto the street—it was raining—I had tears running down my cheeks. It was the last day I would be with Eloy Cruz. In Spanish I asked him, 'How is it that you, being such a tough, he-man, are able to move and influence the lives of people as I have seen you do this week?' He was embarrassed because I had on nice clothes and I had a good automobile and so forth. He finally fumbled through a sentence in

Spanish. It translated, 'Our Savior has hands that are very gentle. He can do much with a man who is hard.'"

Jimmy continued, "It's part of our problem as Christian laymen. We tend to be strong, stalwart, unemotional, proud, hard, when a truer demonstration of strength would be concern, compassion, love, emotion, sensitivity, humility—exactly the things Christ taught us about. I believe if we can demonstrate this kind of personal awareness of our faith individually and as a group that we can provide that core of strength and commitment and unchanging character that our nation searches for and perhaps the world itself."

THE WORLD NEXT DOOR

"There is a sense in which you could say, if you are cynical, that by continuing to do human rights negotiations, by continuing to develop Global 2000 that that is a subconscious way of still playing president. But when you take on local issues like The Atlanta Project or teaching Sunday school, it's something different.

"In the civil rights movement, we were always accused of going in, stirring up trouble and then leaving to go someplace else. People accused us of not having to be accountable for the trouble we stirred up. You could say that about anything international, but you can't say that about a local problem. You can't say that about teaching Sunday school every week.

"I think the grace of Jimmy and Rosalynn Carter is that while they have met the global challenge and responsibility, that is more to be expected of an ex-president; but when you take on a neighborhood, when you take on Sunday school class, that requires real commitment."—Andrew Young, fellow Georgian, former congressman, and former U.S. Ambassador to the United Nations

---

MARY PRINCE

Jimmy and Rosalynn met Mary Prince in January 1971 while she was serving a prison term for manslaughter.

Mary's spiritual journey—with Jimmy and Rosalynn as two of her closes companions—parallels the story of Hagar in the book of Genesis, an Egyptian woman abused and then abandoned in the wasteland. Just as God gave Hagar a promise of security, life gave Mary a second chance in the form of a blonde toddler named Amy and a Georgia governor destined to become president.

Like Hagar sent into the desert, Mary was abandoned to the Georgia penal system in 1970 when she was framed—as two investigations have proven—on charges of manslaughter. She was a young, poor African-American mother of three with no voice in her own plea, her own defense, her own trial.

During her first year in prison Mary proved to be a model inmate, and because she had extensive experience in child care, she was taken one day to the Governor's mansion to try out for the job of nursemaid to the new family in residence. Prison trustees have served as groundskeepers, cooks, housekeepers, and nannies at the mansion since Reconstruction.

Mary sat in my den one Saturday afternoon and described what happened the first time petite, three-year-old Amy Carter walked up to her. "It was my first day there," Mary said. "Amy and I, we hit it off just like that!" The two became so inseparable that Amy would get sick if Mary had to be away for any great length of time.

For Amy, Mary's friendship was welcomed in her being one more trustworthy adult in a fishbowl lifestyle, a tough ally, and a caregiver who, by her own admission, was an "easy touch" when it came to hugs, favor, and candy.

For Mary, Amy and her parents provided a path directly back to Jesus Christ.

Mary attributes her accepting Christ to the influence of Jimmy and Rosalynn Carter. She says that they had a tremendous impact upon her: "Yes, a lot, I mean a lot. 'Cause they read the Bible every morning and every night when they're in bed. And I mean he has just a great influence on me because at one time I wasn't even going to church. And when we lived at the White House, he invited me to go to church one Sunday morning and I ended up getting baptized. Not that Sunday. I made my move that day to become a Christian. And then about two weeks after that I had done a lot of soul-searching and a lot of thinking, and I went on back and I joined the church just like that, and I was baptized the same Sunday.

"Well, you know I'll always be grateful to them, because they trusted me even though I was in jail, and you know people. When you go to jail, people look at you in a whole different manner."

Mary told us how Jimmy learned the facts about her case and gave her a pardon. "They've always treated me like part of the family, even though I was in jail. They used to take me on trips, and he would always say, 'She's a good friend, she's a friend of the family.' He never would say, 'She's our nursemaid' or 'She's our nanny.' He would always say, 'She's a good friend of the family.'

"You know, the Carter family has always treated me as a member of the family and not just as a worker. When they go, I go, and we eat together, we entertain together. I mean we really have fun!"

IGNORING THE POLICY

Although Jimmy Carter adored his father and energetically followed in his footsteps at the peanut warehouse, on the school board, and in the state legislature, the two men were philosophical opposites on at least one issue: race.

Jimmy recalls that the most serious racial argument he had with his father took place in 1950 when he and Rosalynn were home on leave from his submarine duty. Jimmy tried explaining to his father that during a recent stop at Nassau, in the Bahamas, every white crew member turned down an invitation to a special party hosted by British officials because the crew's black members were not allowed to attend. "There was simply no way that I could explain the reasons to my father," Jimmy said. "After that, he and I agreed to avoid racial subjects on my rare and brief visits home."

Although his father could not comprehend Jimmy's racial tolerance, his mother practically passed it on genetically. Lillian Carter often demonstrated for her children a progressive, compassionate view when it came to the relationship between the races.

Amid a hometown environment that was supportive of him, Jimmy recognized at a very young age the disparity between what the world offered to him and the leftovers it gave to his black playmates. One great paradox of Jimmy's childhood was the power of an African-American bishop versus the absurd, unspoken policies of segregation strictly observed throughout the South.

Hundreds of people attended Bishop Johnson's funeral in 1936. Lincolns and Cadillacs from several states descended on Archery, bearing whites and blacks who came to pay honor to this patriarch of the church. Yet, during all the years that the bishop lived in that area, he had to send his driver to the back door of any white person's home—the traditional and unfortunate entrance for African-Americans—and then the occupant came out to the yard for their visit.

In *Why Not the Best?* Jimmy relates his most poignant recollection of this racial anomaly, his being joined in field work by his African-American playmates in tasks that young boys could do.

> . . . all my playmates were black. We hunted, fished, explored, worked and slept together. We ground sugar cane, plowed mules, pruned watermelons, dug and bedded sweet potatoes, mopped cotton, stacked peanuts, cut stovewood, pumped water, fixed fences, fed chickens, picked velvet beans, and hauled cotton to the gin together. . . .
>
> We misbehaved together and shared the same punishments. We built and lived in the same tree houses and played cards and ate at the same table.
>
> But we never went to the same church or school. Our social life and our church life was strictly separated. We did not sit together on the two-car diesel train that could be flagged down in Archery. There was a scrupulous compliance with these unwritten and unspoken rules. I never heard them questioned. Not then.

Despite the black playmates of my youth, I can
remember that I was literally a grown man before I was
thrown into social situations in which I routinely met and
talked with black men and women on an equal basis.

Not only did whites and blacks maintain separate
churches, but they also attended at different times. I suspect
that, since many of the black worshipers had to prepare the Sunday dinner at the homes of their white employers, they and their
families began the custom of having Sunday services in the afternoon. This remains a strong tradition in the South even now.

Alvan Johnson, one of the bishop's sons, who lived and
was educated in New England, was among the first African-
Americans bold enough to ignore the "knock-quietly-at-the-
back-door" policy. He was close to every member of Jimmy's
family except Earl.

"Whenever we heard that Alvan was back home for a visit,
there was a slight nervousness around our house," Jimmy said.
"We would wait in some combination of anticipation and trepidation until we finally heard the knock on our front door. My
daddy would leave and pretend it wasn't happening while my
mother received Alvan in the front living room to discuss his
educational progress and his experiences in New England."

Jimmy often observes that, before integration, the South
was not, as it is commonly said, "separate but equal." Rather, it
was "fearful and constrained." Jimmy is fond of saying that
when African-Americans began claiming equality, it was
impossible to tell which race gained the most from letting go
of foolish standards. One of the first speeches Jimmy made in
the Georgia State Senate was an appeal for the abolition of
those infamous "thirty questions" that had been used to keep
African-Americans from voting. "They had been kept with a
great deal of smirking and pride for generations, questions that
nobody could answer, but which were asked in some counties
to every black citizen who had the temerity to approach a
county registrar and say, 'I want to vote.'"

I remember a man—my boss at the time—telling with
relish what I considered to be a horror story about how the

voting officials in one Georgia county deprived black citizens of the right to register. They were given a piece of waxed paper and a hard pencil and told to show that they could write. They were then given a newspaper in a foreign language and told to show they could read. The story concluded with one black man's statement about the reading part. He said he could not read the text but he could read the headline; it said: "Ain't no black man going to vote in this county."

DOING HIS SHARE
A local unit of Habitat for Humanity gathered several workers one Saturday to replace the roof of the home of an elderly black woman on the south side of Plains. Jimmy had wanted to participate in the work, but his schedule called for him to be away during the week and to fly home that very day. He arrived at the site in the early afternoon only to find that the project was nearly completed. Since he could not share in the roofing work, he went inside, talked to the woman, and learned that the leaking roof had rotted part of the kitchen floor. He returned later, bringing the materials he needed to make the repairs.

Jimmy himself often credits African-American churches in particular with providing the backbone of the civil rights movement. While speaking in Atlanta to ministers of the African Methodist Episcopal Church on June 18, 1976, he said:

> The church is a good reminder that God is indeed with the lowly, the suffering, the deprived. If it hadn't been for the church, that bridge would not have been there. . . . There's another bridge the church has provided—particularly your church. That is the one between black people and white people. There has been an unshakable commitment to human rights, civil rights, justice, concentrated here in Atlanta where the great colleges are. In the years when there was a lot of prejudice, hatred, lack of understanding, difficulty in communication, those great schools provided an unshakable commitment to what was right, what was decent, what was fair, what was just.

In his inaugural address as the Governor of Georgia on January 12, 1971, Jimmy declared: "The time for racial discrimination is over. Our people have already made this major and difficult decision, but we cannot underestimate the challenge of hundreds of minor decisions yet to be made. Our inherent human charity and our religion beliefs will be taxed to the limit. No poor, rural, weak, or black person should ever have to bear the additional burden of being deprived of the opportunity of an education, a job, or simple justice."

Jimmy's comfortable relationship with African-Americans was essential to his winning the White House. He claimed an unprecedented 94 percent of the black vote in 1976. When asked why she thought Jimmy achieved such a large margin, Rosa Parks, the mother of the modern civil rights movement, said in her gentle, understated way, "Simply because he was the best candidate."

The Reverend Andrew Young, a civil rights leader who served the Carter administration as the ambassador to the United Nations, points to Jimmy's childhood as an elemental factor in his popularity among African-Americans. Young told me this story about Jimmy's first meeting with the congressional black caucus, of which Young, at the time a congressman from Georgia, was a member in the mid-1970s.

> There is the Speaker's Room in the House of Representatives, and the Black Caucus used to use that room to meet with all of the presidential candidates. Jimmy Carter was the only one they did not know. He knew only two out of the twenty of us. Every single one of the northern liberals got in the room with twenty black people and were visibly uncomfortable. They'd come in, agree with our overall views, but inevitably they left with no support.
>
> Jimmy Carter came in and disagreed with everybody. He was against the Humphrey-Hawkins Bill on full employment principles. He was against quotas, and he opposed all of the conventional wisdom of the civil rights leadership. But because he had grown up in a community that was more than 80 percent black, he was so comfortable with black people that they trusted him.

The one question he answered better than anybody else was, 'How many blacks are on your staff?' Everyone else had one black staff member, except the most liberal candidate, who was looking for one. Jimmy Carter didn't know how many he had on his staff, and he started listing names of people. Soon we realized there were more than twenty blacks involved at all levels of his campaign. It was also clear to us that Carter hadn't even thought about it in those terms, but that he was practicing what the others were only preaching.

And I guess that is what Jimmy Carter's life boils down to: He practices what he preaches.

The Carters' cabin in the mountains
near Ellijay, Georgia (see p. 75)

An "Unabashed Moralist" in the White House

America didn't create human rights. Human rights created America.

JIMMY CARTER

To understand best how Jimmy Carter won the presidency in 1976 and to comprehend just what he represented to the American public, it is most appropriate to start with the assassination of President John F. Kennedy. Social historians typically point to this event as the beginning of a challenging, exhausting, and demoralizing period in American history. Civil rights. Civil unrest. The Vietnam conflict and its protesters. The murders of Bobby Kennedy and Martin Luther King, Jr. More Vietnam protests. And the crown jewel of political dishonesty: Watergate.

These events formed links in a chain that shackled an American public losing faith in its national leaders, in social justice, and in the moral values of the government.

Then there came, from the Deep South of all places, a reformer, a fresh face, an outsider with a simple message. He promised to eliminate the kind of secrecy in government that had produced Watergate and had created and then escalated the Vietnam War. He promised to open government to the average citizen.

Jimmy Carter promised to try to make his administration "as good and honest and decent and compassionate and filled with love as the American people." America's perception of personal moral character was one of the greatest factors in the election of 1976. While President Gerald R. Ford's lifelong service has proven his own moral character, he was linked with the Nixon administration and could not escape the atmosphere of corruption that surrounded it. In his acceptance speech at the Democratic National Convention, Jimmy sounded the theme, "It's a time for healing. We want to have faith again. We want to be proud again. We just want the truth again. It's time for the American public to run the government, and not the other way around."

A DIFFERENT PERSPECTIVE

When does "being well-prepared and having a mind for details" become a sketch for *Saturday Night Live*, in which the president gives advice on fine-tuning the performance of a copy machine? From the start of Jimmy Carter's administration.

When does every administration become controversial? From the moment the candidate announces plans to seek the office.

When does the honeymoon between the nation and the president-elect end? Almost by the time the ballot booths are returned to the courthouse basement.

History is the final judge of each presidential administration, and history is almost always kinder in retrospect than are the political opponents and the press during the term of office:

- Few of us today remember just how unpopular Harry Truman was when he left the Oval Office. Instead, we know about his strength and his motto "The Buck Stops Here."
- It is even possible that John Kennedy was on his way to completing a mediocre term of office. The murder of the young, handsome president who seemed the embodiment of our own hopes, however, became history's overshadowing image of him.
- A common joke about Eleanor Roosevelt from the early 1940s goes like this: A rural pastor holding a prayer service says to the group before him, "Tonight we have to talk about love. As Christians we are called to love everyone. Let me start by asking, 'Is there anyone you don't love?'"

One farmer in the back slowly raised his hand. "Well, pastor, I don't much love the president."

"Ahh, but can't you at least acknowledge that he answers to a higher power?"

"Yeah, but I don't love her either."

Today Eleanor Roosevelt is held in highest esteem for her dedication to America's poor and powerless. For American citizens too young to remember her long tenure as first lady, it is virtually impossible to understand just how great a target she became.

- A reporter in the fall of 1992 said to Jimmy, "In The White House, you were known as being a man of peace."

  "Really?" responded Jimmy jokingly. "I thought I was known as the man who lost the 1980 election!"

Religion also played a significant role in the campaign. Not since the 1960 contest between Catholic John Kennedy and Protestant Richard Nixon had faith's influence on politics been discussed so thoroughly during a national election. Pollster George Gallup Jr. called 1976 "the year of the evangelical Protestant," a term that applied to both men in the race. President and Mrs. Ford, who are Episcopalians, are both quite articulate about their own spirituality.

On November 2, 1976, the American voters gave Jimmy 40,828,585 popular votes (50.1 percent) to Ford's 39,147,613 (48 percent). Jimmy captured 297 electoral votes (twenty-three states and the District of Columbia) to Ford's 240. It was a narrow victory, but it was greater than John F. Kennedy's in 1960 and Nixon's in 1968.

Jimmy and Rosalynn won the White House by effectively articulating America's frustration with government. They won through sheer ambition and hard work. They won with Jimmy's winning smile and a remarkable talent for organizing. One major news magazine described Jimmy as "the most unabashed moralist" to seek the White House since William Jennings Bryan.

On the very day of Jimmy's inauguration, however, writers in both of the nation's preeminent newspapers used the word *mysterious* in their front-page stories about him: Charles Mohr in the *New York Times* and Haynes Johnson in the *Washington Post*. Johnson wrote: ". . . after tens of thousands of miles traveled, more public appearances than anyone can recall, pitiless scrutiny and constant criticism, he comes to power today still regarded as somehow mysterious."

Jimmy was given the oath of office by Chief Justice Warren E. Burger at two minutes past noon on January 20, 1977. Then the new president began his fourteen-minute inaugural address—one of the shortest ever—by saying, "For myself and for our nation, I want to thank my predecessor for all he has done to heal our land." He reiterated his campaign themes of "a new beginning, a new dedication within our government and a new spirit among us all."

Faith was also an important element in his message that day. He took his oath with his left hand on a Bible that has been in his family for four generations. It was open to a page containing the admonition of the prophet Micah "to do justly, and to love mercy, and to walk humbly with thy God." In his address, he said, "Let us learn together and laugh together and work together and pray together, confident that in the end we will triumph together in the right."

Undoubtedly, Jimmy had followed one of the most unconventional paths to the White House. He was the first president from south of Virginia since Zachary Taylor was elected in 1848. He was the first governor elected president since Franklin D. Roosevelt, forty-four years before him. He was only the third president of the century to turn out an incumbent. Jimmy had never served in the U.S. Congress or Senate. Except for seven years in the navy, he never worked for the federal government. He was not the product of any political machine, and he had few ties to Washington, D.C. He was not a lawyer. Nine months before he was nominated for president, according to *Congressional Quarterly*, three-quarters of Americans had not heard of him.

When Jimmy announced his candidacy in December 1974, the national press virtually ignored him. When regional and local reporters testified to his extremely effective face-to-face campaigning, the national press ignored him some more. His dramatic victory in the Iowa Democratic Caucus on January 19, 1976, finally gained him some media attention, and the expression "Jimmy Who?" accompanied with a hayseed caricature became all too familiar to the American public.

But he won.

One observer noted that when Jimmy and Rosalynn unpacked, they brought along openness, informality, good humor, and austerity. Jimmy immediately ordered the White House thermostats set at 65 degrees and urged all Americans to do the same. At his first cabinet meeting he eliminated the use of limousines by the White House staff and suggested his cabinet members do the same. Overall, he placed a premium on efficiency and tighter management of government. Critics and supporters alike described him as one who was diligent and well-informed, worked long hours, hated small talk and anything that smacked of pomp and circumstance, and was extremely well-prepared.

Hamilton Jordan, the president's Chief of Staff at the White House, said,

> I think the single theme of Carter's presidency and what he will be remembered for is that he went to Washington at a difficult time—in the aftermath of Watergate and Vietnam—and restored confidence. He was a man of integrity, and most importantly, tackled tough issues that had been ignored or side-stepped by recent presidents. Salt II [a nuclear test-ban treaty], Alaskan lands, human rights, everything from civil service reform to deregulation and the energy bill, the Panama Canal Treaty—all of these issues were tough. They were controversial. Very few had a political upside to them, but he did them because they were right. I think that's what he will be remembered for.

The Early Initiatives

Like all presidents-elect, Jimmy laid the groundwork in the transition period for several initiatives he hoped to launch as early as possible during his term of office. His initiatives included an economic stimulus package; a plan to reorganize the federal energy bureaucracy (his first step toward successfully creating a new energy policy); a new ethics code that laid out strict guidelines for his staff, his cabinet officers, and the more than 2,000 political appointees to his administration; and a plan to move his substantial holdings into a blind trust. In addition, he fulfilled a campaign promise in his very first executive order by granting a blanket pardon to all Vietnam draft evaders who had not been involved in a violent act.

This pardon perfectly reflects the nature of the Jimmy Carter I have come to know as his pastor for fourteen years. In his address to the American Legion Convention in Seattle, Washington, on August 24, 1976, Jimmy explained it this way: "Amnesty means that what you did is right. Pardon means that what you did—right or wrong—is forgiven.... I could never equate what they [Vietnam veterans] have done with those who left this country to avoid the draft. But I think it is time for the damage, hatred, and divisiveness of the Vietnam War to be over."

Another initiative, promoting his foreign policy plan to push for basic human rights everywhere, proved to be the hallmark of his administration. I believe it is a sterling example of Jesus Christ's calling us to dedicate ourselves to the least among us.

In Behalf of Human Rights

Frequently during his political career, Jimmy quoted theologian Reinhold Niebuhr as saying, "The sad duty of politics is to establish justice in a sinful world." The thirty-ninth president also rightly observed, "America didn't create human rights. Human rights created America."

One focus of the new president's foreign policy was his repeated expression of concern over violations of human rights in the Soviet Union, Cuba, Uganda, South Korea, and other nations. Less than one month after his term began, Jimmy wrote a letter to the noted Soviet dissident, Andrei Sakharov, saying in part, "You may rest assured that the American people and our government will continue our firm commitment to promote respect for human rights not only in our country but also abroad." This unprecedented move was followed within one week by an administration announcement that aid was being cut to Ethiopia, Argentina, and Uruguay because of their violation of international standards for human rights.

Leonid Brezhnev, then leader of the Soviet Communist party, accused the United States of using the issue of human rights to interfere in his nation's internal affairs. He said it was unthinkable that Soviet-American relations could develop normally as long as Jimmy Carter gave support to Soviet dissidents. But Jimmy never backed down on the issue of human rights.

Andrew Young, who served as Jimmy's ambassador to the United Nations, said, "Human rights is the greatest contribution of his presidency to the world, and it probably was African-Americans' greatest contribution to him. He learned about human rights from Martin Luther King and from African-Americans, and he made human rights the centerpiece of his administration."

Jimmy told Asian officials on October 5, 1977, during his visit to the United Nations, "I've noticed expansion of the definition of human rights in my own consciousness to encompass the right of someone to have a place to work and a place to live and an education and an absence of disease and an alleviation of hunger."

Rosalynn once summed it up this way to me: "I think his faith is one reason Jimmy's human rights program has been so successful. Because people know about his faith and convictions, it has made it possible for us to do so much. People around the world trust him—in the developing world especially. We work a great deal there. They feel that he will be fair and honest to them.

"Many countries don't want Jimmy to say publicly that they have human rights abuses within their borders because a lot of funding from other parts of the world is cut off if they're caught abusing people. They often go out of their way to let Jimmy know they're not abusing anyone. If a human rights organization says to Jimmy, 'We're having a problem with this country,' he will write a letter that says, 'We hear there are abuses. I know you would not do this and you must not be aware of it, but I'm certain you'll correct it.' And they do. Once he won the release of thirteen people who were scheduled to be executed. It was strictly political. These things happen all the time, but he doesn't make it public because then he would lose his effectiveness, and the leaders he's dealing with can't back down."

Religious historians, like political historians, typically highlight this aspect of Jimmy's work. "One of his greatest achievements has been his absolute dedication to this field," said Rabbi James Rudin. "Starting in the 1960s, Jimmy Carter really came through as a man who had genuine rapport with African-Americans in a way no Northerner could and in ways no other Southerners would."

Rabbi Rudin added, "Regarding the Jewish community, one of his permanent legacies, of course, was the Camp David Accord. We recently had the signing of the Middle East peace accords. Had it not been for the Camp David accords and his leadership, it simply would not have happened."

What history may come to show as the most far-reaching achievement of the Carter presidency was the Camp David Accords of 1979. Jimmy persuaded President Anwar Sadat of Egypt and Prime Minister Menachem Begin of Israel to meet with him at the presidential retreat in Maryland. The joint statement issued at the beginning of the Camp David retreat on September 6, 1978, read:

> After four wars, despite vast human efforts, the Holy Land does not yet enjoy the blessings of peace. Conscious of the grave issues which face us, we place our trust in the God of our fathers, from whom we seek wisdom and guidance.
>
> As we meet here at Camp David we ask people of all faiths to pray with us that peace and justice may result from these deliberations.

Despite this opening prayer, both sides arrived at the presidential retreat carrying absolute hatred for the other and a long list of "must haves." Slowly, arduously, through twelve days of negotiations that sometimes broke down in fury between Begin and Sadat, Jimmy had successfully mediated all but one crucial point: the dismantling of Israeli settlements in the Sinai.

Not "Just Being Nice"

When we first came to Plains, the Carters mentioned that they had built a cabin in the Georgia mountains near Ellijay and that we should go up sometime and use it. When Nelle asked me when we were going to use the cabin, I replied: "We're not. They were just being nice. It's a custom here in the South. An invitation is not really an invitation until you put a date on it."

One day when Jimmy and Rosalynn were enjoying homemade vegetable soup at our kitchen table, he asked when we were going up to the cabin. Nelle asked, "Are you serious?" With one voice, they said, "Yes, we are serious." Since then we have enjoyed the indescribable tranquillity of that rustic retreat once or twice a year. There is nowhere on earth more restful and yet exhilarating. Our son and daughter-in-law spent part of their honeymoon there.

Jimmy's White House secretary, Susan Clough, brought him some photographs of Begin, Sadat, and Jimmy. Sadat and Begin had already signed them, and now it was Jimmy's turn. The photos were for Begin's grandchildren, and—because Begin was the one who refused to budge on the last issue—Susan suggested that she get his grandchildren's names so Jimmy could personalize each one.

By many accounts, this was a small gesture, but it achieved world-changing results at the eleventh hour.

Jimmy walked back to Begin's cabin and handed him the photographs. In his memoirs, *Keeping Faith*, Jimmy wrote what happened next: "He took them and thanked me. Then he happened to look down and saw that his granddaughter's name was on the top one. He spoke it aloud, and then looked at each photograph individually, repeating the name of the grandchildren I had written. His lips trembled, and tears welled up in his eyes."

Begin told Jimmy something about every single grandchild. "We were both emotional as we talked quietly for a few minutes about grandchildren and about war."

Nevertheless, Begin pulled Jimmy into his cabin, dismissed everyone else, and in a quiet, sober voice explained that his hands were tied on the last issue.

A dejected, exasperated Jimmy Carter walked back to his own cabin, then found Sadat and told him in private that the plan seemed to be dead. "We realized that all of us had done our best, but that prospects were diminished," Jimmy wrote.

"Then Begin called. He said, 'I will accept the letter you have drafted on Jerusalem.' I breathed a sigh of relief, because it now seemed that the last obstacle had been removed."

Begin and Sadat shared the Nobel Peace Prize as a result of the Camp David Accords.

Footnotes to History

A footnote to this story is that as I was beginning work on my doctorate, Jimmy presented me with a small computer, saying, "You're going to need this." While he was showing me how to use it—which took a little time—he told me how he had used a similar one at Camp David. Whenever negotiations would seem to be bogging down, Jimmy would talk to one man or the other to determine what small point he was willing to concede at that stage the other person would agree to. Jimmy would type into the computer a statement to that effect, print it out on a small battery-operated printer, and have him sign the statement. He then went to the other man with a printed statement signed by the first and would say: "Now he is willing to do this. What are you willing to do?"

Former Vice President Walter Mondale has said, "For me the most exciting moment was when—contrary to everyone's expectation—an agreement was reached at Camp David on the Middle East and Prime Minister Begin and President Sadat and President Carter came home from that meeting and went up to a joint session of Congress that night to announce that an agreement had been reached. That set in motion the peace that's now beginning to move beyond Camp David, but without Camp David it wouldn't have been possible. That night was the finest two or three hours of our administration. There were many others, but they all blur compared to that one."

History will remember Jimmy Carter for having suffered a big defeat in 1980. History will remember him for his moral character, for his skills as a peace negotiator, and for his dedication to human rights and peace. The words of another president, as related by Jimmy in his memoirs, offer a fitting summary:

> Max Cleland (the first Vietnam veteran to serve as Veterans Administration head) came to tell me good-bye. He brought me a plaque with a quote from Thomas Jefferson:
>
> *I HAVE THE CONSOLATION TO REFLECT*
> *THAT DURING THE PERIOD OF MY*
> *ADMINISTRATION NOT A DROP*
> *OF THE BLOOD OF A SINGLE CITIZEN*
> *WAS SHED BY THE SWORD OF WAR.*

An Example for Others

• "Few world statesmen in recent memory have so clearly and unmistakably defined the personal responsibility of people in high government positions. You have recognized that those who make decisions on behalf of the nation must reflect a code of behavior equal to that of the nation as a whole."— King Hussein of Jordan, a Muslim, during a visit to the Carter White House

• "As a former president, Jimmy Carter has set a tremendous example by building houses, promoting peace through his genuine demonstration of family values. All that sets a wonderful example of what a former president should do."—Rabbi A. James Rudin, Interreligious Affairs Director, the American Jewish Committee

• "When our troops were just about ready to invade Haiti, who was it who said, 'Give me another half hour'? As long as there is a challenge, Jimmy Carter will be there to meet it, and the rest of us can be thankful for it. Jimmy and Rosalynn Carter are great Americans and great citizens of the world and more than any figure in public life, we look to Jimmy Carter for example and guidance telling us what we can make of this world if we want to. This is not a bad tribute to a man on his seventieth birthday or at any age."—Actor Kirk Douglas, emcee of an evening in honor of the former president's birthday

• "Jimmy Carter has done more for public service in general—and for the promotion of mutual understanding among nations in particular—than any American chief executive since John Quincy Adams."—Stanley Katz, chairman of the Fulbright International Committee

• "Jimmy Carter is a man who has committed his life to Christ.... He gives the extra measure. If all of us in the world gave an extra measure like Jimmy Carter does in his life, we'd have a much more enjoyable place to live. As an architect, I work with a lot of scales and rulers and, in construction, we work often with tape measures. In our society we have certain standards to measure our success, but I believe we have difficulty understanding the measuring stick the Carters use. Of course, it's not of this world."—LeRoy Troyer, the Carters' house-boss on at least ten Habitat projects

• "I mean no offense to anyone else, but I'm telling you he's the most religious man I have ever known. They read the Bible first thing every morning and the last thing every night. I believe there are angels looking over him seven days a week."—Mary Prince, long-time family friend

Jimmy and Rosalynn walking on
Pennsylvania Avenue to the White House
on Inauguration Day, 1977.

7

FIRST LADY AND FULL PARTNER

The day we got married I thought, "We're gonna have an adventuresome, happy life together!" That turned out to be true, and my life with Jimmy Carter has been more adventuresome that I could ever have dreamed it would be.

ROSALYNN CARTER

Her name is a permanent part of American history. She has been internationally recognized for her work in mental illness, peace negotiations, and childhood immunizations and her advocacy of the mentally retarded. She is remarkably soft-spoken but rightfully earned the nickname "the Steel Magnolia" while she lived in the White House. The thirty-ninth president referred to her as his greatest secret weapon and as a virtual extension of his own heart, soul, and body.

Hers is the story of a straight-A student who grew up in rural isolation, married her hometown sweetheart, and—in the style of Horatio Alger—used hard work and honesty to find herself living one day at 1600 Pennsylvania Avenue.

But from my perspective, and for the purpose of a religious biography, I offer here a viewpoint not likely to be discussed among political historians. While it gets obscured by the windy rhetoric of America's current crop of religious extremists, it is accurate and powerful: Rosalynn Carter's religious journey is an extremely instructive blueprint for women of traditional and moderate religious views who are trying to balance those elements with a dedication to improving their communities through public leadership. In fact, Rosalynn is an icon for anyone trying to hold tightly to traditional values and a Bible in one hand and a gavel, committee roster, and day planner in the other.

JUST ONE OF THE BOYS

Early in my tenure as pastor in Plains, President and Mrs. Carter took time to visit the pastor's home when my wife, Nelle, had most of her family visiting for a weekend. Nelle's mother was celebrating her seventy-fourth birthday. Nelle comes from a large family, and about forty of us were gathered for the party.

One of the children had brought a tape recorder to do an interview with the former president for a school class, but he found that the electrical cord would not reach to the table where Jimmy was sitting. Jimmy simply got up, sat on the floor near the machine, and gave an interview to the nine-year-old.

The Carters waited very patiently afterward while we got all the children out of the house for a group picture.

SERVING "THE LEAST OF THESE"

When Rosalynn entered political life, she brought the reformer's torch with her. "I was taught growing up that everyone you ministered to was important, that every person and every act was significant," Rosalynn said. "I listen to Jimmy every Sunday talk about Jesus and the things He did on earth and how He taught us to walk in His footsteps and then comes the question, 'What does it mean to take care of those who are poor and suffering and sometimes even despised by others?'"

Three weeks after moving into the White House, Rosalynn called a press conference to announce a major review of the nation's mental health system. The *Washington Post* totally disregarded the event, choosing instead to focus on the Carters' decision not to serve liquor on the state floor during formal dinners. Yet, in spite of that unfortunate beginning in Washington, Rosalynn Carter soon established herself as a champion for the country's mentally retarded and mentally ill citizens. She also defended issues important to the elderly, and she fought for the Equal Rights Amendment.

In 1980, she was named Volunteer of the Decade by the National Mental Health Association; In 1982, she received a presidential citation from the American Psychological Association and later was appointed an Honorary Fellow by the American Psychiatric Association.

Edith Mayo, Director of the Political History Division and Curator of the First Ladies Exhibit at the Smithsonian Institution, said of Rosalynn, "Programatically, I think she did a great deal to call attention to the lack of interest in caring for people with mental illness. I think she brought it out from the closet in the way that [former first lady] Betty Ford did for breast cancer and then later for alcohol and drug addiction. It's still thought to be a terrible stigma if someone in your family has some form of emotional or mental illness. I think she did a great deal to bring understanding about that to the American people. I can't even imagine other public figures doing something like that."

In addition, Rosalynn stirred awareness of the need for childhood immunization, and today the Carter Center maintains the ambitious goal of getting every child in the world immunized by age two. Rosalynn's most recent book, *Helping Yourself Help Others*, focuses on the 10 million caregivers in the United States, whose efforts too often go unnoticed and unrewarded in American culture.

As a reformist first lady, Rosalynn was following a tradition well-established by many of her predecessors, such as Ellen Wilson and Eleanor Roosevelt. Edith Mayo observed, "I think her most important legacy has been her decision to continue that long, time-honored tradition of first ladies' helping communities without power, becoming advocates for people who don't have a political voice. I think Rosalynn represents that female reformist strain that has loomed very large in the history of the first lady's role."

ROSALYNN'S STRENGTH

In the nineteenth century, the reformist spirit was inevitably born of religious convictions, and this holds true for Rosalynn a century later. For women reformers especially, social action revealed a belief that nurturing extends beyond one's immediate family and into the community. Temperance, children's welfare, and institutional improvements in hospitals, schools, and libraries were all projects by first ladies. The belief was—and is—that one serves God best by serving "the least of these."

"Rosalynn Carter is a strong woman, and she was not going to be deterred," Mayo observed. "I think that is prompted by a very deep religious conviction. I also think she saw the first lady's role quite correctly as what Teddy Roosevelt called 'the bully pulpit.' She knew she had the power, she knew she had the visibility, she knew she had the legitimacy that the role of first lady conferred. During her term, Mrs. Carter said something like, 'Once you realize that this is there for you, as an opportunity, you'd be a fool not to use it.'"

There is plenty of evidence that Rosalynn courageously and successfully used to good advantage the influence and resources that come with living in the White House. She testified before Congress on mental health issues, was the first of America's first ladies to attend cabinet meetings and—one of the boldest moves of all—served on a special diplomatic mission in the spring of 1977 to seven countries in Central and South America, conveying to those nations the president's hope for a nuclear-free zone. She also went to promote human rights and democracy, a theme that has produced stunning results in that region over the past twenty years through the Carter Center.

Rosalynn maintained a very busy schedule in general as the first lady. The *Washington Star* summarized Rosalynn's activities for the first fourteen months in the White House: She visited 18 nations, 27 American cities, held 259 private and 50 public meetings. She made 15 major speeches, held 22 press conferences, gave 32 interviews, attended 83 official receptions, and hosted 25 meetings with special groups in the White House.

But with every role, especially in that of the first lady, there are overwhelming issues. Rosalynn sized up the problems of high public office this way: "Problems that come to a president or a governor are the difficult ones. After all, if they are easier to solve, they're solved before they get to the governor's desk or the president's desk. One thing that greatly impresses you when you're in the governor's mansion or the White House is just how many problems there are and how many people suffer. The problems you see are the problems that never go away—like the problem of the poor, and the handicapped, and the refugees. These are problems that are just so enormous, and I think you just have to trust God to guide you. So you assume some responsibility, and you ask, 'Why am I in this position?' 'What is expected of me?' 'What can I do to help?'

"What you can do is the *best* you can do," Rosalynn says. "Jimmy's always helped me with that, too, because when he first went into politics the criticisms were very difficult for me. Jimmy used to sit me down and say, 'If you don't think I'm doing the best job I can do, then worry about it. You seek guidance from God to do what's right and best. I think you have to do that constantly because criticisms are constant. It doesn't matter what you do, you are going to be criticized. In the face of criticism you have to be in prayer and just trust God to guide you to do what is best and right for the country.'

"I think if you are deeply rooted in your faith before you get there, it is a lot easier. I was always so thankful for growing up in the church. The whole time we were campaigning and Jimmy was president, one of the worst things that happened to us was Chip's divorce. His wife, and baby, who was about a year old, left the White House, and it was the hardest thing in the whole term. I remember having to pretend that I was smiling and happy and greeting people and so forth when my heart was just breaking.

"I don't see how anybody without faith could maintain any kind of stability or equilibrium when those things happen to you. I think if you do have a deep religious faith then you just fall back on it."

Rosalynn adds that the Scripture verses she memorized and the hymns she sang as a girl help to sustain her in difficult times.

"Jimmy's been such a big help, too. I think sharing faith and Scripture with your spouse is significant. Every morning as he walked to the office through the Rose Garden at five-thirty or six o'clock, he repeated the Bible verse, 'Let the words of my mouth, and the meditation of my heart, be acceptable in thy sight, O LORD, my strength, and my redeemer'" (Psalm 19:14).

GROWING UP IN PLAINS

Like Jimmy, Rosalynn grew up in Plains with a lifestyle that centered around church, family, and school. Like Jimmy, she was extremely bright and proved herself to be a very hard worker. Like Jimmy, she read a great deal and grew up eager to transcend the boundaries of this community.

Eleanor Rosalynn Smith was born August 18, 1927, on the family farm just a few miles outside Plains. She was the first of four children born to Wilbur Edgar Smith, a bus driver and auto mechanic, and Francis Alletta ("Allie") Murray, a seamstress. Reared a Methodist—she became a Baptist when she married—Rosalynn summarized her early church life this way in her autobiography *First Lady from Plains:*

> We had no movie theater, no library, no recreation center in Plains. Occasionally someone would open a restaurant, but it would never last very long. The social life of the community revolved around the churches. My grandmother Murray was Lutheran, my grandfather Baptist, and my parents Methodist. I went to all three churches almost every time the doors opened, it seemed—to Sunday School and regular church service, to prayer meeting, Methodist League, Baptist Girls Auxiliary, and Bible School. We regularly went to family nights at the church and sometimes ate dinner outdoors on the church grounds, and looked forward eagerly to one of the big events of the year, the revival meeting. For a whole week during the summer there would be preaching morning and night, and we never missed a

service. We sang and prayed, and the preachers always came to our house for a meal.

God was a real presence in my life, especially in those revival times. We were taught to love Him and felt very much the necessity and desire to live the kind of life He would have us live, to love one another and be kind to and help those who needed help, and to be good. But we were also taught to fear God, and though I loved Him, I was afraid of displeasing Him all my young life. I didn't think about Him as forgiving God but as a punishing God, and I was afraid even to have a bad thought. I thought if we were good He would love us, but if we weren't He wouldn't.

Just as Earl Carter placed certain expectations on Jimmy, so Rosalynn's parents expected her always to demonstrate the nature of the "responsible oldest sister." She completed a long list of chores every day, learned to sew at a young age, and seemed to be her mother's right hand. But Jimmy grew up on a prosperous farm and securely navigated his childhood and adolescent years under the comforting, supportive guidance of Mr. Earl and Miss Lillian. Rosalynn, by contrast, was forced to surrender some of her childhood and face an uncertain future at age thirteen when her father died of cancer. She had worshiped Edgar Smith—a man who was hard-working and strict by nature but more affectionate toward her mother than any of her friends' fathers were to their wives, the man for whom she prayed day and night to get well.

The loss had spiritual significance for Rosalynn in a couple of ways. Like many adolescents who lose a parent, Rosalynn was struck low by guilt: "Did I somehow cause this?" "Wasn't I being good enough?" "Did God choose me for punishment?" Along with the burdens of doing extra household chores while her mother went to work as the postmistress in Plains and holding a part-time job of her own, Rosalynn felt emotionally paralyzed at times.

Then, also, there was the nature of a small town like Plains when people are in distress. I have not always found it productive to ask "Why?" when tragedy strikes, but I have seen especially in Plains—God's compassion surround us in our darkest moments through the warmth and support of our neighbors and church families. The grieving young woman felt this compassion, as she explained in *Helping Yourself Help Others.*

> Any time there's a crisis, such as my father's fight with leukemia, in a town as small as Plains (with only 600 residents) everyone gets involved. Our friends and neighbors were wonderful. Jimmy's mother, Miss Lillian, was a nurse. She came daily to give Daddy shots or whatever other help he needed. One day, after weeks of trying, she even talked Mother into going to a movie with her.

Further, in *First Lady from Plains:*

> Just before his death, Edgar led a family meeting in his bedroom and gently explained to his children that he wanted each of them to go to college. He instructed his wife to sell the farm if she needed money to pay for it, and he told them his greatest sorrow was that he wouldn't be around to make certain they all got good educations. . . .
>
> In a curious way, my father affected me even more after he died than while he was alive. It seemed more important than ever to do what he had expected me to do. Whenever I was faced with a decision or even a temptation, I would think about whether Daddy would like it or not.

Like Earl Carter, Edgar Smith did not live to see Jimmy and Rosalynn win even their first political victory, but it is a certainty that his oldest daughter has enjoyed a life beyond his greatest hopes and wildest dreams, an exciting life that really took shape as she fell in love with Jimmy.

LIVING IN A WIDER WORLD

Seeking to rebuild her life after her father's death, Rosalynn became absorbed in reading and schoolwork. She played basketball in high school, went out on dates, and attended picnics and parties with her friends. She graduated from Plains High School as the valedictorian of the Class of 1944. That fall, true to the promise she made to her father, seventeen-year-old Rosalynn entered Georgia Southwestern, a junior college in nearby Americus. While she was in college, she began dating Jimmy—her best friend's older brother.

"I had known him for as long as I could remember, the way everyone in a small town knows everyone else, but he was three years older than I and had been away at school for four years," she told me.

Then, when she saw a picture of the Annapolis midshipman on the wall of his sister's bedroom, she was smitten. "I couldn't keep my eyes off the photograph," she said. "I thought he was the most handsome young man I had ever seen."

One summer afternoon in 1945, when Jimmy was home on leave, Ruth arranged for him and Rosalynn to meet at the Carters' pond house. He took to her at once, inviting her to a movie and telling his mother late that evening, "She's the girl I want to marry."

For all her feelings toward Jimmy, however, Rosalynn turned him down at Christmas, the first time he proposed. "It was all too quick," she said. "I wasn't ready to get married."

But Jimmy and Rosalynn pursued their relationship through correspondence, and when she traveled with his parents for a weekend visit to Annapolis in February 1946, he proposed again. This time she accepted. They were married in the Plains United Methodist Church on July 7, 1946, and Rosalynn began her exciting and fulfilling seven-year stint as a navy wife.

Ready to leave behind the small town, Rosalynn suddenly found herself in charge of a household while her husband was away several days or even months at a time. She was soon handling the bills, the living quarters, and the plumbers and landlords with such efficiency, her husband's pride and her own self-confidence grew steadily. As their three boys arrived—John William ("Jack") in 1947, James Earl III ("Chip") in 1950, and Donnel Jeffrey ("Jeff") in 1952—she learned she was a good mother as well.

> As the total wife and mother, I washed and ironed, I cooked and cleaned, mopped floors, even listened to Ma Perkins on the radio. I bought women's magazines and clipped recipes and household tips, bought how-to books

and learned to crochet and knit and make curtains. We had bought a new record player so Jimmy could listen to the collection of classical records he had accumulated at the Naval Academy. Then we added a sewing machine for me so I could make my clothes and the baby's. I paid the bills and saved the money. And I knitted argyle socks for my husband while I waited for him to come home on weekends. I was living the totally conventional life of a young Navy wife in the forties and was more content than I had been in years.

They lived in Norfolk, Virginia; New London, Connecticut; Pearl Harbor, Hawaii; and San Diego, California. If Rosalynn was heartbroken when they received the news in 1953 of Mr. Earl's impending death, she was absolutely devastated when Jimmy announced plans to resign his naval commission and return to Plains to take over his father's business.

"I argued. I cried. I even screamed at him," Rosalynn told me. "It was the most serious argument of our marriage, and I wondered how or if I could hide the way I felt or the tension between us from our families.

"Jimmy said, 'I could stay in the navy and be CNO, chief of naval operations, and never mean as much to the people around me as my father meant to the people of Plains.' He just decided to get out of the navy. I didn't want to go back. I thought I had outgrown Plains—I had gotten a little too big for my britches. I only pouted for about a year after we got home."

Despite a rough transition back to the small town, this phase of Rosalynn's life led to such great adventures that navy life paled by comparison. Jimmy managed his father's business, dealt also with Mr. Earl's estate, and comforted his grieving mother. Meanwhile, as months passed, Rosalynn became comfortable in the community. She rekindled a close relationship with her mother and eventually found she could balance housework with office duties at the warehouse.

Then, in the spring of 1955, Jimmy called me one afternoon to ask if I could come and answer the telephone for him so he could get out of the office and visit some customers. I went that afternoon, taking the children with me, and soon I was going one day a week, then two. Before long I began making out bills for the customers, posting sales to the farmers' accounts, and paying the bills. It was a pleasant change for me. I felt I was doing something more important than cooking and washing dirty blue jeans, and the children couldn't wait to climb on the bags of fertilizer and seed in the back of the office and ride in the big trucks with their father.

"FAIR AND HONEST"

Some reflections from Rosalynn on Jimmy's achievements for human rights:

"Because people know about his faith and convictions, it has made it possible for us to do so much. People around the world trust him—in the developing world especially. We work a great deal there. They feel like he will be fair and honest to them.

"Many countries don't want Jimmy to say publicly that they have human rights abuses within their borders because a lot of funding from other parts of the world is cut off if they're caught abusing people. They often go out of their way to let Jimmy know they're not abusing anyone. If a human rights organization says to Jimmy, 'We're having a problem with this country,' he will write a letter that says, 'We hear there are abuses. I know you would not do this and you must not be aware of it, but I'm certain you'll correct it.' And they do.

"Once he won the release of thirteen people who were scheduled to be executed. It was strictly political. These things happen all the time, but he doesn't make it public because then he would lose his effectiveness, and the leaders he's dealing with can't back down."

Community service increased for both of the Carters as well. Jimmy became project chairman of the Plains Lions Club, a director of the county Chamber of Commerce, and a member of the library board, the hospital authority, and the county school board. Rosalynn joined the PTA and the garden club. They both taught Sunday school at Plains Baptist Church and at the Baptist Training Union. The Training Union was a Sunday night organization intended for teaching subjects other than strictly Bible study, which was the purview of the Sunday school. It provided both a time for learning about the ways Baptists do things and a social hour just before the evening worship.

All this time, Jimmy and Rosalynn were laying the foundation of a political partnership that met its first test in Jimmy's hard-fought battle for the state legislature in 1960. When Jimmy took his seat in the Georgia State Senate in Atlanta, Rosalynn's world expanded again.

THE ROAD TO THE WHITE HOUSE

Rosalynn took to political life with the same vigor and determination she had demonstrated in so many other endeavors.

> I liked being a political wife. A number of the other senate wives went with their husbands to Atlanta during the session to enjoy the social activities; others stayed home to take care of the children. Some felt burdened with all the responsibilities while their husbands were away. I stayed at home and took care of the children, but I never felt burdened. I had an important task. I had to keep the business running while Jimmy was gone. I liked the feeling that I was contributing to our life and making it possible for him to pursue a political career. I was more a political partner than a wife, and I never felt put upon. During the next four years [Jimmy was re-elected in 1964] I only had to call him home once, when one of our old brick warehouses collapsed, dumping several hundred tons of peanuts into the street!

After one unsuccessful bid for the Georgia governor's post, Jimmy announced on April 3, 1970, that he would again be a candidate. Rosalynn proved to be an effective and hard-working campaigner, and together they shook hands with more than 600,000 people—half the voting-age population of the state.

Despite the jubilation of victory, the governor's mansion proved to be one of the most challenging environments for Rosalynn.

"Going from Plains to the governor's mansion was harder for me than going from the mansion to the White House," she wrote. "In Plains I had worked in a farm supply business, and I had been taking care of children. All of a sudden I was in the governor's mansion without any good help at first, and it was really distressing."

Rosalynn had many achievements in Atlanta—from prison reform to vast improvements in the state's mental health program—but the roles of superwife, supermom, and super-hostess eventually took a toll. She once told me that she had lived in the mansion about eighteen months when she became exhausted and depressed. She felt she had no emotional, spiritual, or even phsyical privacy. She wrote in *First Lady from Plains*, "I snapped at my children, at the maids and the security men. And I found myself in long and continuous arguments with Jimmy over everything, especially my discontent."

Rosalynn responded the same way my own wife would—the same way many of the women in my congregation would. She joined a Bible class, thinking it would help get life back on track.

This led to spiritual answers which, she says, changed her life in a powerful, healthy way—but not, however, before she encountered an unfortunate episode all too common in the lives of Christian women.

She wrote,

> I learned from the teacher that a well-known evangelist would be in town; I paid $60 to hear him teach a course on Christian living. It was the wrong thing to do. I argued in my mind with almost everything he said. He taught sub-servience by the wife and mother and children, with no acknowledgment or thought of mutual respect and sharing and love within a family. Subservience and discipline. There's more to life than that, I thought, and there's more to living the life Jesus wants us to live than being punishing and rigid and afraid. . . . I got up and left.

Feeling guilty, feeling certain *she* had been the one in error, feeling like giving the program one more chance, she went back the next night—and managed to stay for twenty minutes.

Shortly after this, a friend from Rosalynn's Bible class asked to come to the mansion to talk to the trustees about Jesus. Rosalynn wrote,

> I was glad to have her come. The prisoners might need Jesus, and I needed Him, too. I especially needed to be reassured after my conflict with the evangelist. Had she sensed that? I'll never know. "Jesus love you. You are precious to Him," my friend said to the prisoners, and me, assembled in the ballroom. "It doesn't matter who you are are or where you are or what you have done, He loves you. Everyone in this room is precious to Him. I am precious. Mrs. Carter is precious. Every one of you is precious to Him. He wants all of us to be happy. He wants to take away our problems and our cares, and He will—if we'll only let Him."

Rosalynn told me she made the profound decision that day to release her challenges and frustrations—through prayer—to Christ, a choice she insists saved her life. "It was a burden lifted," she wrote. "Things didn't change suddenly. It took a while for me to work through all the problems I'd saved for myself, and each day I'd find something else to give to Jesus. Sometiems I'd have to say, 'Here, take this one again,' when I couldn't seem to let go."

JIMMY AND ROSALYNN'S SPIRITUAL RELATIONSHIP

The image that best represents the political relationship—and the spiritual relationship—between the Carters is their walk to the Capitol on the day of James Earl Carter's inauguration as the president of the United States. They strolled side by side, hand in hand, surrounded by their family as they faced a new adventure as a team.

"I thought that was a very symbolic image of the two of them," observed Edith Mayo, "the Carters, walking back to the White House hand in hand on the first day, minutes after the inauguration. In many ways they were announcing a political partnership. Though it could have caused him a great deal of problems in his administration, he made it no secret that Rosalynn was going to be a political partner in the White House."

Jimmy has been quoted more than once as saying of Rosalynn, "She's an extension of me." While in the White House, he once told a reporter, "There is very seldom a decision that I make that I don't discuss with her, tell her my opinion, or seek her advice. . . . On matters where her knowledge is equal to mine, she prevails most of the time."

Jimmy invited his wife to sit in on cabinet meetings, quoted her frequently to his other advisers, and constantly sought her comment by using memos and a scribbled note, "Ros, what think?"

Press Secretary Jody Powell once told a reporter, "Everything they've done has not been a case of Jimmy Carter doing it with a supportive wife. It has been Jimmy Carter and Rosalynn Carter doing it as a team."

When she was asked which first ladies she most admired for their spirituality, Rosalynn chose Eleanor Roosevelt because of her dedication to the poorest Americans and Lady Bird Johnson for her dedication to the American family.

Edith Mayo observed that in regard to the religious faith of the first ladies, Rosalynn is most like Lucy Hayes, who lived in the White House exactly one hundred years earlier. I find this to be an extremely perceptive comment.

Like Rosalynn, Lucy Hayes was a strong social reformer whose convictions came directly from her religious faith. Like Rosalynn, she was a Methodist; and she was soft-spoken and quick-witted and a genuinely gracious hostess.

Although Lucy did not fulfill the role of president's political partner to the degree that Rosalynn did, only a fool would underestimate either of these women. Both were especially effective at social reform because each woman vowed not to be deterred when facing what she felt was a social evil.

Lucy often said that she wished she could have "served Mr. Lincoln with a garrison of women at Fort Sumter." The only correct response to slavery, she observed, was total rebuke.

Both first ladies were absolutely dedicated to children, the elderly, education, and health care. Both were extremely effective in advancing their agendas in ways the press never realized.

Edith also compared Rosalynn to Martha Washington in their views of social equality and their service to the less fortunate. "Both have Southern backgrounds, a strong sense of gentility, and both greeted everyone on equal terms, which is a very crucial part of any administration's public perception.

"Martha extended a great deal of interest and attention to soldiers when she visited her husband at his various encampments. She would darn socks, mend shirts—it's really quite extraordinary. You can't picture Mamie Eisenhower in Europe while her husband is the commander-in-chief, darning soldiers' socks. It is a charitable and almost motherly, protective kind of gesture. The fact that she did it and it was so talked about was quite extraordinary for its time. And I think in the sense that Rosalynn and Jimmy welcomed all comers is a latter twentieth-century expression of what Martha was doing earlier."

A reporter once asked Rosalynn, "How will history books describe you?" She responded, "As an ordinary woman, who never for one moment doubted she was anything but an ordinary woman, who did the very best she could, and took advantage of every opportunity that came her way."

Maranatha Baptist Church

"ALL ARE WELCOME HERE"

*Christian hospitality . . . is primarily the cre-
ation of a free space where the stranger can
enter and become a friend instead of an
enemy. Hospitality is not to change people,
but to offer them space where change can take
place. . . . Hospitality is not a subtle invitation
to adopt the lifestyle of the host, but the gift of
a chance for the guest to find his own.*

HENRI NOUWEN

Imagine a rural town of 700 people suddenly flooded—
absolutely overwhelmed—by up to 10,000 visitors every single
day. Great crowds began coming to Plains from the moment
Jimmy Carter won the Democratic nomination in July 1976—
all seeking to learn who this man was and whence he had
come. The resulting stress of the situation was one of several
factors in the creation of Maranatha Baptist Church.

Life was a logistical nightmare around Plains. Visitors
couldn't find restrooms, adequate parking, or other facilities
expected in a tourist site because Plains had never before been
one. Local residents hardly knew how to respond to the
onslaught of outsiders—especially the press, who camped out
in "TV City" under the town's water tower. Some village folk
developed short fuses with outsiders and with each other.

In the summer of 1976, some 110 reporters were stationed
here and expected to file a daily story. They recorded every tiny
detail of Plains, every bark of the dog, every snap of a twig.

Nothing seemed too insignificant for the evening broadcast. If someone in Plains sneezed, it made the Associated Press.

Residents of Plains couldn't leave their own driveways because tourists had them blocked in. Locals couldn't shop in the village because visitors filled the stores. On Sunday morning, members of the Plains Baptist couldn't attend church because tourists already had the place packed.

The media reported that segregation alone caused the eventual split in the church, but it was not nearly that simple. It is accurate that some members of Plains Baptist didn't want African-Americans in the church, but they were generally the same people who didn't want *any* outsiders to enter their sanctuary. While it is important to understand the race issue as it applied to Plains Baptist, the problems extended far beyond skin color.

Jimmy described the church in *Why Not the Best?*

> In our own church at Plains, we had historically invited black neighbors to attend special services like weddings, funerals, and sometimes baptisms, but it had not been the custom for many years for blacks to attend the regular worship services. Earlier in the history of our little church, following the War Between the States, black and white worshipers attended the same services, but then the churches split into separate congregations and from that time forward they were segregated.
>
> I was a deacon in our church and missed one very critical deacons' meeting during this period [in 1965]. On that occasion, the other eleven deacons and our pastor voted unanimously to propose to the church congregation that if any blacks attempted to enter the church on Sunday they would be blocked and excluded from the worship service. I heard about this vote later, after the meeting, and it disturbed me deeply.

In a subsequent church meeting, Jimmy urged the congregation to consider allowing blacks to attend the church. His proposal was soundly defeated.

The issue remained unchanged until October 24, 1976— the last time Jimmy and Rosalynn attended church in Plains before the presidential election. Between Sunday school and the church service, one reporter bluntly asked Jimmy whether blacks were welcome here, and he said he believed that if they wanted to, they could join the congregation now.

The Reverend Clennon King, a black activist from Albany, Georgia, challenged Jimmy's comment by writing the church and informing them he would gladly join them the following Sunday for worship—the Sunday before the election.

In response, the deacons canceled the church service. At a news conference in Sacramento, California, reporters besieged Jimmy about the controversy. He told them, "I think my best approach is to stay within the church and to try to change the attitudes which I abhor. Now if it was a country club, I would have quit. But this is not my church. It's God's church. I can't quit my lifetime habit of worship and commitment because of a remnant of discrimination which has been alleviated a great deal in the last ten years."

Shortly after the election, on November 21, the congregation officially voted to open the church to "all people who want to worship Jesus Christ." Following the vote, Jimmy offered this prayer of reconciliation:

> Our Father, we come together with humble hearts and thankful hearts, realizing how You have blessed us, recognizing our sinfulness, weakness, shortcomings, failures, as measured by the perfect life of Christ.
>
> Help strengthen our commitment to observe the Bible teachings so we may help the humble, poor, despised....
>
> Bind our church in close fellowship, help us overcome our difficulties in this church, brought about by recent events. Let this be a place of pure and inspired teachings of God's Word. May those who come here come with hearts yearning for truth and love; let other motives for coming to our church be wiped out.

On February 13, 1977, during his first visit home after his inauguration, Jimmy offered this prayer for Christian love in the men's Sunday school class at Plains Baptist:

When so many hearts are turned to Thee, let us realize the permanence of Thy teaching and the characteristics that are reflected in Jesus' life: simplicity and humility and compassion and love and truth.

We thank Thee for giving Him to us, and as we study about this Christ, Your only Son, might we decide how far short we fall of His perfect example and with Thy forgiveness and Thy love for us even though we are sinners, that we might be encouraged to admit our sins and repent of them, and turn toward Thee, trying always to pattern our lives after Jesus' life.

Draw us near to Thee, to God, and to Thy Christian love. Let us see we are brothers and sisters to all our fellow human beings. And in the spirit of a close-knit family, let us be drawn to one another in a realization of common purpose, common needs, and common blessings that come from Thee. Forgive us this morning our sins and receive our grateful thanks for sending Your Son to this earth.

However, a divisive spirit remained in the Plains Baptist Church. Not long after the inauguration, and with Jimmy in Washington, a more serious controversy erupted. Some church members wanted to fire the pastor. Others wanted to vote to decide just who could attend the worship services. Reporters covered every frustrated expression, every sigh, every look of disgust, and church members rightly felt that all the eyes of the world were watching their enormous, internal struggle.

A SEARCH FOR RECONCILIATION

Jimmy knew his own presence had created a challenge for the church. On Easter Sunday 1977, while visiting the First Baptist Church in Calhoun, Georgia, Jimmy told the men's Sunday school class: "We have a little problem worshiping as a First Family. Large crowds follow me around. It's almost done severe damage to our little church in Plains. I hope you'll pray for them. They've had a lot of problems. It gives me a sense of humility that my own shortcomings are significant because I am president.

"I enjoyed being a student this morning," he told the crowd. "I know that sometimes when we come to visit a church, it disrupts the service and causes unnecessary furor. It brings a lot of people to church and Sunday school who don't normally attend. I'm just like you are. The fact that I was elected president doesn't make me any better than you are or closer to God."

ALONG FOR THE RIDE

The Carters became interested in "Mike," a sixth-grader who received little family nurture and had been befriended by one of his teachers. Once, on a church outing, Jimmy and Rosalynn let Mike ride in the van with them and the Secret Service agents. Not only was this special to him, but the Carters came by our home the next morning to allow Mike to go jogging with them. Later they autographed a Bible the teacher was giving Mike for his birthday.

The Plains Baptist Church did vote to fire the pastor, Bruce Edwards, who had stood clearly in support of both Jimmy and desegregation. The congregation divided in April 1977.

The twenty-nine founders of the new Botsford Baptist Mission were intentional about hospitality from the very first service, which was held May 22 in a vacant church building belonging to the Lutheran church in Plains and located about six miles south of town on Georgia Highway 45. Among the leaders at the new church were Hugh Carter, Sr., who had been the songleader and the congregation clerk at Plains Baptist.

Like any difficult separation, this one left many Baptists angry and deeply wounded while most non-Baptists watched in curious fascination to see who landed in which church once the dust settled. No one doubted that Jimmy knew what was happening, and most figured that he had been kept informed day by day during the worst of the crisis. But everyone in Plains—Baptist or not, townspeople or media—pondered the

103

same questions: What will Jimmy and Rosalynn have to say when they come home? Which church will they attend?

The questions hung in the air throughout the summer of 1977 until the weekend of August 7, when the Carters returned home for Rosalynn's annual Murray family reunion. Now the village could have an answer.

Jimmy and Rosalynn attended both churches, setting about to see what they could do to heal the obvious wounds. The Carters went first to Plains Baptist, where Jimmy offered this prayer at the men's Bible class:

> Our Father, we come together in Thy house for worship. Let each one search our hearts, help us remove thought of jealousy, lack of compassion and love for our fellow human beings.... Deal with those who look to us for leadership as Christians. Help us realize and personify what Christ our Savior is and was, and realize that we are to set a pattern as Christ set one for us. God is love, and this feeling of friendship and spirit of companionship and love is a central part of Christianity. Bless all the members of this church and Christians around the world who share brotherhood and sisterhood in God by Christ. We ask Thy blessings on this country as we struggle for the right to have a decent way of life. Let our nation have the humility to recognize our shortcomings and failures. Bind our hearts together and help us serve you every day of our lives.

Then the president of the United States traveled six miles out of town to deliver this benediction at the newly formed church:

> O Father, bless this small and new church. Separate it, we all pray, not out of a sense of alienation and hatred but out of love and rededication to Thee. Help all tensions to be alleviated. Let there be a genuine search for reconciliation with the Plains Baptist Church. Let it not be a sign of weakness in Thy kingdom, but a sign of strength. Let there be a permanence based on love and forgiveness and rededication.

The Carters continued this pattern whenever they returned home—prayer at the Plains Sunday school, benediction at the new church (which was eventually named Maranatha, a biblical term that means, "Come, Lord"). On Christmas Day 1977, Jimmy offered this touching benediction at Maranatha Church:

> Our Father, we know nothing could be more appropriate on this birthday of the Prince of Peace than for us each to seek that feeling in our own lives and all human beings. We pray we might remove from our consciousness any feeling of divisiveness or hatred or misunderstanding, or an absence of an ability to communicate on a level of compassion and understanding.
>
> You sent Your Son to be with us, to set an example for us, and we are deeply thankful for this opportunity to learn about Him. With Christ as part of our lives we have an opportunity to exhibit what belief in You means: subservience to Thy will, a desire to think of others and not of ourselves, an absence of pride, a realization of our need for humility, a desire to have brotherhood and sisterhood exemplified throughout the world.
>
> So in Your holy name we pray this morning that we might realize peace on earth and good will to all human beings who join to us and with us in worshiping Thy name.

While they lived in the White House, Jimmy and Rosalynn traveled between the two churches as a gesture of hospitality and friendship to each congregation and as a way of extending his hope and personal assistance to bring healing between them.

In 1978 the Maranatha congregation built the present church building on eleven and a half acres at the edge of the village. Our numbers grew from the original 29 to a current membership of about 128, with an average of about 147 visitors per week. On most of the Sundays when Jimmy and Rosalynn are present, visitors outnumber members. On some occasions, the ratio is four-to-one or higher.

Until 1994, the church averaged about 100 visitors every time Jimmy taught Sunday school—about 3,600 visitors a year. After his peacekeeping trips to North Korea and Haiti and the publication of *Always a Reckoning*, the number of visitors rose to about 250 each time he teaches. The total number attending his class during 1995 was 7,632 persons. The mission of the church has grown exponentially, and we are of a mind that America's fascination with Georgia's native son will only get stronger.

Returning from the White House to live in Plains, the Carters joined Maranatha Baptist Church on January 25, 1981. I was not called to serve as Maranatha's pastor until several years after the Carters joined. People sometimes would inquire why the Carters chose this church; I made a decision not to ask them so that I could honestly reply, "I really do not know. I just cannot say."

FORM AND FREEDOM

Life offers all too few rare privileges, and one of mine had to do with Jimmy's preparations for his book of poetry (*Always a Reckoning*). As with any form of art, we need feedback from others in order to make sound judgments about the merits of our work. Jimmy told me he had written some poems and wanted my opinion.

Jimmy would write a few poems, then come by and stick an envelope with copies into my newspaper box. I would read them and pass my comments back to him. I had no idea how much he knew about the mechanics of poetic form, and the poems were a blend of blank verse and free verse. I took one and recast it into iambic pentameter. He responded with a note: "If you change my poems too much, they will no longer be my work." The fact is, his version came out far better than mine, and after seeing the finished book with its glowing word pictures of experiences that so often resonate powerfully with my own memories, I appreciate all the more the honor his request conferred on me.

A MINISTRY OF HOSPITALITY

Jimmy and Rosalynn do more at Maranatha than just attend church when they are home on a weekend. Rosalynn, who formerly taught a young people's Sunday school class, now is among a group of volunteers who clean the building, and Jimmy takes his turn mowing the grounds in the summer months and, of course, helping me recruit new members. The two of them have given Maranatha a number of handcrafted gifts—wooden offering plates, a table for the younger Sunday school students, and even some bookshelves for the pastor's study.

Undoubtedly, however, the greatest gift the Carters have presented to this congregation is the unique ministry of hospitality. The covenant between Maranatha and her most famous members, as you can imagine, produces some amazing results and takes us down an adventurous path in our service for Christ.

Standing at the back of church one Sunday, Rosalynn told a reporter, "I think we have a wonderful ministry because we have people coming to our church who are really dedicated Christians, such as those who work with Habitat for Humanity, and then we have a number of visitors who have never been in a church before, so it makes for a wonderful witness.

"We have had some very special visitors. I remember Jimmy and I were out riding our bicycles one day, and we rode past a migrant camp and stopped to invite them to our church. And they came. It was thrilling."

The migrant workers entered the church and, as was their custom, the men sat on one side and the women and children sat on the other. Jimmy stood up at the beginning of the worship service and explained to them, in fluent Spanish, that they could sit together in families if they liked.

As a Maranatha tradition, I ask visitors at the start of worship to introduce themselves and tell us where they are from. A spokesman for the migrants stood to introduce the group and said, "We came because we were told we would be welcomed here."

It was a poignant moment. Many of us were moved to tears by the profound realization that this group of people had been overlooked for so long that a simple and sincere invitation to church fellowship meant the world to them.

At Maranatha, only 20 percent of the visitors are Baptist. We have opened our doors to Hindus, Muslims, Jews, Christians of every stripe, atheists, Druids, and agnostics. The traditional prime directive of Southern Baptists remains missionary witness. But unlike other missionaries, who often go far distances to reach the masses with the Gospel, we sit tight, for—as one visitor observed—"If he teaches, they will come." One Sunday in 1988 they came from fourteen different nations; during a massive Habitat "blitz build" in April 1993, they arrived from thirty different states of the U.S. Over the years, nearly 50,000 visitors representing more than eighty countries have joined us for church.

While doing graduate study in ministry after I became the pastor at Maranatha, I began looking for other congregations in the United States that draw hundreds of visitors because of a celebrity member. I simply could not find one. The houses of worship that perhaps come closest to our experience are Saint Peter's Basilica in the Vatican in Rome, Westminster Abbey in London, and the National Cathedral in Washington. However, tourists are not usually there during times of worship. When they come to Maranatha just to see Jimmy Carter, they usually attend Sunday school and the worship service.

Today the opening prayer in Sunday school and the benediction at worship may be offered by an Episcopalian, a Jesuit, a Presbyterian, or even a rabbi. Requesting prayer from a visiting religious leader is a wonderful gesture of hospitality, and we have been blessed by their words. On one Sunday, Jimmy asked a United Methodist pastor and seminary professor from South Korea to offer the opening prayer. The visitor did so in his native language, and at the end Jimmy confessed, "I understood three words: Jimmy, Carter, and amen."

Many international students studying at nearby Georgia Southwestern College visit our church. One Japanese student wrote to me that her positive experience at Maranatha had caused her to seriously consider accepting Christ. She wrote later, saying, "I became a Christian in May at First Baptist Church at Valdosta in Georgia. It was the greatest experience for me since I came to the United States."

Obviously, this is one of my most exciting rewards as pastor of Maranatha, although we usually never know what impact we have had on visitors.

I hear it often: "I have seen many Christian churches, but this is the first time I have ever been inside one." I mentioned this to a woman whom I was greeting at the close of a service, and she said: "Yes, and I am one of them."

Because we meet many people like this, we make it a point in each worship service and Sunday school class to promote three primary messages:

- You are very welcome here.
- We believe Jesus Christ is the Son of God, and we hold Him as Lord, Savior, and model for our individual lives.
- The best way to serve Jesus is by serving others.

THE RISKS OF HOSPITALITY

For all of its rewards, however, hospitality also involves risk. There is always the chance that a stranger will exploit an offer made in good faith, that the visitor will not or cannot fit into our expectations or group social dynamics.

A bag lady I will call Julia hitchhiked into Plains all the way from Louisiana, believing that if she could just meet Jimmy one time, her problems would be over forever. Because she was a paranoid schizophrenic, her thinking was disjointed, and she struggled to complete a logical sentence. But when she camped out in the church's toolshed for three days and spoke constantly of Jimmy, we understood her intentions thoroughly.

We phoned Jimmy at home on a Wednesday, and he made a special trip to the church that evening to visit her. His gentleness and respect were touching. However, poor Julia—so consumed by an inner agenda—couldn't understand that she was actually getting her wish—to meet Jimmy Carter. Only after their visit did she seem to realize she had just met the former president.

Julia remained in the toolshed four more nights, explaining that she wanted to stay for church on Sunday and have her picture taken with the Carters afterward. My wife, Nelle, and I brought a

Polaroid camera on Sunday so Julia could see the photo immediately. Jimmy presented her with a Bible from our church, and
several of our members offered money to help her travel to relatives or a safe destination. She flatly refused the money.

Julia wanted me to keep both the Bible and photo for her,
fearful that someone would steal them during her travels. I
insisted she take them, and the last thing we knew, Julia was
headed down the road with her canvas bag and the two items
she collected in Plains—a Bible and a photo that would likely
stun her future therapists and caretakers.

Maranatha Church, in turn, has received many gifts from visitors. Some ship us Bibles to distribute wherever they are needed.
Some enter the sanctuary with incredible musical talents. Rarely
do we receive the type of gift PLO leader Yasser Arafat sent us in
the fall of 1993—a stunning carved icon made of mother of pearl.
One scene depicts the Nativity; another depicts the Last Supper.
The icon is framed in olive wood from the Holy Land.

Yet I believe that the greatest gift we receive from our
guests is a renewed commitment to our own legacy of hospitality and to a larger worldview. The apostle Paul wrote to the
Christians in Rome, "Welcome one another, therefore, just as
Christ has welcomed you, for the glory of God" (Romans 15:7
NRSV). In Christ, the sinner is no longer an enemy of God but
one who receives a welcome and a place of hospitality. No one
is outside God's love. Cultural barriers must fall. If congregations take seriously Christ's demand to make disciples of all,
they cannot reject anyone.

Unfortunately, the phrase "Southern hospitality" is a relative expression regarding church services. The observation of
the Reverend Martin Luther King Jr., "Sunday at 11:00 is the most
segregated hour in America," remains largely true even today.

The good news for Plains, Georgia, however, is that the
relationship between Maranatha and Plains Baptist churches
has healed nicely, and today we combine our efforts for min-
istries such as local revivals and Vacation Bible School. But for
us, the greatest news is that we serve Jesus, and we welcome
all to Maranatha. It is more than our ministry; it is genuinely
our privilege.

Jimmy teaching the adult Bible class at
Maranatha Baptist Church

A LEGACY IN THE CLASSROOM

Any visitors today? (Laughter) That's my best laugh line ever.

JIMMY CARTER

Many visitors recall to mind the television images of the late 1970s as they drive into Plains in the 1990s: the depot that served as campaign headquarters, the late Billy Carter's gas station, and a giant, smiling peanut statue (which Jimmy cheerfully despises) reminiscent of a Carter-Mondale campaign button that read, "The grin will win."

Other visitors recall the images of state dinners, Secret Service escorts and a string of White House limousines and, as they drive by the Carters' home—modest, but obscured by a compound fence, guardhouse, and separate quarters for security personnel—wonder whether they really can attend church with the couple who live inside.

It is not only possible to worship with the Carters at Maranatha Baptist Church, but, in fact, the entire ministry is tailored—with Jimmy and Rosalynn's help—to serve just such an experience.

By the time visitors arrive at our church door Sunday morning, we are prepared for a variety of comments:

"Is he actually going to teach this morning?"

"You know, I have just got to tell them I voted for him—twice!"

"We're Habitat volunteers from Michigan and worked with them in Eagle Butte."

113

"What is Amy doing these days?"

"I simply never dreamed I would meet a president. Are the Secret Service intimidating?"

Families relate how they planned their vacations around his teaching schedule, high school students tell us how they surely will earn extra points for *this* history essay, and fall visitors describe the peanut shipments they followed on their way into Sumter County.

As visitors arrive, we greet them, give a tour if there is time, and then direct them to our fellowship hall, which seats about 110 on folding chairs. They share rows with the regulars, including Millard and Linda Fuller, co-founders of Habitat for Humanity; Jimmy's first cousin, Hugh Carter, and his wife, Ruth, and others from the community who have known him since his first bid for public office thirty years ago.

The fellowship hall is rather sparsely decorated. There is a folded partition on several sides and a podium in front, along with a standing map of ancient Israel. The decor is admittedly plain, but first-time visitors don't notice at all. As the clock approaches 10:00 A.M., they glance at each new person entering the room, hoping it will be Jimmy. When the crowd overflows the room—which has become constant for now—the class is moved into the sanctuary.

Of Christ and Service

Conversations stop abruptly, a few flashbulbs pop, and everyone looks up to see Jimmy enter the room and take his place in front.

"Welcome to our church," he says. "I'd like to know where the visitors are from."

At this moment Jimmy stands before a curious mix of tourists, lifelong friends, Secret Service agents, and political supporters who can spit out the word "Republican" like an olive pit. Some in suits, some in sneakers and blue jeans, the visitors take turns talking to Jimmy, while others snap more photos, smile broadly, and whisper urgently to the next one over, "Lordy mercy, but that grin brings back memories!"

"Where's Rosalynn? I don't see her."

"Fourth row back at the opposite end."

Jimmy asks if any clergy are present, and several hands go up. One is a Jesuit priest, another a Mennonite, and a third one a Presbyterian. When the last visitors introduce themselves, Jimmy says, "I'm eager to get to today's lesson, but—as part of an agreement I have with the regulars—I will take a few minutes first to bring them up to date on what I have done since the last time we were together."

FULL MOON

Not long after I had become pastor of Maranatha Baptist Church, I received a telephone call from Jimmy asking me to go to the church with him to get his Sunday school teacher's book. It was Saturday evening before the first Sunday in a quarter; he had been out of town, and he needed to study the lesson for the next day. We retrieved the book and were leaving the church when he looked up and said, "Hmm. Full moon."

I quipped, "Does it make you want to howl?"

He playfully answered, "I'm too old to howl, but I might moan a little."

What follows is anybody's guess. It could be an account of climbing Mount Fuji, a ski trip out west with underprivileged youth as part of the Atlanta Project, a confrontation with State Department officials, the threats of an angry crowd in Guyana who menaced Jimmy while he was monitoring their elections, or a conversation with a Communist dictator about Jesus.

The Sunday School lesson itself is about forty-five minutes long. While Jimmy remains dedicated to the assigned lesson and Scripture text from the curriculum, the themes that seem most profoundly reflected in his personal life and work surface naturally and inevitably: "How do we respond to people we despise? How do we love people who are unlovable?" he asks frequently in class.

Or he might say, "Because we are human, we succumb to fear, and we have doubts about our own ability and doubts

CLASSROOM QUOTES

- "This is my church; if there's one thing that gives stability and continuity to my life in the hurly-burly and pressure of a political campaign, it's coming home to Plains every weekend, coming to my church and listening to my teacher."—Men's class at Maranatha Baptist on September 5, 1976, on the eve of his formal campaign as the Democratic nominee for president

- "You took us in, you've given us stability in a position that is inherently sometimes unstable, and you've given us a sense of belonging. Quite often a president of our great country can be isolated from the surrounding world. Whether you're a lonesome farm boy in Plains, Georgia, fifty years ago, or in the White House now reaching out for human understanding across the ocean, or a candidate looking for a common ground to understand one another, the thing that ties them together is a common belief in Christ."—First Baptist in Washington during an annual dinner of the couples' Sunday school class he taught about one week in six

- "The separation of church and state has been a divisive issue since the time of Christ. In some Christian groups . . . there are prescriptions for who is a good American. People who disagree with them on a particular issue, therefore, are not good Americans. All of us have the tendency to believe that our way of worship is obviously the best way. . . . But when we start trying to force—through government laws—others to worship as we do or treat them as secondary citizens without equal rights, that's when we become like the Pharisees."—Adult class at Maranatha, July 1994

- "God's law doesn't change, no matter if one is in Plains, Georgia, Washington, the Soviet Union, China, or Pakistan. Congress meets and goes home. God's law doesn't change."—The first Sunday school class Jimmy taught at First Baptist in Washington, February 20, 1977

- "Suppose we kneel down at our bed at night and say, 'Lord, forgive me of all my sins.' I don't believe it works unless we're willing to say, 'God, today I was not kind to my husband or wife, my children. God, today in a business transaction I cheated a little bit. God, today most of the time I was separated from you. God, today I told two or three lies or misled people a bit. God, today

116

I had a chance to do some kind things or I had a chance to forgive someone I had hatred for and who hurt me. I didn't.' Enumerate them. Call them by name. Under those circumstances, all your sins are wiped away."—Couples' class at First Baptist in Washington, April 24, 1977

- "When is wanting wrong? The Tenth Commandment may be at the base of all the other commandments: 'Thou shalt not covet what is thy neighbor's.' If any commandment is uniquely applicable to the United States and our materialistic society, this is the one. Which is more important—freedom or equality?

  "If I were teaching this class in the ghetto of New York, where parishioners can't go to church in an automobile and worry about what their children will have for supper, I think they'd say 'equality.' There is a natural preference for the powerful and the rich and the good to say 'freedom,' but for many people in the world who are deprived, all they want is to be equal. There has always been a conflict between these two things."—Couples' class at First Baptist in Washington, September 25, 1977

- "A Christian must have the willingness of a soldier to give his life, the discipline of an athlete to train, and the patience of a farmer who plows in hope."—Couples' class at First Baptist in Washington, June 12, 1977

- "We can talk, attend Sunday school, sing hymns, put on a pious attitude, and not prove, thereby, that we really love Christ. We love ourselves. We love the approbation that comes to us from Christians as we pretend to love Christ. Love is an active thing, a demonstrable thing. We can isolate ourselves, not do anything, not hurt anybody—that would not be an expression of love. Love is a precious thing, and, like almost every other precious thing, it has a lot of counterfeits."—Couples' class at First Baptist in Washington, January 29, 1978

- "We're not saved because we're Americans. We're not saved because we come from a community that's stable. We're not saved because our parents were Christians. We're saved because God loves us. We're saved by grace through one required attitude. That is faith in Christ. We're saved by grace through faith in Christ." —Men's Bible class at Plains Baptist, June 20, 1976 about the future. Unfortunately, we let the 'busy-ness' of life and the preoccupation of daily things get the best of us. Our own selfish ambitions—the accumulation of money, social standing, and personal success—separate us from God and the purity of our relationship with Jesus."

With Jimmy Carter, each lesson leads back to Jesus Christ and to the service of others.

"How would Christ define a successful life for us?" he asks. "Humility, service, suffering if necessary, and a life full of compassion for unlovable people."

EVER A TEACHER

Following the lesson and the worship service, he and Rosalynn do not leave the church grounds until every visitor gets a chance to meet them and have a photograph taken with them. He sometimes even instructs the photographer in how to use a visitor's camera.

Over the years I have had many conversations with Jimmy about his faith. We have discussed it in the local restaurant, at my kitchen table, even in my little red Volkswagen. But one of the most memorable conversations took place in Jimmy's living room the Sunday after his historic trip to Haiti in 1994. We talked about everything from General Raoul Cédras to Jimmy's views on teaching the Bible.

On that day, this is what he said regarding the church and his role in it:

"I'm personally sitting within the moderate wing of the Southern Baptists, but there is no arch-conservative fundamentalist church member who would come into my Sunday school class and be shocked by what I teach. I teach fundamentalist Baptist theology, and not in an exclusive way but in a way that was stated to me when I was a child and a young man, all the way through my life. I don't believe that I've changed in my basic beliefs.

"I started teaching Sunday school when I was eighteen years old at the Naval Academy. I taught every Sunday in the Naval Academy chapel to the young, junior-aged daughters of the officers and the men assigned permanently to Annapolis. Later, when I was on ships, we didn't have regular services on Easter or sometimes on Christmas if we were at sea, so I would conduct a brief religious service right there between the torpedo tubes of the submarine. It was for a few enlisted men and officers who might come.

"And then when I resigned from the navy and came home, I immediately started teaching the junior boys at the Plains Baptist Church in 1953. Later I taught the whole junior department and was the junior department superintendent, but I still taught the boys. We would meet and have a brief assembly, and then we'd split up. I taught the boys while Rosalynn taught the girls.

"Then I went to the governor's mansion and joined the Northside Baptist Church [in Atlanta]. I was a deacon there, and I taught some, but not a great deal because we had a very strong and respected Sunday school teacher who preferred to teach.

"When we got to the White House, again we joined the Baptist church nearest the White House just to save a squabble—everybody wants the president to join their church. We went regularly. Every Sunday that we were in Washington we went to the First Baptist Church; but if could get away, we went up to Camp David [in Maryland]. I'd say about a third of the time we attended First Baptist. At Camp David, a military preacher would come to give us a sermon and bring a tape recorder with the music and then go back as a chaplain of a nearby military base and preach the same sermon to the them.

"We had a very good Sunday school teacher at First Baptist in Washington, but I think I taught on fourteen Sundays during the four years. When I left the White House, the church gave me tape recordings of the lessons. Then, when we came home and joined Maranatha, there was already a teacher, so for about a year I didn't teach. I didn't want to interrupt."

Jimmy began teaching at Maranatha in 1982. And that's where you will still find him on any Sunday when he's home in Plains.

Jimmy Carter and Betty Godwin aboard a private jet on the way to the doctoral ceremonies for the Reverend Dan Ariail (see p. 123)

10

A WARRIOR FOR PEACE

There is no nobler calling on this earth than the seeking for peace.
JIMMY CARTER AT THE WHITE HOUSE
ON FEBRUARY 8, 1978

When Jimmy Carter left the Haitian presidential palace on September 18, 1994, with a signed agreement preventing a military confrontation in the island nation, Americans claimed that he should be awarded the Nobel Peace Prize.

It was Jimmy's second major achievement toward international peace that year and came just three months after his North Korean trip that defused a crisis over nuclear policy.

The flurry of attention was actually quite embarrassing for Jimmy, and he dismissed his own nomination and predicted that PLO President Yasser Arafat and Israeli Premier Yitzhak Rabin would win the Nobel. Jimmy said, "I haven't had to endure political consequences or physical danger, whereas Arafat, I think, has put himself in physical danger and Rabin is subject to tremendous political fallout."

(Whether intentionally or not, Jimmy was poignantly understating his situation. Those of us in Plains who watched live television coverage that weekend were horrified to learn that an invasion force was on the way to Haiti even while Jimmy remained in the country. Obviously he and I disagree on the term "physical danger.")

Meanwhile, historians noted that if he had won the Nobel Prize, he would be only the third U.S. president—and the first former president—to do so. In 1906, Republican Teddy Roosevelt became both the first American and first sitting U.S. president to receive the award. Democrat Woodrow Wilson became the second president to be so honored when he received the award in 1919.

I have discovered many things in common between Jimmy Carter and various Nobel Peace Prize recipients:

- Like the Reverend Martin Luther King Jr., Jimmy is a Baptist and supporter of civil rights in the South.
- Like Dr. Albert Schweitzer, Jimmy supports his own humanitarian organization financially, through money raised in public appearances and book sales.
- Like Jane Addams, the social worker who founded Hull House in Chicago but fell from grace for her opposition to World War I, Jimmy was rejected by the American public in the 1980 election.
- Like Dr. Elie Wiesel, a survivor of Buchenwald and Auschwitz who has written extensively about the Holocaust, Jimmy is a university professor.
- Like Mother Teresa, who is renowned for her service among the urban poor of India, Jimmy is articulate about describing how his faith influences his concerns for society.

Alfred B. Nobel was a Swedish chemist, industrialist, and inventor whose greatest invention, dynamite, earned him a fortune. Knowing that this explosive was responsible for thousands of deaths, including that of his younger brother, Nobel willed his massive wealth to establish the annual Nobel Prizes in five fields. The prizes for physics, chemistry, physiology or medicine, literature, and peace were first awarded in 1901. (A sixth prize in economics was initiated in 1986.)

The most famous prize, the one for peace, sprang from Nobel's fear that if humankind didn't find a way to end wars, it would "fall back into barbarism." Nobel called war "the greatest of all crimes" and even described weapons like the ones he invented as "instruments of hell."

DOCTOR OF MINISTRY

When I began serious work on my doctorate with Southern Baptist Theological Seminary, I half-jokingly asked Jimmy if he would speak at my graduation. He replied: "If you graduate, and if I'm in the country, I'll speak at your graduation." And he did.

As graduation time neared, the seminary president, Roy Honeycutt, invited Jimmy to address the graduating class. He also asked me how best to arrange things in order to make it possible for Jimmy to accept. I told him about the problems of travel, how the Carters often must waste a lot of time at the airport waiting for commercial flights—not to mention the many people who want to meet him and ask for autographs. I suggested that if the seminary could arrange for a private jet to get the Carters to and from Louisville, Jimmy would be much more likely to accept the invitation. Fortunately, a benefactor of the seminary and friend of Dr. Honeycutt owned a jet and made it available to fly out from Americus, Georgia.

Betty Godwin, a close friend and fellow church member, wanted very much to attend the graduation. She knew that we would be already in Louisville, that the Carters would fly up, and that she would have to drive for more than twelve hours to get there. I knew the kind of accommodating person Jimmy is, so I asked Betty: "Why don't you just ask Jimmy if there is an extra seat on the jet?" She felt this would be much too bold, but she really wanted to go. Finally, after a lot of prodding from Nelle and me, she got up the courage to ask. The Carters were glad to have her and her daughter, Gail Allegood, accompany them.

When I asked Jimmy what it would mean to him as a Christian to receive the Nobel, he said, "If I should ever get it, that would obviously be a great honor for me. It's the ultimate honor for someone who works in the field I do. And I would be grateful, and it would exalt my ability to do things that are compatible with my Christian faith. There's no doubt about that. Just as having been in the White House gives me access to anyone on Earth—any kind of leader—the Nobel Peace Prize would give me a broader base of stature or more influence—

not just having been a politician who was elected president of the United States, but someone who was elected president and also got the Nobel Prize."

NOT FOR ACCOLADES

Jimmy has received many prestigious humanitarian and peace awards, including the Gold Medal of the International Institute of Human Rights, the Martin Luther King Jr. Nonviolent Peace Prize, the Albert Schweitzer Prize for Humanitarianism, and the Fulbright Prize for International Peace Keeping.

From Jimmy's spiritual perspective, however, he is involved in conflict resolution, traveling to hostile environments, and talking with unfriendly leaders, not because of the accolades they often bring but because the teachings of Jesus Christ require it.

"We have a need," he told me one day in his living room, "to meet with, understand, and communicate with people who are condemned by our government and by American society, including Communist dictators and fundamentalist Muslims that we call fanatics and so forth. Our ministry is with people who live under the domination of people like that. Just because a society has an unsavory leader, we don't abandon that society. We go in, meet with him, but then we immunize the country's children, we eradicate diseases in their villages, we help them grow more food grains and feed the people, and in the process get to know these leaders who are almost universally condemned and even demonized in our own press.

"These leaders are regarded as having no redeeming features, and this encompassed Yasser Arafat, who was known by most Americans and by all Israelis as a terrorist only. I have known him well. He's got his faults and attributes as I do. It's the same way with General [Raoul] Cédras in Haiti and President Kim Il-Sung, whom no one would talk to in North Korea, and General [Muhammad Farah] Aidid in the streets of Mogadishu in Somalia when we were trying to hunt him down and kill him, and President [Hafez Al-]Assad in Syria when we would not even send an ambassador to Damascus.

"We deal with people of all religious beliefs and all political philosophies and all political choices. You don't have to be a moderate Southern Baptist to believe in humanitarian projects or in God."

The Sunday after he returned from Haiti, Jimmy told me, "I was just watching television, and George Will said I was the worst president since way back because I was so gullible and because I was willing to forgive the crimes of people our country labels as terrorists. Fidel Castro calls me when he wants to, and Cédras and so forth. Will said I betrayed my country by going in and letting this person convince me he is a real human being instead of a demon.

"I had a conversation with a North Korean ambassador this past Monday who said that he could never forgive the president of South Korea because he had forbidden anyone from North Korea now living in his country from expressing condolences when Kim Il-Sung died. When some students did indeed express condolences, he had them imprisoned.

"The ambassador from North Korea said, 'We'll never forgive them for that.'

"I tried to draw a distinction between being unforgiving and unforgetting. I asked him, 'Do you understand the Christian faith?'

"He said, 'Yes I do. I've made a study of it.'

"I said, 'We are taught to forgive, and unless you are willing to forgive this insult to your departed leader, there is no need for me to try to come to Korea and work out the differences between you two.'

"Begin and Sadat forgave each other, but they never forgot what happened. I tried to explain to the ambassador how I dealt with people who were at war anywhere from twenty-five years in the case of the Egyptians and Israelis, to fifty years in the case of the Koreans.

"You've got to understand that all of us are fallible, and God doesn't want us to judge each other but to forgive."

WAGING PEACE ON TWO FRONTS

While his motivation as a peacemaker is religious—the standards of Jesus as reflected through mercy, justice, and kindness—Jimmy Carter has developed his peacekeeping efforts into an exact science by battling the evil of war on two distinct levels. He resolves conflict directly with the warring sides, and he plants the "seeds of peace"—food, shelter, health, and democracy.

Jimmy points out often in his speeches, as also in his book *Talking Peace*, that "the existence of war is incompatible with our basic needs as human beings: a stable home, food, and health care, a life free from fear and persecution. The tragedy is that often most national leaders and the news media pay little attention to conflict around the world until wars cause such destruction and starvation that they can be ignored no longer."

I have also heard Jimmy lament the lack of interest and media coverage because a particular conflict involved "no white skin or oil." An absence of those two key features, according to Jimmy, leads the American public and media nearly always to conclude that the United States has no connection with that problem or motivation to help solve it.

The evidence suggests he is right. American ignorance about conflicts throughout the world is shocking. If you were to guess how many different military conflicts are going on throughout the world right now—conflicts that have cost a thousand lives or more—what number would you pick? 20? 40? 80?

Try more than 130. That includes 25 major conflicts of the scope of the civil wars in Bosnia and Somalia and more than 100 smaller but still devastating and costly conflicts.

Jimmy monitors these situations at the Carter Center in Atlanta, through his International Negotiation Network (INN), which is part of the larger Conflict Resolution Program. Designed to "marshal the expertise of peacemakers worldwide to address the suffering caused by armed conflicts," the CRP, upon request, offers advice and assistance to resolve disputes.

By its own definition, the INN "includes world leaders and experts from international organizations, universities,

foundations, and others who seek peaceful ways to end conflict."
The INN Council includes several international heavyweights:
Nobel laureates Oscar Arias Sanchez, former president of Costa
Rica; Desmond Tutu, Anglican archbishop of Cape Town, South
Africa; Javier Perez de Cuellar, former Secretary-General of the
United Nations; Elie Wiesel; and the Reverend Andrew Young,
former U.S. ambassador to the United Nations.

The INN focuses on the world's deadliest wars. Guided by
Jimmy, the INN has brought together experts in annual con-
sultation to address conflicts in Angola, Armenia, Azerbaijan,
Burma, Cyprus, Kosovo, Liberia, Macedonia, Sudan, and Zaire.
Without a well-indexed atlas at hand, most of us are left asking,
"Just where are these countries?" The members of Maranatha
Baptist Church are an exception—both because of Jimmy's
reports in Sunday school and because some of our visitors
have come from these countries.

In 1989, Jimmy and the INN hosted peace talks in Atlanta
and Nairobi, Kenya, between the Eritrean People's Liberation
Front and the government of the People's Democratic Republic of Ethiopia. In addition, the Carter Center is working with
opposition parties in Ethiopia to build strong human rights protections, to help the country develop a democracy, and to
improve public health.

In 1993, the Carter Center hosted a meeting with the
Sudan People's Liberation Army United to explore possibilities
for peace between that group and the opposition. This is an
extremely complicated war, and this story involves Maranatha
beautifully. The head of one faction brought a small delegation
to attend Jimmy's Sunday school class in the late 1980s, and
that is how the group first met the Carters. Jimmy relates what
happened during the 1993 meeting:

"Later, Rosalynn and I went there, and we spent six days
and nights negotiating between the two groups. One reason we
went into Sudan was to increase their production of sorghum,
but then we found out what they really needed was wheat. We
couldn't get it into the south, the region controlled by the Christians, because you simply can't go in there. It's a battle zone. In

the northern part, controlled by Muslims, we increased their wheat production from 160,000 tons per year to 1.2 million tons per year, and then we withdrew because they had all the wheat they needed."

Since 1992, the INN has worked to increase international attention on Burma as a step toward resolving the conflict there. During a 1993 consultation, INN Council members Tutu and Arias Sanchez traveled with several laureates of the Nobel Peace Prize to Thailand to urge the release of fellow laureate Daw Aung San Suu Kyi, who had been held under house arrest in Burma since 1989.

Jimmy and Rosalynn have also had an ongoing role in the Liberian peace process. After civil war began in Liberia in December 1989, the INN became involved, sending representatives to summit meetings on the Ivory Coast and then hosting representatives from Liberia at the Carter Center in 1992.

Jimmy said, "We expect to play a major role, together with other U.S. and international organizations, to promote reconciliation, civic education, and free and fair elections under the terms of the Cotonou agreement," the peace treaty negotiated in 1994 between the two major factions in Liberia.

THE TACTICS OF NEGOTIATION

In contrast to a military general, who studies conflict to learn the most effective ways to engage his troops, Jimmy Carter monitors wars to look for opportunities to stop them. He has made conflict resolution a science by identifying the common elements of conflicts, studying the particular quirks and personalities of the individual leaders who have the power to negotiate a settlement, and then seeking an opportunity to persuade them to move toward the conference table.

Jimmy's negotiating success is linked to his determination to work directly and only with top officials who can implement the promises they make. He spends a great deal of time studying the cultural and personal history of the combative leaders and typically becomes involved in many preliminary talks to identify for the leaders the benefits of peace for their citizens, resources, and economic base.

He lays the groundwork for possible talks and is known to begin negotiations by saying, "Let us agree we will not leave this place until we have a peaceful settlement."

The former president is also known for beginning individual sessions by demonstrating how much the two enemies have in common and identifying all the elements successfully negotiated to this point. He explains, "I described in *Talking Peace* the rudiments of the causes of conflict and that could be between you and your spouse or you and your parents or within a church group or on a school campus or inside a country or between nations. The basic elements of a dispute that deteriorates into actual conflict or combat are similar no matter where they are—as are the other deprivations of human needs that cause people to become desperate.

"I would take up arms if I had a government that made it impossible for me to feed my wife and children. I mean, I would do something rather than sit there and pout and hide. I would do whatever was necessary to get food or firewood or water for my family. When a society deteriorates to a degree that people are starving—particularly if they identify rightly or wrongly their political leaders as the cause—they take up arms and try to overthrow the government. So we go into a country to try to analyze the problems, talk to the ruling party, and try to increase food production. We are not there to save that ruling party from overthrow but just to alleviate suffering."

Dr. Irwin Abrams, distinguished professor emeritus and former chair of the history department at Antioch University in Yellow Springs, Ohio, has nominated Jimmy for the Nobel Peace Prize several times.

In one of his letters to the Nobel committee, Abrams wrote, "After leaving office with his prestige as an ex-president and with universal respect that exists for his moral stature, he had made a remarkable contribution to the peace of the world in ways quite unprecedented. When they [President and Mrs. Carter] founded the Carter Center, they established it on the principle that everyone on earth should be able to live in peace. . . .

"Peace, to him, is not just a matter of ending conflict. It means developing the conditions for peace: having enough to eat, having enough medicine, water and just conditions for work. True peace can only be built upon a just society in which each individual is free to realize his or her potential."

Abrams, the author of *The Nobel Preace Prize and the Laureates: An Illustrated Biographical History, 1901–1987*, cited Jimmy's achievements in increased crop production in Third World nations along with economic and political reform and medical achievements, such as the eradication of the deadly guinea worm in Africa.

"The fact that he's independent of government gives him the kind of freedom an ambassador can't have," Dr. Abrams wrote. "It's unprecedented what he's done. Other presidents could have done it but didn't."

Abrams also said that those who criticize Jimmy as one who has compromised his own morals by meeting with international villains have completely missed the point. "They don't understand what a mediator does. A mediator is talking to two sides and really has to understand the other person. In the case of Haiti, he was between President Clinton and General Cédras.

"You don't just dismiss someone as something of the Devil. As Quakers, we think there's something of God in everybody. Quaker mediators and others speak to the best in the person they are talking to."

THE BLESSINGS OF PEACE

Through the Carter Center, Jimmy has undertaken many attempts to bring reconciliation and restore harmony in trouble spots around the world. Some of these trips have been widely publicized, and others have not. Jimmy traveled to Syria in 1987 to meet with President Hafez al-Assad, he traveled to Nicaragua in 1988 to assist in that country's democratic election, and he monitored the 1989 elections in Panama that were later nullified by Manuel Noriega. In 1992 he was menaced by an angry mob while monitoring an election in Guyana.

But Jimmy's efforts in Haiti demonstrate his persistence and passion for peace and human rights perhaps better than any other venture.

In 1990 Jimmy traveled to Haiti to assist in the peaceful election won by Jean-Bertrand Aristide. But despite an over-whelming victory in which he claimed 70 percent of the vote, Aristide soon fell from grace in the beleaguered Caribbean nation that has suffered politically and economically under one dictator after another. In *Talking Peace*, Jimmy explained the reasons for Aristide's downfall:

> Although deeply religious and dedicated to the well-being of the poorest people of Haiti, who had given him their support, Aristide had little understanding of politics or governing. It was almost impossible for him to compro-mise on any issue, and he failed in his efforts to reach out to Haitian financial, business, education and social lead-ers to join him in the long-overdue reforms. Not trusting the army, he began to organize his own armed security force. There was little cooperation between the new pres-ident and the elected members of the parliament.

Eight months later, General Cédras overthrew Aristide. Jimmy observed, "Haiti, already the poorest country in our hemisphere, is sinking even further into disorder and poverty."

As the political situation in Haiti worsened, public pres-sure grew for Aristide to be restored to his rightful place as president. General Cédras and Acting President Emile Ges-saint had steadfastly insisted that any attempt by Aristide to return, enforced by United States military forces, would be met with armed resistance. Jimmy was apppointed by President Clinton to lead a negotiating team in an attempt to resolve the impasse. The other members of the team were General Colin Powell, former chairman of the Joint Chiefs of Staff, and U.S. Senator Sam Nunn of Georgia.

The Carter entourage arrived in Port-au-Prince on Sep-tember 17, 1994—sixteen years to the day after then-President

Carter announced the Camp David Accords with Anwar Sadat and Menachem Begin. There are striking similarities between the two events.

Both took place under the constant eye of the American media—although Camp David is secluded, and CNN was broadcasting live from Haiti, barely giving air time to commercials. Both were considered extreme long shots, given the resolute animosity between the opposing parties. And both produced dramatic, last-minute victories.

From Haiti, Jimmy phoned the White House several times to ask for more time on the island. When he called the last time that night to ask for just thirty more minutes, President Clinton said, "I will grant this, but we've been friends a long time, and I'd hate to have to order you out of there." Jimmy understood the implication, and this is how he described the dramatic final moments in Haiti to his Sunday school class:

"I did not know when the invasion was going to take place. I found out later that General Powell did know, but he didn't tell me, and I didn't ask anyone. We were meeting when General [Philippe] Biamby came running in the room, and he said, 'You are traitors to our country because you kept all of us here in this room. Our troops are not alerted, and I just learned from Fort Bragg, North Carolina, that paratroopers are on their way to attack our nation.'

In fact, sixty-one planes were on their way, but General Cédras and General Biamby agreed to continue discussions with Gennesaint—a man whom the U.S. government dismissed as an inept president, but whom Jimmy saw as a wise elder statesman of his country.

"We talked to this fine old gentleman," Jimmy continued. "He is eighty-one years old, tall, gangly, a very dark, black fellow. He had been the chief justice of the supreme court for many years. He went into retirement. They called him back to write a new, democratic constitution for Haiti in 1987 when 'Baby Doc' [Jean Claude] Duvalier was forced out the country.

"He said we would have peace and not war. All of his ministers stood up and said, in effect, that they would resign. They would not accept his decision. His defense minister said, 'I resign as of now. You'll have my resignation in the morning.'

"Gennesaint was perfectly at ease. He said, 'Okay, I'll accept your resignation. We already have a weak government. It won't be that much weaker if you leave.'

"At this point the ministers said they would go into the other room and decide the true fate of the nation, but Gennesaint said very casually, 'The decision is already made. The decision is peace.'

"We finally got the deal signed. When I told President Clinton it was concluded, he said four words: 'Thank God. Thank God.'"

Jimmy also explained to the Sunday school class how the entire mission for peace turned on a single conversation with the wife of General Cédras.

"She was and is a remarkable woman," Jimmy began. "She is a very, very powerful force in their family." Jimmy drew laughter with an aside: "This was a situation I had never before encountered in my own family."

"But she brought her children in, a seventeen-year-old boy, a thirteen-year-old girl, and a ten-year-old son who had had his birthday the day before. I gave him a little pocket knife for a birthday present. The thirteen-year-old came in and showed me a picture she and I had made together in 1990 when they held their election down there. She was very proud of this picture.

"And then Mrs. Cédras, who was very uptight, told her children to leave. General Cédras sat mute, and his wife spoke. A very neat-looking woman and carefully groomed, she said she'd been up all night getting ready for our visit. And she spoke in the most fervent terms, saying that we didn't understand her country.

"She said, 'You don't even know the grandeur of Haiti,' and she pointed out that Haiti is the oldest black republic on earth. It became independent in 1804 when just a small group of slaves under inspired leadership, defeated France's army, the finest in the whole world.

"She also deplored the poverty of her country and the division that had created strife among its people, and she said her father and grandfather had been offered the presidency of Haiti, but they refused to go into politics because they wanted to serve their people in other ways. And she also said they—all Haitians—had great pride, that there was no way any Haitian with any self-respect could permit foreign invaders to come into their country without offering his or her life.

LESSONS ON PEACE

- "With all the difficulties, all the conflicts, I believe that our planet must finally obey the biblical injunction to 'follow after the things which make for peace.'"—Address in Charleston, South Carolina, July 21, 1977, quoting Romans 14:19
- "A great, strong, sure person need not prove it always. That's the way it is with Christ. And that's the way it is with Christians. When you're sure of your strength, you can exhibit compassion, emotion, love, concern, equality—and even better than equality—the attitude of a servant."—Sunday school class at Plains Baptist Church, July 18, 1976
- "Have we created chasms around ourselves that separate us from those who need and hunger for the gospel of Christ? Is our primary goal in life as Christians to husband to ourselves the mercy of God, the forgiveness of our sins, the knowledge of Christ that gives us truth? Or is it to tear down barriers, to reach out and share, to affect other people's lives in a benevolent way and an unselfish way, and, at the same time, to expand our own lives, instead of being narrow?
- "Sometimes the church creates a barrier itself because we tend to encapsulate ourselves in respectability, security, goodness, decency, religious commitment. Amos said, 'I hate and I despise your feasts and your institutions' (5:21). He was talking about the church of his day. He said, 'Let justice roll down like waters, and righteousness like an ever-flowing stream' (5:24 RSV). It was hard back in those days for justice and righteousness to roll down like waters out of the church, and it's hard today. Where is the water, where is the ever-flowing stream that can roll down out of the church, filled with righteousness and mercy? Where is that water? Ourselves. We are the rivers of water. We are the

ever-flowing stream."—Couples' class, First Baptist Church of Washington, November 6, 1977

- "Among the many who marched and suffered and bore witness against the evil of racial prejudice, the greatest was Dr. Martin Luther King, Jr. He was the son of Georgia and a spiritual son of Mahatma Gandhi.

  "The most important influence in the life and work of Dr. King, apart from his own religious faith, was the life of Gandhi. Martin Luther King took Gandhi's concepts of nonviolence and truth-force and put them to work in the American South.

  "Like Gandhi, King believed that truth and love are the strongest forces in the universe. Like Gandhi, he knew that ordinary people, armed only with courage and faith, could overcome injustice by appealing to the spark of good in the heart of the evildoer.

  "Like Gandhi, we all learned that a system of oppression damages those at the top as surely as it does those at the bottom. And for Martin Luther King, like Mahatma Gandhi, nonviolence was not only a political method, it was a way of life and a spiritual path to union with the ultimate.

  "These men set a standard of courage and idealism that few of us can meet, but from which all of us can draw inspiration and sustenance. The nonviolent movement for racial justice in the United States, a movement inspired in large measure by the teachings and examples of Gandhi and other Indian leaders, changed and enriched my own life and the lives of many millions of my countrymen."—Address to the Parliament of India, New Delhi, January 2, 1978

"She also told all of us that the previous night, quite late when her husband didn't come home, she brought her three children in the room where we were sitting and that they took an oath of death—that they would not leave their home but they would instead stay there and die. She said, 'I know the Americans have our house targeted because I have seen your clandestine troops around our house several times. There is no way we would yield.'

"Obviously we thought our mission had failed. You cannot imagine how powerful a force this woman was. Cédras hadn't said anything. I nodded to General Powell, who is respected superbly by the Haitian soldiers, and he said that there were two choices a commander could make when facing overwhelming forces. He could either commit suicide, in effect, by offering his life and the lives of all those others, or he could exercise judgment and wisdom and yield to the superior forces and preserve his troops for another day.

"Then I came in and pointed out the difference between waging peace and waging war. I said, 'It's very difficult to wage peace because you make a decision that's going to be examined for years by historians and your own people. The questions are difficult to answer. You've got two choices to make. You never know in your own mind, 'Did I make the right choice?' It's a very difficult thing to do because you also have to accommodate the needs, the beliefs, and the philosophy of your adversary. But in waging war it's quite simple. You stand and say, 'I will give my life. I will die for my country. I will also commit my family and those who look to me for leadership to pledge to die also.'"

"Mrs. Cédras was taken aback. She sat there silent for a long time. We didn't know what was going to happen. Finally she looked at her husband, and she kind of nodded her head. He said, 'OK, we will meet you in our headquarters in about an hour,' and from there we moved on."

Jimmy understands but has always been reluctant to employ, the role of military force that is required at times in the delicate process of waging peace. During his term as president, he ordered United States armed forces abroad only twice. The first was in Zaire in 1978 when U.S. military aircraft provided logistical support to Belgian and French rescue operations. The second was in Iran in 1980, when six U.S. transport planes and eight helicopters were used in a failed and fateful attempt to rescue American hostages. By contrast, former president Ronald Reagan ordered troops oversees eighteen times during his eight years in the White House, and former president George Bush did so twelve times during his four-year term.

Ironically, it was aboard the nuclear submarine *Sea Wolf* that Jimmy Carter first acknowledged his passion for peace. As he relates in *Talking Peace*, "As a submarine officer in the U.S. Navy and later as president of the United States, I learned first-hand about the terrible nature of war. This knowledge strengthens my personal commitment to work for the blessings of peace."

Many people still believe that Jimmy Carter deserves the Nobel Peace Prize for his achievements such as those in Haiti. The Nobel was, in fact, awarded just three weeks after Jimmy's return from Port-au-Prince. But not to Jimmy. Instead, the recipients were—as Jimmy predicted—Yasser Arafat and Yitzhak Rabin, along with Israeli Foreign Minister Shimon Peres.

Yet, Jimmy's commitment to peace, deeply rooted in his Christian faith, remains undiminished. Jimmy gave perhaps the best and simplest expression of that commitment in a statement he made as president on February 8, 1978, after a visit with President Anwar Sadat of Egypt: "There is no nobler calling on this earth than the seeking for peace. For it is that reason which caused the Bible to say that peacemakers shall be called the sons of God."

Ron and Debby Haynes of Plains with the
Carters (see p. 140)

Making a Difference

The Carter Center is now so massive and so diverse in its functions that it is almost indescribable.

JIMMY CARTER

Faced with the overwhelming problems confronting the human race from war, hunger, and pestilence, many people would throw up their hands in despair. Not Jimmy Carter.

Many people feel powerless and defeated by the sheer magnitude of the task—despite the persistent admonitions of Jesus Christ that we cannot serve God without serving our fellow humans and seeking to improve their lot in life. Not Jimmy.

Jimmy's response to Christ's call and the problems of humanity brings to my mind a sermon illustration about a little boy who runs down to the beach every morning to toss starfish back into the surf. They wash up on shore, and the boy knows they will die there in the sun as the day wears on, so he casts them back to the sea.

An old cynic sitting on the beach yells at the boy, "I don't know why you're doing that. You can't save them all, you know! You aren't really making a difference!"

"It's true I can't save every last one," said the boy, holding up a fine specimen and studying it with admiration. "But I can save this one, and it sure makes a difference to him!"

While that spirit has governed much of Jimmy Carter's adult life, he more recently has created a means to enlarging that commitment on a grander, worldwide scale: the Carter Center.

My conversations with visitors suggest that most people associate the spirituality of Jimmy and Rosalynn first and foremost with Habitat for Humanity International. That seems natural, considering that Habitat's international headquarters is just ten miles from Plains, that many of its volunteers in the region visit Maranatha church often, and that the Carters have been so visibly identified with the organization. While Habitat is an interdenominational, Christian housing ministry that the Carters and Maranatha support enthusiastically, it is accurate to say that the large majority of the Carters' Christian social service is actually provided through the many programs of the Carter Center.

A NEIGHBORLY VISIT

The couple had just moved to Plains and were living amid a houseful of packing boxes and crates. It was autumn Sunday afternoon, and Ron and Debby Haynes, along with Debby's mother, Virginia Harrison, who was visiting from Cornelia, Georgia, were in kitchen, shelling pecans. Their work and conversation were interrupted when the doorbell rang, and Ron went to the front door to answer it. When he didn't return right away, Debby commented to her mother, "I wonder what's taking him so long? We don't know anybody here."

Her mother casually ventured, "Well, you know there is one famous person who lives here"—she paused—"and that sounds like Jimmy Carter's voice!"

Debby remarked, "It couldn't *possibly* be! Jimmy Carter in our house? He doesn't know us. No way!"—just as Jimmy and his pastor entered the kitchen.

The new residents were almost in a state of shock. Ignoring the packing boxes and wearing blue jeans, Jimmy contentedly sat down in the kitchen and started getting acquainted. To Ron's delight—since he is an avid fisherman—Jimmy took note of the Jack Wingate fishing shirt Ron was wearing and mentioned that he and Wingate were fishing buddies.

Later in the conversation, Jimmy and I invited the Haynes to visit Maranatha Baptist Church and Jimmy's Sunday school class. When they seemed interested, Jimmy asked, "Would you like to see the church right now?"

What can you say to a question like that from a former president of the United States? We all piled into Jimmy's van, and he chatted about several local businesses they passed on the way. When they reached the one-story brick building nestled in a large pecan grove, Jimmy and I showed them the physical plant along with the tables, bookcases, shelves, and walnut offering plates that had come from Jimmy's home woodworking shop.

For the Hayneses and Mrs. Harrison, it was a memorable afternoon. For me, it was just another example of a world figure, used to flying to the remote parts of the earth, demonstrating that he remains a down-to-earth, unself-conscious Christian once he is back home in Plains.

A Life of Its Own

The center is located on a thirty-five-acre site about two miles from downtown Atlanta. Four circular, interconnected pavilions, totaling nearly 100,000 square feet, house offices for Jimmy and Rosalynn and the center's programs. The complex also includes the nondenominational Cecil B. Day Chapel, conference facilities, and administrative offices. Additional offices are in the nearby Kirbo Building. The Jimmy Carter Library, which is operated by the National Archives, adjoins the center.

Most of the center's employees work in Atlanta, but field representatives are stationed in Guyana, Liberia, Ethiopia, Nicaragua, and elsewhere.

With an annual budget of nearly $26 million and 250 full-time employees as well as 100 student interns, the center offers profound evidence that an organization intelligently and stubbornly dedicated to improving life for the least among us can take on its own life form. The center's activities are focused on promoting political democracy and economic development, global health, and urban revitalization. It encompasses thirteen core programs in more than thirty countries. In just a little over a decade it has grown into an internationally respected nongovernmental, nonsectarian organization. Most important, the center gets results.

141

"Our method everywhere is twofold," Jimmy once told me. "First, we identify creative ways to address problems that affect the most vulnerable people—those who have the fewest resources. Then we build partnerships to implement solutions that achieve lasting improvements.

"Because the center and its programs are not aligned politically with any particular party, group, or government, we can step in where governments and other agencies cannot go and mobilize world leaders and other eminent people to effect change. As president of the United States, I was uniquely placed to take measure of the terrible problems plaguing our world. But I also had the opportunity to see that solutions can be found—solutions that sometimes fall little short of extraordinary. We're committed to forging the links among people and ideas that make such progress possible."

The mission statement for the Carter Center concludes: " . . . by fostering collaboration and avoiding duplication of existing efforts, and by combining effective action plans with research and analysis, the center can achieve goals beyond the reach of single individuals or organizations. The center is guided by the principle that people, with the necessary skills, knowledge and access can improve their own lives and the lives of others."

What does the Carter Center do? Many things.

DEMOCRATIZATION AND DEVELOPMENT

One phase of the center's work includes the African Governance Program, the Commission on Radio and Television Policy, the Global Development Initiative, the Human Rights Program, and the Latin American and Caribbean Program.

The African Governance Program

In the United States we learn through grade school history and civics classes what it means to live within a democracy and to enjoy the privilege of voting. We study the special challenges faced by women in the 1920s and African-Americans in the 1950s who successfully crusaded for the right to cast their ballots.

Imagine, though, a country not born a democracy but trying to recreate itself as one. How does the transformation occur? Who teaches its citizens about their responsibilities?

The African Governance Program advocates democracy in sub-Saharan Africa by monitoring elections, by promoting human rights and civil liberties as essential elements of democracy, and by assisting governments, political parties, and citizens' groups in making the transition. This requires a variety of skills—from negotiating the anticipated shift in power to aiding polling workers with the logistics of fair voting practices. The number of sub-Sarahan countries the Carter Center classifies as having introduced democracies has jumped from four in 1989 to fifteen by 1993. There are three profound examples:

- Zambia: In October 1991, Jimmy led an international observer team to monitor registration and voting processes and to verify the first free and fair multiparty elections in Zambia's history. The Carter Center continues to assist the fledgling democracy.
- Ghana: In November 1992, a Carter Center observer team monitored that country's first democratic presidential election in more than thirty years.
- Liberia: The Carter Center is helping the country rebuild its democracy after years of civil war by providing technical assistance on election, civic, and voter education and advice on postelection consolidation.

The Commission on Radio and Television Policy

The Carter Center is helping radio and television broadcasters in Russia and the fifteen new states of the former Soviet Union to redefine their roles and professional standards in the face of political transition in their countries.

In 1990, as a result of talks between Jimmy and former Soviet leader Mikhail Gorbachev, the Commission on Radio and Television Policy was formed to address the social, political, and economic impact of television in the United States and abroad. Chaired by Jimmy and Eduard Sagalaev, president of Russia's first independent TV station and the Confederation of

Journalists' Unions, the commission includes media specialists from the U.S. and all the new independent states.

Since the Soviet Union broke apart in 1991, nearly five hundred TV and radio stations have begun operating in Russia alone, with another hundred on the air in the Baltic states. One of the commission's most significant achievements has been to offer these stations models of fair coverage—a relatively new concept in Russian media.

The Global Development Initiative

There is a terrible gap—some would say a chasm—between one nation and another when we compare economic, social, and political development.

Development aid—also called resource assistance—from stronger nations and private international agencies is essential to securing basic human rights for citizens of the developing countries. In the past, monetary aid given to such nations has faced several obstacles: The aid was often inadequately coordinated by donor agencies, recipient countries were sometimes ill-equipped to use the funds they received, and "success" was frequently measured too narrowly by economic growth rather than political, environmental, or social factors. These problems are exacerbated today by shrinking aid budgets and by the persistent political and financial instability of the countries. (Consider, for instance, the economic, political, and social shifts that occurred with the dissolution of the former Soviet Union.)

In December 1992, Jimmy Carter and the secretary-general of the United Nations, Boutros Boutros-Ghali, co-chaired a conference to help international donor agencies and recipient countries to create a more effective model for the development aid process. This led to the creation of the Global Development Initiative.

Guyana, on the northern coast of South America, has proved to be the most dramatic success story, beginning with its first democratic election in sixty years. Jimmy was on hand to monitor the balloting, and at one point he was threatened by an angry crowd but deliberately put himself in harm's way in order to force an honest election. The incident received little publicity in the media. (In fact, it ranks as number two among the least-known episodes in Jimmy's public life, the foremost being the time when, as president, he fooled the press at Camp David and went off fly-fishing in Pennsylvania for two days— a tale that needs more telling.)

Through the Global Development Initiative, Guyana secured $320 million in new aid, considered a significant step toward a stronger democracy and more secure environment for the citizens of that country.

"Public Christians"

Leonard Sweet, professor of church history and chancellor of United Theological Seminary in Dayton, Ohio, said, "In historic perspective, Carter is a classic, pre-Civil War evangelical, and for him, the personal gospel and social gospel are one and the same. Carter is cut from the same cloth as Charles G. Finney, an evangelist in the 1830s and '40s, who implemented the altar call. He said to people as they approached the altar to commit their lives to Christ, 'You must also commit yourself to improving your country. Here is the American Bible Society. Here is the American Anti-Slavery Society. Join them.

"Like Carter, those early antebellum evangelicals were public Christians, and the Jesus moment absolutely meant the integration of one's faith to one's engagement with the world. The personal and social gospel are so intermingled, you can't tell the difference. He's structured his whole life so there is no divorce between the private and public person. African-American Christians would say, 'He walks the talk.'"

Human Rights Program

Basic human rights—which include adequate food, shelter, access to medical services, and personal security and safety—remain essential to peace and democracy. The Carter Center's Human Rights Program provides technical assistance to help countries establish these safeguards. The Center is working, for instance, with the transitional government of Ethiopia to write human rights protections into its new constitution. Guyanese leaders have asked the staff to conduct police training workshops on human dignity and community policing based on the success of this program in Ethiopia.

A distinctive feature of the program is the direct intervention Jimmy and Rosalynn have made on behalf of individuals who are being persecuted.

In 1986, philanthropist Dominique de Menil and Jimmy established the the Carter-Menil Human Rights Prize, a $100,000 award to honor individuals or organizations for achievements on behalf of human rights, typically at great personal sacrifice. The award enables human rights activists to continue their work and focuses global attention on their struggles. Winners have included the Native American Rights Fund of Boulder, Colorado; the Haitian Refugee Center of Miami, Florida; and the Group for Mutual Support of Guatemala.

Latin American and Caribbean Program

Jimmy Carter understands networking, and this is a fascinating and innovative example of his ability to pull the right people together to affect an entire region of the world. The Latin American and Caribbean Program seeks to strengthen relationships among the nations in this region.

The program also serves as the headquarters for the Council of Freely Elected Heads of Government, a group of about twenty-five current and former leaders from the Western Hemisphere who promote democracy and the peaceful resolution of the region's conflicts. Council members include the presidents of Chile, Haiti, Venezuela, Uruguay, and Argentina; Oscar Aria Sanchez, former president of Costa Rica; Joseph Clark, former prime minister of Canada; and Gerald R. Ford, former president of the United States.

This council is a pioneer in mediating and observing elections—so far in Panama, Nicaragua, Haiti, the Dominican Republic, Guyana, and Paraguay. The council's significance is evident from this account filed by the Associated Press on May 10, 1993:

146

Paraguayans streamed to the polls Sunday to choose a civilian president in the country's first truly democratic election in 182 years of independence.

For 53-year-old Sixto Zaracho and thousands of others, voting was not just a novelty. It was deeply satisfying personally.

For the first time, no one handed Zaracho a ballot he was expected to use. No one looked over his shoulder as he marked it. And he left the voting booth without already knowing who would win.

GLOBAL HEALTH

Another major component of the Carter Center programs is global health concerns.

Agriculture

Several developing countries have enjoyed remarkable progress in health and agriculture thanks to the efforts of Global 2000, a nonprofit organization incorporated separately from the Carter Center. The program strives to increase cereal grain production by teaching farmers to use better farming practices and improved seeds and fertilizers. In Ghana, farmers increased national corn production by about 143 percent from 1985 to 1993. In Sudan, farmers raised 500 percent more wheat in 1991–92 than in the 1986–87 production year. The program has also aided farmers in Zambia, Tanzania, Benin, Togo, Nigeria, and Ethiopia.

Sub-Saharan Africa poses some of the most urgent agricultural challenges on earth. One-fourth of the people are underfed. More than 75 percent of Africa's food production is still accomplished through village farming using hand-held hoes and sickles. The food supply is not keeping pace with the population growth. Extension agents work with farmers in a few villages to teach them how to improve their production. In exchange, those farmers agree to share their experiences with at least ten neighbors during the growing season.

Guinea Worm Eradication Program

Thanks to the work of the Carter Center, guinea worm last year became the second disease in human history to be eradicated from our planet. Smallpox was the first, a feat achieved in the 1970s through the efforts of the World Health Organization of the United Nations (WHO).

As recently as 1990, guinea worm—a painful, devastating parasite—infected as many as 2 million people per year and put more than 100 million others at risk in India, Pakistan, and sixteen African countries. People become sick when they drink water contaminated with microscopic guinea worm larvae, which migrate through the body before emerging a year later in an ankle as thin, threadlike worms up to a yard long. No effective treatment has ever been discovered, but health education and water purification have broken the worm's life cycle.

Global 2000 employed local health workers to monitor cases, prevent infected villagers from contaminating drinking water sources, and apply larvicide to stagnant pools. They also taught how to filter and boil drinking water. Before the eradication project began, Ghana and Nigeria ranked first and second worldwide in the numbers of cases of the disease. From 1989 to 1993, however, the two countries reduced guinea worm by 90 percent from 820,000 to 82,000 cases. In 1993, only two cases were reported in all of Pakistan.

Environmental Initiative

Various environmental conditions hinder human well-being in many parts of the world, but none is more significant than the fact that forests are disappearing at a rate of more than 40 million acres each year. One of the newer programs of the Carter Center is the Environmental Initiative, formed in 1991 with the following goals:

- To prevent and reverse environmental degradation
- To promote equitable and environmentally sound public policy
- To encourage sustainable population policies

148

Interfaith Health Program

"Wouldn't it be wonderful if faith groups—a Baptist church, a Catholic mission, a Jewish congregation, a Muslim center—adopted one close-by geographical area and made sure that every single child in the neighborhood was immunized against the basic diseases? That there was no hungry person in that area? That every person had a basic medical exam? That every woman who became pregnant would get prenatal care? That every elderly person was contacted daily?

"Suppose these congregations convinced parents and children to fight the presence of guns. Suppose they made a commitment to provide the kinds of alternatives needed to reduce violence that afflicts the poorest among us. These are very exciting and very redemptive options for the faith groups and our nation, but are they possible?

"We believe the answer is yes."

This declaration is Jimmy's favorite way to introduce the Interfaith Health Program (IHP) when he discusses it in public appearances.

A great gulf exists between the current level of public health and the potential to improve the length and quality of life in America. To help fill that gap, the Carter Center created the Interfaith Health Program, designed to help religious groups in the U.S. to provide health education in their communities. In times past, faith groups led the way in establishing hospitals and clinics. Today, the battle for good health is also fought through education, prevention, and public policy.

"People of faith know that religion sometimes is perceived as strident and divisive. Religious virtue, once synonymous with humility, is becoming confused with self-righteousness. Even while religion is being devalued, the world cries out for credible demonstrations of hope, for a competent and compassionate future," Jimmy says. "The answer is not *less* faith, but *more*. Those of us who are part of a faith community must demonstrate that faith leads toward the service of others. Nowhere is the need for leadership by faith groups so appropriate as in the field of health, as it draws together age-old commitments to wellness with the most current scientific insight."

The IHP gives churches information about creative community health models and preventive health-care ideas such as

- Recruiting a volunteer nurse to check blood pressures once a month after a church service
- Developing a system to check in daily with the shut-in members of the church
- Educating youth and adults about the dangers of cigarette smoking and an unhealthy diet while promoting discipline through regular exercise and proper eating
- Educating church members about the dangers of guns and other weapons used in violent acts
- Discussing with members the importance of preventive health care through regular checkups
- Contributing time or money to low-cost clinics or organizations offering and promoting immunization among children

"Imagine what would happen if the 145 million members of faith groups in the United States served just their immediate neighborhoods," Jimmy implores.

Mental Health Program

Today, more than one out of five Americans has a diagnosable mental disorder, yet most of these people do not seek help because they do not understand mental illness, fear the stigma associated with it, or lack access to treatment.

The Carter Center addresses public policy on this issue through its Mental Health Task Force and the annual Rosalynn Carter Symposium on Mental Health Policy. As a culmination of her longstanding public service in behalf of mental health, Rosalynn established the symposium to promote coordination and intercooperation among mental health organizations nationwide. The annual symposia have examined topics such as

- Mental illness and the elderly
- Emotional disorders of children and adolescents

- Support to families of patients with mental illness
- Financing mental health services and research
- Stigma and mental health
- Mental health within health-care reform

Rosalynn founded the Mental Health Task Force in 1991 to identify major issues; provide networks for mental health providers, patients, and family members; develop strategies for reducing stigma and discrimination against people with mental illness; and promote generally the mental health of Americans. Priorities set by the Task Force include

- Equitable inclusion of mental health in health-care reform
- Early intervention and prevention programs for children and their families
- Accurate portrayal of mental health issues in the media
- Improving treatment services and support to people with mental illness and to their families

Tobacco Control Program

The U.S. Centers for Disease Control and Prevention (CDCP) estimates that direct use of tobacco kills more than 8,300 Americans each week. This is roughly twice the number of all deaths caused by alcohol, car accidents, AIDS, suicide, homicide, fires, crack cocaine, and heroin.

The Carter Center is attempting to prevent tobacco-related diseases and promote smoke-free environments through educating Americans and influencing public policy. In recent years it has advocated a higher excise tobacco tax to deter tobacco use, especially among teens. (In Canada, an increase in tobacco taxes resulted in a sharp drop in the number of teenage smokers.)

In an editorial published in the *New York Times* on February 16, 1993, Jimmy wrote,

> The single most effective way to reduce tobacco use and nicotine addiction, especially among children, is to increase substantially the price of tobacco products. Health groups

estimate that a $2-a-pack increase would reduce smoking rates enough to save nearly 2 million lives—more than the total lives lost in all US wars combined.

This proposal would raise more than $30 billion a year in new revenue, which could be put to good use paying for health care reform, childhood immunization efforts, and other high priorities. In this way, tobacco could begin to pay its fair share of the tremendous costs it imposes on our society.

Developing countries also are responding warmly to ideas for reducing tobacco use. Joining forces with the WHO and the CDCP, the Carter Center has shared models of tobacco-control legislation with African nations and encouraged them to develop school health curricula that teach the dangers of tobacco use.

THE ATLANTA PROJECT

In 1992 the Carter Center created The Atlanta Project (TAP) to help urban communities gain access to the resources they need to solve the problems of violence, poverty, and inadequate housing. According to the center's staff, "This unprecedented grass-roots project has brought together thousands of volunteers, who are working with residents in twenty 'cluster' communities to identify needs and to create avenues for change in education, housing, community development, economic development, public safety and health."

After the clusters were established, they were paired with twenty-four major corporations and twenty-three colleges and universities that can offer assistance. TAP is working with the Atlanta Housing Authority to renovate public housing and has begun an antiviolence campaign known as TAP Into Peace. Among the other efforts through which TAP is helping Atlanta residents:

- A job-training program enlists corporate sponsors, who give special opportunities to residents in their assigned clusters

- Washington Cluster volunteers assist in criminal rehabilitation by serving as probation officers
- Southside Cluster has joined a food co-op, staffed by volunteers, to enable residents to buy groceries at discounted prices
- Brown Cluster residents can receive credit counseling from the NAACP Community Development Resource Center, which was created through TAP
- Positive Generations, in the Central DeKalb Cluster, helps children born to single mothers by getting both of the parents involved in child care
- Recreational centers in the Therrell Cluster provide youth with an alternative to crime through seminars, workshops, forums, and after-school activities
- Volunteer instructors help Douglass Cluster residents to stay fit by teaching free aerobics classes at the local high school

TAP's first full-scale program involving all the clusters was a massive Immunization/Children's Health Initiative in 1993. The goal was to have 7,000 volunteers identify up to 6,000 preschool children who would either receive free immunization or have their records updated. The results far exceeded expectations: By the time the immunization week ended, 12,000 volunteers (60 percent of whom were residents of TAP clusters) had provided for 17,000 children to be immunized or updated.

TASK FORCE FOR CHILD SURVIVAL AND DEVELOPMENT

An independent organization that works in close partnership with the Carter Center is the Task Force for Child Survival and Development, which was formed in 1984 to coordinate and expand global immunization efforts. Working with its major sponsors—the Rockefeller Foundation, WHO, UNICEF, the World Bank, and the United Nations Development Program—the task force successfully raised the immunization rate of the world's children from 20 to 80 percent in just six years.

Achieving that marvelous success, the task force expanded its goals to conquer the following by the year 2000:

- The global eradication of polio
- A 90 percent reduction in measles cases and a 95 percent reduction in deaths from measles
- A 70 percent drop in deaths due to diarrhea
- A 25 percent decrease in deaths from acute respiratory infection in children under age five
- A 50 percent reduction in maternal mortality rates

The task force oversees several other programs.

Attacking River Blindness

Nearly 10 million people in Africa and Latin America are no longer at risk from river blindness because of the joint efforts of the task force, the Carter Center, and Merck & Co., an American pharmaceutical firm. River blindness is caused by parasites borne by blackflies that breed in fast-flowing rivers. When the flies bite humans, they deposit the larvae of parasitic worms. As the worms mature, they produce millions of microworms, which can scar the eye. The WHO rates river blindness as a leading cause of blindness in Africa and Latin America, affecting 18 million people and threatening another 126 million worldwide.

Merck has made unlimited donations of the drugs available. Just one dose of Mectizan each year prevents the disease. The task force oversees Mectizan distribution to community groups in twenty-three endemic countries in sub-Saharan Africa and all six endemic nations in Latin America.

ON HUMAN RIGHTS

From a Sunday school class:

"In large measure, the beginnings of the modern concept of human rights go back to the laws and the prophets of the Judeo-Christian traditions. I have been steeped in the Bible since early childhood, and I believe that anyone who reads the ancient words of the Old Testament will find ... the idea of equality before the law and the supremacy of law over the whims of any ruler; the idea of the dignity of the individual human being and also the individual conscience; the ideas of service to the poor and to the oppressed;

154

the ideas of self-government and tolerance and of nations living together in peace, despite differences of belief.

"The Old Testament offers a vision of what that kind of peace might mean in its deepest sense. The lines from the prophet Micah—who is still one of my favorites—are words to which no summary or paraphrase could possibly do justice:

> "But in the last days it shall come to pass, that the mountain of the house of the LORD shall be established in the top of the mountains, and it shall be exalted above the hills; and people shall flow unto it. And many nations shall come, and say, Come, and let us go up to the mountain of the LORD, and to the house of the God of Jacob; and he will teach us of his ways, and we will walk in his paths: for the law shall go forth of Zion, and the word of the LORD from Jerusalem. And he shall judge among many people, and rebuke strong nations afar off; and they shall beat their swords into plowshares, and their spears into pruninghooks: nation shall not lift up a sword against nation, neither shall they learn war any more. But they shall sit every man under his vine and under his fig tree; and none shall make them afraid: for the mouth of the LORD of hosts hath spoken it. For all people will walk every one in the name of his god, and we will walk in the name of the LORD our God for ever and ever (Micah 4:1–5 KJV)."

All Kids Count

Developed by the task force in 1992, All Kids Count promotes the tracking of childhood immunization. "The need for such monitoring systems became clear in 1990 when a measles outbreak caused 44,000 hospitalizations and 64 deaths nationwide," according to task force officials.

Unfortunately, many Americans do not realize that children should receive all the important childhood immunizations by age two. The CDCP reports that only 44 to 63 percent of preschoolers are properly immunized. In some U.S. cities, the rate drops as low as 10 percent.

Through All Kids Count, seventeen health sites throughout the country have received funds to develop computer systems that will track all children under age six. The systems will be linked to hospitals, schools, public health agencies, and physicians' offices with the hope that children at risk for measles, mumps, rubella, polio, and other diseases will be vaccinated.

Every Child by Two

In 1991, Rosalynn joined forces with Betty Bumpers, the wife of U.S. Senator Dale Bumpers, to create Every Child by Two, which emphasizes the importance of early immunization. The program seeks to educate parents, promote long-term policy changes to ensure vaccination for all U.S. children by age two, and encourage health departments to expand access to immunization services.

The program is now established in about forty states, many under the sponsorship of the governors' spouses. Every Child by Two also joined with the American Nurses Association to enlist more than seventy national organizations to become partners in the immunization campaign.

Program Against Micronutrient Malnutrition

Three critical nutrients—vitamin A, iron, and iodine—have a profound effect on child survival, women's health, learning ability, adult productivity, and general resistance to disease. It is estimated that at least 4 million children's lives could be saved each year by increasing their intake of vitamin A alone. PAMM was created to help countries control micronutrient malnutrition.

The Responsibilities of Power

All these programs and initiatives of the Carter Center grew out of Jimmy and Rosalynn Carter's commitment to serving Christ through serving humanity. Rosalynn told me,

> When we came home from the White House, we realized we still had vast resources. I mean anybody will help you with anything because you were President. All you have to do is ask them, and that puts a huge responsibility on what you do with that power. Especially because of our Christian religion, I think, it was important to us to help

those less fortunate. It was the religious underpinnings which motivated us in this direction—to create the Carter Center—when we realized we had this kind of influence.

Then when we started the Carter Center, it developed into something we never dreamed it would be.

Elie Wiesel frequently observes that evil has outdone itself this century, using technology as its toy. Consider the mustard gas used in World War I, the concentration camps and gas ovens of the Nazi era, and the development of the atomic bomb.

Although Jimmy agrees with Dr. Wiesel—or perhaps *because* he agrees—he remains determined, energetic, and quite certain we can change the lives of those around us and especially the lives of the world's poorest and most oppressed. In fact, while most of us may feel drained and exhausted at hearing the latest reports from Somalia or Korea or the latest account of some madman with a rifle, Jimmy responds by insisting that we *must* act and *must* commit ourselves to making a difference.

Dan Ariail, Rosalynn and Jimmy Carter, and Cheryl Heckler-Feltz

REDEEMING THE TIME

I have one life to live. I feel God wants me to do the best I can with it.

JIMMY CARTER,
DURING THE PRESIDENTIAL CAMPAIGN OF 1976

In the 1976 presidential campaign, a reporter asked Jimmy, "When your life is over, for what do you want to be remembered?"

Jimmy replied, "I would like to have my frequent prayer answered that God let my life be meaningful in the enhancement of His kingdom and that my life might be meaningful in the enhancement of the lives of my fellow human beings. That I might help translate the natural love that exists in the world and do simple justice through government. I believe that the almost accidental choice of politics as part of my life's career will have been a very gratifying part of realizing that prayer. I've never asked God to let me win an election or to let me have success in politics. I've just said, 'Lord, let my action be meaningful to You and let my life that You've given me not be wasted. Let it be of benefit to Your kingdom and to my fellow human beings.' If I had that prayer answered, I think I would be very gratified."

The New Testament tells us that the primary agency for advancing God's kingdom in this world is the church, but Jimmy's life demonstrates that an individual servant of God can make a profound difference as well. For those seeking a stronger spiritual awareness of God's world, Jimmy's legacy is dedication to the highest standards of service, a reminder that making every minute count is essential in the life of a Christian, and finally, awareness that the journey of a Christian begins with a personal decision to choose Jesus.

Jimmy doesn't just ask, "Did I serve God today?" He asks, "Did I serve God to the best of my ability?" The difference between these questions is as great, as Mark Twain would say, as the difference between lightning and the lightning bug.

For residents of Plains, for residents in shacks rebuilt by Habitat, for residents of the twenty Atlanta Project clusters, for residents of the nations experiencing brand-new democracy and peace, for residents of Africa no longer suffering from guinea worm or river blindness—for all these, Jimmy Carter has been a bolt of lightning.

The world nearly lost Jimmy when he was in the navy. He describes this episode in *Why Not the Best?*

> In the middle of one night—during a heavy storm—we were on the surface and I was on the submarine bridge about fifteen feet above the level of the ocean itself, holding on as tightly as I could to an iron pipe handrail inside the bridge shelf.
>
> An enormous wave rose around us to a level of about six feet or so above my head. I lost my grip as the force of the wave tore my hand from the handrail, and I found myself swimming literally within the huge wave, completely separated from the submarine itself.
>
> After I swam for a good while—it seemed forever—the wave receded, and I landed on top of the five-inch gun located about 30 feet aft of where I had been standing. I clung desperately to the gun barrel and finally was able to lower myself to the deck and return to my watch station. Had the currents been even slightly broadside instead of from forward to aft, I never would have landed on the ship as the wave receded and would undoubtedly have been lost at sea in the dark storm.

It saddens me to think what we—here in Plains and the world at large—would have lost that night. But that brush with death is a crucial reminder of the biblical injunction to "redeem the time" (Ephesians 5:16). This is another key element in the spiritual legacy of Jimmy Carter.

Although he is the oldest of four siblings born to Earl and Lillian, Jimmy is the sole survivor of his family of origin, and in his family, only his mother—who died at age eighty-four—surpassed his present age of seventy-one.

Andrew Young described to me a frightening episode when someone attacked Martin Luther King Jr. at a civil rights event and stabbed him in the chest. "Martin used to say that every morning when he brushed his teeth and looked in the mirror he was reminded that this day might be his last," Young said. "Everybody in Jimmy Carter's family has died of pancreatic cancer, and that usually means that within three months after the discovery, they are gone. I think that's one of the motivations that people don't understand. Jimmy Carter knows just how valuable time is."

This awareness of "making the most of every opportunity"—as the *New International Version* renders Ephesians 5:16—has been a persistent and consistent theme throughout Jimmy's adult life.

When asked by newsman Bill Moyers in 1976, "What do you think we're on earth for?" Jimmy gave this response:

> ... I could quote the biblical references to creation, that God created us in His own image, hoping that we'd be perfect, and we turned out to be not perfect but very sinful. And then when Christ was asked what are the two great commandments from God which should direct our lives, He said, 'To love God with all your heart and soul and mind ... and love your neighbor as yourself' (Mark 12:30–31). So I try to take that condensation of the Christian theology and let it be something through which I search for a meaningful existence.
>
> But the truth is, I don't worry about it too much anymore. I used to when I was a college sophomore, and we used to debate for hours and hours about why we're here, who made us, where shall we go, what is our purpose. But I don't feel frustrated about it. You know, I'm not afraid to see my life ended. I feel like every day is meaningful. I don't have any fear at all of death. I feel I'm doing the best I can, and if I get elected president, I'll have a chance to magnify my own influence, maybe in a meaningful way.

In the Sunday school classroom, Jimmy frequently points out that the length of one's life is not as significant as the fact of making the journey with Christ:

"Physical life is not the most important thing in God's eyes. We attach great importance to death, funerals, bereavement, and so forth. If we are Christians, that's the beginning of our promised life with Christ. What Christ was saying was, the destruction of a human being's relations with one another, relations with God, are much more important than even the loss of one's life."—Couples' class, First Baptist Church in Washington, D.C., August 28, 1977

"If we think that our existence on earth is the most important of all, then to lose it is one of our most important losses. Christ's death and resurrection proved to us that there's life after death, but it also proved to us that preoccupation with the present human life should not be ascendant in our consciousness."—Couples' class, First Baptist Church in Washington, D.C., January 29, 1978

On still another occasion he told the couples' class at the church in Washington:

"What difference is it if we live fifty-six or fifty-eight years or seventy-three years or eighty-four years?

"Sometimes we have such an intense fear of death that we can't really live. The meaning of life is not in the number of years on earth. Martin Luther King Jr. died a young man. John Kennedy died, a young man. The average age of those who wrote the Declaration of Independence was about forty. Christ's ministry only lasted for three years.

"We tend to think that to exist seventy, seventy-five years is a great achievement and very important. But Christ is trying to show us that victory over death can give meaning in our lives. We should not be preoccupied with physical death; we should not be preoccupied with physical health. We should not be preoccupied with fame and reputation and social status.

"When does eternal life begin for us? At death? Are we partaking now of part of our eternal life? Yes.

"We have too much tendency to say, 'Someday, later on, I'm going to be a meaningful person. I'm going to do the things

I've always known were right. I'm going to prepare for my life with Christ—someday. But for the time being, I'm going to cling to things given me—security, status, competence, happiness, gratification.'

"Let's not wait until the day of our death to start to join the presence of Christ. A lot of people say this: 'After death, I'll be with Christ. After death, the Holy Spirit will be part of my existence. After death, I'll know the meaning of God.'

"Christ says, forget about death and enjoy and appreciate and understand the meaning of life. We don't have to wait until we die, or to come back to life, or a miracle occurs, to know joy, exaltation, fullness of life, celebration, because God has already given it to us. To the extent that our life isn't full, but if filled rather with fear or trepidation or doubt or insecurity, we're wasting it.

"It's a symbol of selfishness to concern ourselves about the limit of our physical existence. Paul said that all those who believe in Christ have eternal life. Life begins now.

"Our relationship with Christ is of greater significance to our life than the shortness of our life, the absence of our life.

On the day we know Christ our eternal life begins, and the rosy future that we set down when we are going to restructure our lives is now."

When asked another time during the presidential campaign how he wants to be remembered, Jimmy answered, "It's not an unpleasant sense of being driven. I feel I have one life to live. I feel God wants me to do the best I can with it. And that's quite often my major prayer: Let me live my life so that it will be meaningful."

His life before, during, and after his presidency is a testimony that that prayer has been answered in many, many ways since 1976. The life of Jimmy Carter has proved to be fruitful beyond what most of us can grasp, and he remains one of the most fascinating and admired people in America.

Plains Baptist Church

APPENDIX: YOUR TRIP TO PLAINS

The village of Plains had it beginnings in the 1840s several miles northwest of the present location at a lovely spot still known as Magnolia Springs, in the southwest corner of Sumter County. When the railroad serving nearby Americus, Preston, and Lumpkin expanded its line in the 1880s, the folk relocated next to the railroad. A new town sprang up and in 1884 took the name "the Plains of Dura." The designation, taken from a biblical quotation in Daniel 3:1, aptly describes the flat landscape of the region. Eventually the name was shortened to "Plains."

The 1920s were good times in Plains. Not only was a future president born here in 1924, but the village experienced an economic boom and reached a population of six hundred. Services that decade included two banks, two drugstores, a cotton gin, a hotel, a dentist, and an undertaker. Unquestionably, the most prestigious and famous establishment was the Wise Sanitarium, a cancer hospital that drew patients from three states.

Plains always has been a rural town, serving as the center of commerce for the surrounding farming community. Six-to-ten thousand bales of cotton were shipped annually from Plains during the 1920s. But the town's rapid growth ended during the depression years of the 1930s, and the population has remained near seven hundred ever since.

When Jimmy Carter began his campaign for the presidency in December 1974, national attention was focused on this town for the first time, and the crowds of people who came were beyond imagination. Now that Jimmy is no longer in public office, the crowds are thinner, but steady as people come hoping to see the Carters at church or just to see the small town that gave the United States its thirty-ninth president. More than any other president in recent decades, Jimmy Carter is closely identified with his hometown.

In 1987, Congress created the Jimmy Carter National Historic Site and Preservation District, which is under the direction of the National Parks Service (NPS) and includes four sites: Plains High School, Plains railroad depot—which served as the presidential campaign headquarters, Jimmy's boyhood home in Archery, and the Carter compound (Jimmy and Rosalynn's current home, the adjacent lot, and Secret Service headquarters). The NPS has produced a comprehensive management plan for these sites, and I encourage you to see all these when you visit.

Plains is within 170 miles of the Gulf of Mexico, which accounts for the town's mild climate. An average January day offers a low of 40 degrees and a high in the 60s. Snow is rare. August is hot.

The population of Sumter County is estimated at 30,000. The county seat of Americus has about 18,000 residents.

Atlanta, the state capital, is 134 miles north of Sumter County. Columbus is 60 miles northwest, Macon is 70 miles northeast, and Albany is 35 miles south. If you are flying into Atlanta, allow at least three hours to travel between the airport and Plains. Our village is located about one hour west of Interstate 75 near the Vienna Exit and about ninety minutes east of the Alabama state line near Eufaula.

The closest accommodations are found at the Plains Bed and Breakfast, housed in a turn-of-the-century building with period furnishings and a beautiful, wide verandah. On a historic note, this is where Lillian and Earl Carter were living when they discovered they were expecting the future president.

Two places in Plains offer meals for the visitor. On weekdays, Scarlett's, which is part of the Petal Pushers flower and gift shop, offers sandwiches, salads, and soft drinks at the lunch hour. This shop is in the main group of storefronts in Plains and is owned by Marijane Woodward and Kathy Johnson.

The main restaurant in town is the Kountry Korner, amanged by Beck Dale. Right on U.S. 280, the Kountry Korner is open for lunch on Tuesday through Sunday and for dinner on Friday and Saturday. Mrs. Dale features an economical Sunday buffet and, on Friday and Saturday evenings, an all-you-can-eat seafood dinner of farm-raised catfish or mullet.

The Windsor Hotel, built in Americus in 1892, is a restored castle-like hotel with fifty-three guest rooms, including an elegant fourth-floor bridal suite and the Carter Presidential Suite. It was here that motion picture stars Jessica Tandy, Hume Cronyn, and Esther Rolle stayed while filming the Hallmark Hall of Fame production *To Dance with the White Dog*.

What to See and Do in Plains

Plains High School is the building where the future president and first lady got their education, all the way from first grade through high school. Now part of the National Park Service, it has only recently been restored to look as much as possible as it did when Jimmy and Rosalynn were going to school there. Displays and video presentations explain how things once were, and there are National Park personnel and volunteer guides.

The Depot Museum was once a CSX Railroad depot and served as the first headquarters of the Carter presidential campaign. All of his local speeches for the public and media were given from the loading platform facing Main Street. It has displays and a gift shop and is also operated by the National Park Service.

Plain Peanuts, located in the heart of the village, is now a store, but it was in this building that Earl Carter had his peanut warehouse office for many years. The store sells a variety of peanut products and offers a thirty-minute tour that takes visitors past more than twenty-five sites, including the First United Methodist Church, where Jimmy and Rosalynn were married; TV City, where hundreds of reporters "camped out" for five years; and Billy Carter's gas station. The store, owned by Bobby Salter, is in the main group of commercial buildings on Main Street.

Hugh Carter's Antiques, also located on the main strip, is owned by Jimmy's first cousin, who himself served as a state senator for many years in the same seat once held by Jimmy. As youngsters, Hugh and Jimmy sold ice cream and hamburgers in Plains; today they both serve as deacons at Maranatha Baptist Church. The store offers antiques, books, and souvenirs—and some presidential memories from Hugh.

WHAT TO SEE AND DO OUTSIDE PLAINS

Koinonia

Koinonia Farm is a pioneering Christian community founded in 1942 by Dr. and Mrs. Clarence Jordan. He and Florence led this group to live by the New Testament model of the early church as depicted in Acts 2:44–45 and 4:32. Koinonia, which takes as its name the Greek word for "fellowship" in the New Testament, was an experiment in commonality, meaning "they had all things common." It also involved putting aside barriers of race, therefore bringing down the wrath of many in the vicinity. Despite the hatred shown to its residents and the hardships they endured in being different, Dr. Jordan insisted that they turn the other cheek, saying, "We're God's people. He gives us the strength to love our enemies—and even to help them if we get the chance."

Koinonia is about eight and a half miles south of Plains on Georgia Route 49. Visitors are welcome, and tours can be arranged.

Americus

Founded in 1832, Americus was a major cotton center during its early days and the site of three hospitals for Confederate soldiers during the War Between the States. At one time Americus was the eighth largest city in Georgia and one of the first in Georgia to have electric streetcars. Downtown Americus is a classic example of the fanciful Victorian commercial architecture of the 1880s and the "gay '90s."

The Habitat for Humanity International Headquarters is located in the newly renovated Rylander Building on West

Lamar Street in Americus. This Christian-based organization has built more than 40,000 homes for the less fortunate in more than forty countries. Habitat has also been responsible for improving the looks of the area through its Sumter County Initiative, created to end substandard housing in the county by the year 2000.

The Brickyard Plantation Golf Club is a picturesque course with twenty-seven holes and is located on U.S. 280 east of Americus.

Andersonville

The Andersonville National Historic Site is the location of an infamous Confederate military prison where 13,000 Union prisoners died during the fourteen months it was in existence during 1864–65. It includes a national cemetery and is the home of the National POW Memorial, commemorating all the prisoners of war in United States history. It is located on Georgia Route 49.

The Civil War Village of Andersonville is a quaint community that served as the supply center for the Andersonville Confederate Prison. It includes a pioneer farm, Civil War museum, historic log church, antique and craft shops, restaurant, RV campsite, and a bed-and-breakfast. It is also on Georgia 49.

The Andersonville Trail is a seventy-five-mile sight-seeing loop tour off Interstate 75, including quaint hometowns and Main Streets, historic homes, museums, two National Historic Sites, antiques, shopping, camping, fishing, hunting, watermelons, peaches, peanuts, and pecans.

Buena Vista

The Elvis Presley Collection Museum, located on the town square, is the world's largest private collection of Elvis memorabilia, which is valued at more than $3 million. Stage clothing, musical instruments, personal items, jewelry, guns, cars, and furniture from Presley's Hollywood home and Graceland estate all are on display.

The National Country Music Museum is housed within a hundred-year-old cotton warehouse that has been beautifully restored on the town square. The collection includes more than a hundred exhibits representing the biggest names in country music. Stage clothing, furniture, and even automobiles used by entertainers such as George Jones, Merle Haggard, Johnny Cash, Dolly Parton, and Kenny Rogers are displayed.

Columbus

The Columbus Museum displays American art and regional history exhibits. Permanent exhibitions include the Chattahoochee Legacy and Transformations, a hands-on discovery gallery.

The Columbus Riverfront offers a scenic view of the Chattahoochee River along the new Riverwalk-Promenade complete with gazebos, benches, and fountains. Located adjacent to Uptown and the Columbus Historic District, this is a great place for walkers and runners.

The Confederate Naval Museum, located at 202 Fourth Street, displays the salvaged remains of the Confederate ironclad *Jackson* and the gunboat *Chattahoochee*, along with other exhibits relating to the history of the Confederate States Navy.

Cordele

The Georgia Veterans Memorial State Park was established as a permanent memorial to the veterans who served, fought, and died in America's wars. Two museums are located in the park. The indoor museum has exhibits that interpret American wars and battles from the eighteenth-century French and Indian War through the Vietnam conflict. The outdoor museum is composed of planes, cannons, and tanks of World War I through Vietnam. Located near Lake Blackshear, the 1,300-acre site includes eighty-five tent and trailer sites, a swimming pool and beach, an eighteen-hole golf course, ten rental cottages, and a winterized group shelter. It is located just west of town on U.S. 280.

Griffin

Downtown Griffin is an award-winning Main Street city listed on the National Historic Register. There are unique specialty shops and restaurants in a Victorian atmosphere.

Lumpkin

Providence Canyon State Conservation Park is also known as "Georgia's Little Grand Canyon" and is one of the seven wonders of Georgia. There is an Interpretive Center, and the park offers hiking, picnicking, a pioneer campground for organized groups, a backpack trail for overnight camping, and an enclosed group shelter. It is located on Highway 39C, seven miles west of Lumpkin.

The Village of Westville, on South Mulberry Street, realistically depicts Georgia's preindustrial life and the culture of 1850. There is a blacksmith shop and various craft shops for baking, making candles, syrup, and soap.

The Bedingfield Inn is a restored stagecoach inn and family residence with period furnishings, dating to 1836. It is located on the town square and offers guided tours.

Pine Mountain

The Callaway Gardens and Resorts feature the John A. Sibley Horticultural Center, an indoor-outdoor display garden complex; the Day Butterfly Center, a glass-enclosed tropical conservatory filled with more than a thousand butterflies in free flight; Mr. Cason's Vegetable Garden, a seven-acre demonstration garden that is the home of Public Television's *Victory Garden South*. The resort offers bicycling, boating, fishing, tennis, and golf. It is located on U.S. Highway 27 just south of Pine Mountain.

Franklin D. Roosevelt State Park, along Georgia Route 190, is a 10,000-acre mountain park with 21 cabins, 140 tent and trailer sites, a swimming pool, two lakes, fishing, horseback riding, family and group picnic shelters, and thirty miles of hiking trails.

The Pine Mountain Wild Animal Park houses exotic animals from every continent of the world at its 500-acre site. The two-section park features a drive-through wilderness area plus a walk-through area that includes a petting zoo, old McDonald Farm, and a serpentorium. It is located at 1300 Oak Grove Road, five miles north of Pine Mountain.

The Pine Mountain Campground, on U.S. Route 27, has 154 sites, 48 pull-throughs, swimming pool, jacuzzi, volleyball court, horseshoe pits, stocked fishing ponds, and children's playground.

Vienna

This small rural town boasts a historic driving tour show-casing structures built during the Victorian era and points of interest such as the Walter F. George Law Office Museum and an 1892 courthouse that is listed on the National Historic Register. There are also antique and craft shops and agricultural tours.

Warm Springs

The "Little White House" is a historic cottage where President Franklin D. Roosevelt stayed while undergoing polio therapy. He died there on April 12, 1945.

The Antique and Crafts Mall Unlimited contains 114 shops and is located two miles north of Warm Springs.

Special Events

The Plains Country Day is held the third weekend of May and includes arts and crafts booths, a one-mile fun run and 5K race, a parade, and food stands.

The Dogwood Trail Tour of Homes is held in Americus in April.

The Andersonville Arts, Crafts, Antiques & Civil War Artifacts Fair falls on Memorial Day Weekend.

The Andersonville Historic Weekend is held in October.

The Callaway Gardens' Spring Celebration is held mid-March through mid-April at Pine Mountain.

Tourist Information

Many of the sites and events describes in this appendix require admission fees.

Additional information may be obtained from the following:

- Americus-Sumter County Chamber of Commerce, 400 W. Lamar St., PO Box 724, Americus, GA 31709. Telephone: 912–924–2646
- Visitors Center, Plains, GA 31780. Telephone: 912–824–7477
- Andersonville Welcome Center, Andersonville, GA 31711. Telephone: 912–924–2558
- Presidential Pathways Travel Association, PO Box 2768, Columbus, GA 31902

AT THE CHURCH

Visitors are welcome anytime at Maranatha Baptist Church, but here are some tips for those who wish to attend Jimmy's Sunday school class and have a photograph taken after the worship service:

- Plan your trip no more than four or five weeks in advance. The Carters' schedules sometimes change abruptly, and the church typically schedules one month at a time. Jimmy was able to teach on thirty-seven of the fifty-two Sundays in 1994.
- Call the church at 912–824–7896 to learn which weeks he will be teaching. Please phone again during the week of your visit to be sure his schedule has not changed.
- It is best to arrive at the church by 9:45 A.M. for the Sunday school class, which begins at 10:00. The worship service is at 11:00.
- You are welcome to bring a camera, but please keep your pen in your pocket. Jimmy and Rosalynn will pose after church for photos with guests but will decline requests for autographs. Please be prepared to take just one photo.

Sources

The authors and publisher acknowledge that this listing may not be complete and regret any omissions.

INTRODUCTION

God's Trombones (New York: Penguin Books, 1972), p. 20.

CHAPTER 1

The verses in Spanish are from *Santa Biblia Version Riena-Valera, Revisión de 1960.* The verses quoted in Spanish are John 1:1 and John 1:51; in English, Exodus 33:14.

CHAPTER 2

Always a Reckoning: And Other Poems (New York: Random House/Times Books, 1994).

Why Not the Best? (Nashville: Broadman Press, 1975), pp. 15, 17–18, 23, 26, 31, 35–36, 48. Used by permission of the author.

Jimmy's school essay was published in *Yankee From Georgia* by William Lee Miller (New York: Times Books, 1978), pp. 114–15.

Quotations from personal, taped conversations.

CHAPTER 3

Personal interviews with Martin E. Marty, Rabbi James A. Rudin, the president, and others.

CHAPTER 4

The epigraph is from *Why Not the Best?*, p. 172.

Ruth Stapleton Carter, *Brother Billy* (New York: Harper & Row, 1978).

Press conference on March 19, 1967.

Interview with Bill Moyers, Public Broadcasting Service, May 6, 1976.

The quotation of Bert Lance comes from *A 70th Birthday Tribute to President Jimmy Carter* (30 September 1994 celebration), DeTournay Productions, Woodland Hills, California. Used by permission.

Letter from Leonard Sweet to the authors.

Chapter 5

Transcriptions from adult Bible class at Plains Baptist Church.
Personal interview with Mary Prince.
Why Not the Best? Pp. 42–44. Used by permission.
Personal interviews with Andrew Young.
Address to ministers of the African Methodist Episcopal Church in Atlanta, June 18, 1976.
Inaugural address as Governor of Georgia, January 12, 1971.

Chapter 6

The quotations of Hamilton Jordan and Walter Mondale come from *A 70th Birthday Tribute to President Jimmy Carter*. Used by permission.

Keeping Faith: Memoirs of a President (New York: Bantam Books, 1983).

Chapter 7

Photo of Jimmy and Rosalynn Carter © 1977 by AP/Wide World Photos. Used by permission.

The information about Lucy Hayes is from Edith Mayo and from Kenneth W. Leish, *The White House*, Wonders of Man Series (New York: Newsweek, 1972), pp. 70–71.

Rosalynn Carter with Susan K. Golant, *Helping Yourself Help Others: The Caregiver's Handbook* (New York: Random House/Times Books, 1994), 17.

First Lady from Plains (New York: Houghton Mifflin, 1984), pp. 10—11, 18, 29, 39, 53, 93–94. Used by permission.

Conversations with Rosalynn Carter and Edith Mayo.

Chapter 8

Epigraph is from Henri Nouwen, *Reaching Out: The Three Movements of the Spiritual Life* (New York: Doubleday, 1975), pp. 71–72.

Why Not the Best? Pp. 78–79. Used by permission.

CHAPTER 9

Personal conversations with the president.

CHAPTER 10

Personal conversations with the president.

Taped sessions of the adult Bible class at Maranatha Baptist church.

Telephone interviews with Dr. Irwin Abrams. The publisher of *The Nobel Peace Prize and the Laureates: An Illustrated Biographical History, 1901–1987* is Macmillan, 1988.

Talking Peace, (New York: E. P. Dutton, 1992), p. 140.

CHAPTER 11

Much information in this chapter comes from a Carter Center publication entitled "Waging Peace Around the World."

Letter from Leonard Sweet to the authors.

CHAPTER 12

Why Not the Best? Pp. 57–58. Used by permission.

Interview with Bill Moyers, Public Broadcasting Service, May 6, 1976.